The Care of Reptiles and Amphibians in Captivity

Revised Edition

Chris Mattison

BLANDFORD PRESS
POOLE · NEW YORK · SYDNEY

First published in the UK 1982 by Blandford Press, Link House, West Street, Poole, Dorset, BH15 1LL.

Copyright © 1982 and 1987 Chris Mattison

Reprinted May 1983
Reprinted December 1983
Revised edition 1987
Reprinted 1987

Distributed in the United States by Sterling Publishing Co., Inc., 2 Park Avenue, New York, NY 10016.

Distributed in Australia by Capricorn Link (Australia) Pty Ltd. PO Box 665, Lane Cove, NSW 2066.

British Library Cataloguing in Publication Data

Mattison, Christopher
  The care of reptiles and amphibians in
  captivity — Rev. ed.
  1. Amphibians   2. Reptiles
  I. Title
  639.3'76   SF459.A45

ISBN 0 7137 1826 9

Typeset by Permanent Typesetting Co., Hong Kong

Printed in Great Britain by Butler and Tanner Ltd., Frome and London

Contents

PART TWO: DESCRIPTIONS OF SPECIES AND THEIR MAINTENANCE

Scincidae — Skinks
Cordylidae — Zonures
Gerrhosauridae — Plated Lizards
Lacertidae
Teiidae — Tegus and Whiptails
Anguidae — Slow-worms, Glass Lizards and Alligator
     Lizards
Varanidae — Monitors
Amphisbaenidae

Acknowledgements

Over the years I have benefited enormously from advice and information freely given by amateur and professional herpetologists too numerous to mention. In the same way, I have sought, and found, answers in many magazines, journals and books, some of which are listed in the bibliography. However, several people and institutions have contributed directly towards the contents (but not the shortcomings) of this book, and their help is especially appreciated: Chester Zoo, Chris Howard of Twycross Zoo, Dennis Lee, Nick Nyoka of Knaresborough Zoo, Mrs J. Parkin, John Pickett, Phil Reid, James Savage, Norman Snelling and the University of Sheffield for allowing me to photograph animals in their care; C. Bath of Paignton Zoo, Tony Mobbs, and Louis Porras of 'The Shed', Miami, for dealing promptly and succinctly with specific enquiries; Paul Hodges for the line drawings; David Hollingworth for valuable advice on processing certain of the monochrome photographs; and the editors of Blandford Press for advice, encouragement and patience.

Special thanks are due to John Cooper who critically read the manuscript, John Pickett who also read part of the manuscript and who has helped in so many other ways, both before the book's germination and during its development, and to my father, Ron Mattison, who expertly corrected, and suggested improvements to, the first draft. Finally, nothing would have been possible without the assistance of my wife Rosemary, who, apart from sharing her home with a wide (and sometimes weird) assortment of amphibian and reptilian lodgers, has constantly provided ideas and discussion, as well as companionship, throughout.

Introduction

The care and management of captive animals is a science based upon a sound knowledge of the biology, ecology and behaviour of the same animals in the wild state. The interplay of many factors creates the environment for which each species is best suited. Some factors are essential, others are not, and as our knowledge increases and we become more experienced in providing correct conditions for a particular species some factors can be disregarded or simplified, whereas others must be considered and duplicated. Thus, to keep a budgerigar it is not necessary to re-create an exact replica of its Australian environment, but to arrange only for a suitably balanced diet and protection from extremes of weather. With reptiles and amphibians our expertise is very limited. Several species can be kept alive under the most basic conditions (for example the African Clawed Toad, *Xenopus laevis*, requires only a few centimetres of clean water and two meals every week) but others have defied the most elaborate and ingenious attempts to induce them to thrive in captivity. The reasons for these anomalies may be summarised in the term 'adaptability', and the adaptability of a species has been one of the major considerations when deciding which species to include in the accounts that form the second part of this book.

Part I deals with the basic principles of reptile and amphibian management, such as housing, feeding and so on, which are common to every species. In addition, the sections in Part II dealing with each family are introduced by supplementary information relating to its members, and in some cases more detailed notes are provided on those species or groups of species which have more specialised requirements.

Because the re-creation of an animal's environment is a complicated procedure, the most important factors of light, heat, humidity and 'furnishings' are dealt with under separate headings. It should not be forgotten, however, that under natural circumstances these factors are closely inter-related and, furthermore, alter throughout each day and from season to season. Therefore, there are few species for which a simple step-by-step 'recipe' can be provided; but by giving information on the basic requirements of selected species, coupled with an account of the techniques by which the environment can be controlled, it is hoped that a sufficiently accurate set of values can be achieved. Further experimentation with one or more factors may be required before 'ideal' conditions are formulated.

Since this book is intended primarily for the use of hobbyists and school or college laboratories, all equipment described can be easily and cheaply bought or made. For the same reason, little space has been allocated to the subjects of display or presentation, which are more applicable to zoological gardens. It should be borne in mind, however, that animals which are attractively set up are likely to hold the interest of their owner for longer, and thus encourage more conscientious attention.

Many species of reptiles and amphibians are threatened with extinction, mainly through pollution and the destruction of their habitats. As the vast majority of animals in the pet trade are taken from these dwindling populations, vivarium-keepers have a moral obligation to care for their animals in a serious and humane way, and not to look upon them as easily-replaced novelties. An irresponsible attitude by even a small minority will certainly be rewarded by ever more stringent regulations concerning the collecting and keeping of many popular and common species along with the acknowledged rarities.

In this vast subject, I have tried to provide accurate and easily understood guidelines for the care of reptiles and amphibians as a whole. Much of the information is first-hand, gained through many years of keeping several thousand individuals, from tadpoles to tortoises. The remainder has been gathered from papers, articles and lectures, and from conversations with amateur and professional herpetologists of many countries, and I would recommend personal contact as the most important means of increasing one's expertise in this fascinating field.

Finally, it is sincerely hoped that the effect of this book will not be to encourage the casual and unthinking confinement of wild animals for reasons of idle curiosity or exhibitionism, but rather to promote a better standard of care, resulting in fewer mortalities and more reproductive successes and hence a stemming of the flow of animals from dwindling wild populations.

Introduction to the Revised Edition

In the six years which have passed since this book was first written, many aspects of keeping reptiles and amphibians have changed. Sources of animals have been reduced, mainly due to legislation in Europe, North America and South America, resulting in the loss of several popular species from the hobby, whereas demand has grown steadily, and 'new' species have been introduced to meet this. For example, the ban on importing tortoises into Northern Europe was rapidly followed by a sustained influx of North American Box Turtles. Not all of these new introductions are good choices for the vivarium, and even those which are often arrive in poor condition, especially animals from the Far East.

Reptiles have suddenly become big business and, as such, the 'profitability' of a species has become every bit as important as its 'adaptability' – perhaps even more so. For this reason, it is now more important than ever to be selective when choosing a reptile or amphibian – I am continually being asked for advice by beginners who have bought animals which they have almost no hope of keeping alive for any length of time. Often, the dealer who sold them the animal had assured them that it was easy to care for – they are hardly likely to say otherwise – but the fault must lie with people who buy an animal on impulse and worry about its maintenance afterwards.

On the brighter side, the lack of imported specimens of some of the more desirable species has led to a more serious approach to captive breeding. It is encouraging to see that several people are able to make a living from breeding, rather than collecting or importing, reptiles and amphibians. Indeed, many species are now much more readily available through this means than ever was possible through collecting. Furthermore, their prices have dropped to levels where many more people can afford them, the animals are strong and healthy and, perhaps most importantly, the techniques necessary to breed these animals are becoming more refined, adding to the pool of knowledge which is an essential part of our hobby.

Finally, I wish to thank those people who have pointed out errors or omissions in the first edition or who have provided me with additional information which will, I hope, make this book more useful.

PART ONE
General Care

1
Some Biological Considerations

This is not the place to deal with the biology of amphibians and reptiles in its entirety — this information can be obtained from a number of excellent text books, some of which are listed in the bibliography. In order to appreciate certain requirements of captive animals, however, it will be necessary to be familiar with some relevant information at the outset. The most important aspects of the biology of amphibians and reptiles from the point of view of the vivarium-keeper are behavioural adaptations to the environment, particularly in relation to temperature, and social behaviour.

In brief, amphibians and reptiles form two separate classes of the vertebrates, or back-boned animals. The other classes of vertebrates are the fish, which are more primitive than the amphibians and reptiles, and the birds and mammals, which are more advanced. Collectively, the amphibians and reptiles number almost 10,000 known species — about the same number as there are species of birds. Amphibians evolved from fish about 350 million years ago and were the first vertebrates to colonise the land, although they were still dependent on water for breeding purposes. This disadvantage was overcome 50 million years later with the development of the shelled egg. At about the same time, the animals' dependence on water was further mini-mised by the production of a hard, scaly skin — which meant the first reptiles had appeared. From these primitive beginnings, amphibians and reptiles have diversified to fill many niches in the order of living things. Many, such as the dinosaurs, have been superseded by later, better adapted forms, but in spite of several limitations almost every part of the world has its share of amphibians and reptiles.

THERMOREGULATION

The most important of these limiting factors is temperature. Like all animals, amphibians and reptiles operate most efficiently at certain optimum temperatures which may vary from one species to another; unlike birds and mammals, however, they are not able to produce heat internally, but are dependent on outside sources for it, and are thus labelled 'ectotherms' or 'poikilotherms'. For this reason, the greatest concentrations, both of individuals and of species, are to be found in the tropics, with the numbers dropping off quite rapidly as the poles are approached.

In general, amphibians tolerate, indeed prefer, lower temperatures than reptiles, and are usually found to be at about the same temperature as their surroundings. Certain reptiles, however, have one or two methods by which they can elevate their body temperature above that of their surroundings. These species bask for part of each day in order to absorb solar heat; and some of them increase their efficiency by developing dark colours when cool and becoming paler when the correct temperature is reached, or by flattening and aligning their bodies to the direction of the sun's rays early in the day in order to warm up, and thereby becoming active more quickly. Once the desired body temperature has been achieved, the animal may move into the shade to prevent over-heating. Thus emerges a pattern of basking, followed by activity, followed by more basking.

Fig. 1   A cage set up to provide a thermal gradient, with a 'hot-spot' and an area of shade.

16

Fig. 2   A small lizard (*Podarcis milensis*) taking up a basking position beneath a heat source.

This routine is easily observed if a small group of diurnal lizards is kept in a cage with a single light bulb at one end. Shortly after the light goes on in the morning there will be a jostling for the prime basking sites, followed by the gradual dispersal of the group as each individual reaches its preferred temperature. The time taken will depend on (among other things) the size of the individual — large bodies take longer to warm up than small ones. Other activities, such as feeding, drinking and courtship, are then pursued, with periodic returns to the basking site in order to keep the body temperature 'topped up'. Shortly after the light is extinguished in the evening, all the lizards will again be found around the basking site, this time pressing their limbs and bodies against the rocks and logs in order to soak up the last few remaining degrees of warmth retained there. It follows from this that species which habitually bask, mainly certain snakes, lizards and turtles, should have some form of radiant heat source and conveniently-placed basking 'platforms' on to which they can climb to absorb the heat.

Non-basking forms, such as nocturnal and fossorial (burrowing) species, are less able to thermoregulate, and it is to be expected

17

that their captive quarters will have to be more closely adjusted to their preferred ranges. Nevertheless, burrowing species probably move through the substrate in order to find the most satisfactory place to rest, and nocturnal species may adjust their period of activity slightly according to the prevailing temperature; for instance, they may emerge from their retreats during the early part of the night while the substrate is still warm. Unfortunately, the preferred temperature ranges for many species have not been established, and conditions in captivity must sometimes be the result of intelligent guesswork. Many species have optimum ranges which are much higher than may perhaps be anticipated, and in the past captive animals have been kept far too cool as a consequence. On the other hand, species which come from tropical regions do not necessarily require high temperatures, especially if they hail from regions of high altitude or from cool micro-habitats (for instance, in the spray of a waterfall or in an area of permanent shade). Some species have ranges which stretch from the tropics to well within temperate regions; individuals coming from one end of the range may have different preferences from those from the other.

All of these factors have to be considered when deciding which animals are to be accommodated and how their temperature requirements are best met. It should not be thought, however, that the majority of species are difficult or demanding to cater for in this respect: amphibians and reptiles are, on the whole, a remarkably tolerant and adaptable group of animals, and the parameters within which they live are to some extent flexible. This means that they will live (for a while at least) under less than ideal conditions, and provided that the means of adjusting the temperature is available losses should not occur. The behaviour of the animals is a pointer to their well-being: if they spend all of their time under the heat source they are being kept too cool, but if they retreat into the corner furthest from the source soon after it has been switched on it is too hot. The power-rating of the heat source, the amount of time it is kept on and the insulation of the cage must be attended to accordingly.

SOCIAL BEHAVIOUR

No animal lives out its life without some influence on, and by, other members of its own species. These encounters may be infrequent or continual (as with species which live in colonies), and they result in what may be loosely termed 'social behaviour'. Under natural conditions most animals are, to some extent, territorial. Territoriality is the means of sharing out resources, consisting of food, water, mates, basking sites, etc. In the wild, all these resources are strictly limited, and although in captivity they may be provided in abundance, the instincts for territorial jousting are unlikely to become suppressed. It is therefore important to provide adequate and suitable territory for each animal in order to prevent stress in those individuals at the bottom end of the pecking order, and in extreme instances this may take the form of a separate cage. Males are usually (but not always) far more territorial than females, particularly during the breeding season, when if they are to attract a mate or mates it is important that they occupy territory which will keep them well fed and in good shape. During this time, the dominant male's colours may be intensified, identifying him as an eligible territory holder.

Species which normally live solitary lives are best kept this way in captivity except when mating is to take place, but species which usually form colonies may do better if a number are kept together. If nothing else, the interactions between the various individuals will provide interest for the vivarium-keeper, and his observations will have more relevance to conditions in the field. Naturally, the limitations of space prevent the maintenance of large species in quantity, but the keen herpetologist should consider whether, given a certain amount of cage space, it is preferable to house a group of small animals rather than one or two large ones.

The successful keeping and breeding of amphibians and reptiles depend on two things: a careful study of the animals' requirements and how they can best be duplicated in the vivarium; and the animals' adaptation to an artificial environment. Thus, the so-called 'difficult' species are those whose requirements are poorly understood or which are so specialised that they cannot easily be reproduced, and the 'easy' species are those which are tolerant of a variety of conditions, or which have requirements which have been investigated and can be duplicated. Many species in the former category will hopefully become transferred to the latter one as information relating to these important factors is gathered and made available to others.

2
Obtaining Specimens and Making a Start

There are four common methods of obtaining reptiles and amphibians. They are as follows.

MAIL ORDER

Several dealers send out regular lists of reptiles and amphibians which they have in stock, together with a varying amount of auxiliary information such as size, country of origin and so on. A reputable dealer will guarantee live delivery and offer advice on housing, feeding, etc, and should also be able to provide a back-up service of food and equipment if required. The disadvantages of mail ordering are that you cannot see what you are buying, or select specimens of particular size or colouration. The dealer may offer to send particular sexes where this is possible, but there may be an extra charge for this.

PET SHOPS

Many pet shops have a fairly limited range of reptiles and amphibians, usually the commoner and more popular species. Although they may not be able to give specialised advice on caring for these, you can at least select healthy specimens and should be able to pick out the sex(es) you require. A few pet shops specialise in reptiles and amphibians (and these may also do mail order); if you are fortunate enough to have such an establishment in your area, you will have the opportunity to see a good variety of species over a period of weeks or months and so form a good idea of where your main interest lies. You can also take note of how the proprietor cares for the various species, and provided that he is not pestered continually he should be prepared to advise on all aspects of reptile and amphibian maintenance.

OTHER HOBBYISTS

By joining a society, or by personal contact, it may be possible to find a hobbyist who can offer animals for sale or exchange. His surplus stock may come from importing a group of animals not obtainable through the usual channels because they are too specialised, from a collecting trip, or through captive breeding. Animals obtained from the latter source are probably the best because they will be free from parasites and disease, and will almost certainly adapt to captivity better than wild-caught individuals. In addition, the practice of buying and selling captive-bred stock should be encouraged in order to reduce the pressures of collecting on wild populations, although captive-bred animals may be slightly more expensive owing to the considerable investment in time and resources which is often necessary to produce young animals successfully. Whatever their origins, animals from another hobbyist will usually be in good condition and should come complete with sound advice based on personal experience.

COLLECTING

Collecting reptiles and amphibians, both at home and abroad, is a separate subject from maintaining them, and is somewhat controversial. However, we are only concerned here with collecting for one's own personal use, and therefore in moderation. The advantages of collecting, as opposed to buying, specimens, are the knowledge gained of the animals' natural surroundings and habits, and of obtaining specimens which are almost certainly in excellent health and which, if treated correctly, can be brought home and housed with the minimum of stress. In order to collect effectively, a sound knowledge of the animals' range, habitat preferences and habits is necessary, as well as some measure of physical fitness, cunning and stealth. Certain items of equipment, such as snake-sticks, torches, bags, boxes, etc, will need to be made or purchased beforehand. Most importantly, documentation may be required (*see* Appendix I).

SELECTING SPECIES

Of the 10,000-odd species of amphibians and reptiles, only a relatively small proportion are suitable or available for vivarium culture. The reasons for this are manifold: many species are rare; some may be common but rarely seen; others may require a type of food which is difficult to obtain, or they may grow to a size which is not easily accommodated. Many would make excellent captives but are dull in appearance and uninteresting in habits (or may appear so to dealers and are therefore infrequently imported).

The suitability of those which are available varies according to the facilities and resources on hand. Remember that the initial purchase price is only the beginning of the demand on your purse or pocket — the animal still has to be accommodated, heated, and fed, and vets' bills may also be incurred.

As a general rule, do not buy a reptile or amphibian unless you can: accommodate it satisfactorily; still accommodate it when it has grown; provide the correct temperature, lighting and humidity for it; provide suitable food for it regularly. To enable you to do all of these things you will have to: know what it is called; find out about its natural history; or know someone who has kept the same species successfully.

Remember that some species make far more demands on your space, time and pocket than others. Choose one which suits your circumstances.

The following list contains species which are less demanding than some others and are therefore especially recommended for beginners. They are not necessarily the most attractive or desirable species of reptiles and amphibians, but they represent a cross-section of types which should thrive in the care of anyone who, though perhaps lacking in expertise, is prepared to care for his or her animals regularly and conscientiously. Most of them are inexpensive to purchase and require fairly basic accommodation and equipment. Experience gained with them will provide a good grounding, after which other, more specialised, kinds can be attempted. Furthermore, many of them will breed readily in captivity.

Newts and Salamanders

Axolotl *(Ambystoma mexicanum)*
Alpine Newt *(Triturus alpestris)*
Marbled Newt *(Triturus marmoratus)*
Red-spotted Newt *(Notopthalmus viridescens)*
Rough-skinned Newt *(Taricha tortosa)*
Japanese Fire-bellied Newt *(Cynops pyrrhogaster)*

Frogs and Toads
Clawed Frogs *(Xenopus* spp.*)*
Yellow-bellied Toad *(Bombina variegata)*
Oriental Fire-bellied Toad *(Bombina orientalis)*
Green Toad *(Bufo viridis)*
European Green Tree-Frog *(Hyla arborea)*
Grey Tree-Frog *(Hyla versicolor)*
Green Tree-Frog *(Hyla cinerea)*

Turtles and Tortoises
African Mud Turtle *(Pelusios subniger)*
American Mud Turtles *(Kinosternon* spp.*)*
Musk Turtles *(Sternotherus* spp.*)*
Carolina Box Turtle *(Terrapene carolina)*

Lizards
Leopard Gecko *(Eublepharus macularius)*
North American Skinks *(Eumeces* spp.*)*
Wall Lizard *(Podarcis muralis)*
Alligator Lizards *(Gerrhonotus* spp.*)*

Snakes
Corn Snakes *(Elaphe guttata)*
Rat Snake *(Elaphe obsoleta)*
Prairie Kingsnake *(Lampropeltis calligaster)*
Common Kingsnake *(Lampropeltis getulus)*
Gopher Snake *(Pituophis melanoleucus)*
Common Garter Snake *(Thamnophis sirtalis)*

It will be noted (perhaps with astonishment) that none of the larger spectacular snakes or lizards are included. This is because few beginners realise the spacial requirements for examples of these species once they are fully grown and I can see no point in obtaining an animal which will have to be disposed of (often with difficulty) before it attains full size. Nor is there any pleasure to be gained from seeing an animal in a cage which is much too small for it. Of the species listed, some are not always easily available – membership of a society will greatly improve the chances of finding species in which there is little commercial traffic.

On the other hand, dealers may stock a variety of species which have an immediate appeal to the beginner. Many of these should be avoided like the plague because they rarely do well, except in the hands of experienced keepers, if then. Examples are: large active frogs, which easily damage themselves in small containers; baby tortoises and turtles, which have dietary requirements which are not easily catered for; Chameleons; Agamas; large lizards such as Iguanas, Spiny-tailed Iguanas, Tegus and Monitors; large boids such as Anacondas, African, Reticulated and Indian Pythons; Asian Water Snakes *(Enhydris, Erpeton, Acrochordus)*; and of course all venomous species – lizards of the genus *Heloderma*, large back-fanged colubrids, Vipers and Cobras.

LEGAL ASPECTS

Various laws and regulations are concerned with collecting, dealing in and keeping reptiles and amphibians. Some are based on the protection of rare species, some on the conservation of complete areas and habitats, and some are concerned with the health and safety of the keeper and the public. All of these laws vary according to locality, and furthermore are in a continual state of flux; but a brief summary of the relevant information is given in Appendix I. It is vital that you establish your legal position before you attempt to collect, import or keep any reptiles or amphibians.

As an aside, it is an unfortunate fact that by listing certain species as endangered, and affording them legal protection, the authorities may give the impression that species not listed are, by omission, common, and fair game to collectors. This of course is not necessarily so, and care should be taken not to patronise the trade in rarities, whether protected legally or not.

SELECTING SPECIMENS

The selection of each specimen should be carried out with the same amount of care as the selection of species to be kept. The things to consider, in order of importance, are health, sex, age and markings. Animals in good health will be alert and lively, their eyes will be bright, and they will have no pieces of unshed skin adhering, nor large numbers of ectoparasites (*see* Chapter 7). Amphibians in particular should be free from wounds caused

24

by rubbing or rough handling — these easily become infected and are difficult to treat. The natural reaction of a wild animal when handled is to try to escape, hide or, in the case of turtles and tortoises, withdraw into their shell. Be suspicious of an animal which does not act thus, unless it is a long-term captive or of a normally bold species. If possible, ascertain that prospective purchases are feeding (a poor appetite is usually the first symptom of an ailing reptile or amphibian), but bear in mind that some species are easily put off their food for reasons other than disease.

For many species it is important to select compatible sexes even if breeding is not to be attempted; males may not live together peacefully. It may also be necessary to ensure that there are no great discrepancies in size, either within species or, if a community of species is concerned, between species. Smaller, hence younger, specimens adapt better to captivity and live longer, but may be difficult or impossible to sex, and may require a small size of food which is not readily available. Their markings and colour may not be fully developed, although in some species the juveniles are more attractive than the adults.

For species having large ranges, it may be helpful to establish the approximate site of capture of the example offered, as this could have a bearing on its temperature requirements, breeding season, or even food preferences. Similarly, with captive-bred specimens, information relating to age, previous care, and origins of the parents may be useful, if available.

PREPARATIONS

Having chosen a species which appeals to you, and which you may legally keep, and having ensured that its requirements can be met, subsequent preparations are mainly common sense. A reliable food supply must be arranged, the vivarium should be set up at least a week beforehand so that temperature, humidity and so on can be monitored, and, just as importantly, you should become familiar with the species by reading as much as possible about it, and by discussion with other hobbyists.

If the animal(s) is to be added to an existing community, either of the same or other species, it should be kept for a suitable period in a separate cage where its behaviour with regard to feeding may be observed, and where it can be examined for ecto-parasites or other signs of illness. If the animal is particularly valuable it will be worthwhile sending faecal samples to a laboratory for screening, via a vet, and many collectors like to give prophylactic treatment for certain common ailments during this quarantine period (*see also* Chapter 7). The temporary cage should be arranged as simply as possible in keeping with the animal's requirements, and precautions should be taken to prevent cross-infection whether or not disease is apparent, i.e. separate instruments should be used for cleaning, handling, etc, the cage should be as far away from the main collection as possible, and any servicing should be carried out *after* maintenance of the other animals has been completed. The actual period of quarantine is difficult to establish, but in two weeks most common problems should have become noticeable, although longer periods, perhaps up to twelve weeks, may be necessary before an animal can be cleared of disease with any degree of certainty.

The stress of moving an animal to a new environment will often affect its appetite and behaviour for a few days, so if it does not feed or is particularly restless or shy during this period this is not necessarily a sign of ill health.

3
Accommodation

The general requirements governing the accommodation of reptiles and amphibians are that the cage should be escape-proof, it must provide sufficient space for the animals to move about and behave in a natural manner, and it must allow for some measure of control over temperature, lighting and humidity, in keeping with the natural environment and preferences of the species concerned. In addition, it should be easily serviced and cleaned, and it should be designed to complement, rather than detract from, the attractiveness of its inhabitants. These stipulations are met only by careful consideration of the materials to be used, the size and shape of the cage, its furnishings, and the equipment with which its environment will be controlled.

CAGES

The best approach to the problems of designing, buying or building, and eventual setting-up of the cage, begins with an investigation into the habits and habitat of the species you wish to keep, along with reference to others who have successfully kept that species. Armed with these facts, it should not be too difficult to arrive at a suitable and practicable design; but, of course, unless a collection consists solely of closely related forms, a rather heterogeneous selection of cages will be necessary. Reptiles' and amphibians' requirements are far from standard, hailing as they do from a wide range of latitude, longitude and altitude, and having adapted for an equally wide range of climate, habitat and food. There is also a huge diversity of size within the group.

The range of vivaria which can be purchased is limited to containers for aquatic species (in other words, aquaria, with their back-up of excellent equipment for heating, lighting and cleaning), and a few basic designs for terrestrial species. By necessity, most of the latter cater for the 'average' specimen, but it may be that the species, or group of species, to which you are attracted require certain special conditions if they are to thrive. Even if an aquarium tank is appropriate, the lid with which it is supplied may not be escape-proof or well enough ventilated, and will need to be modified or replaced with something better.

One valuable spin-off from the tropical fish hobby has been the introduction of silicon sealer, and its use in the construction of all-glass aquaria and vivaria. This has opened up a whole range of possibilities in designs which would previously have been impractical or costly to implement. Using silicon sealer it is possible to make low cages for desert-dwellers, tall cages for tree-dwellers, cages consisting of land and water in various propor-tions, cages to fit into odd-shaped alcoves and corners in the home, as well as the 'conventional' rectangular cages.

The construction of a straightforward 'shoe-box' type of cage is extremely simple, especially if the glass is ordered cut to size. When ordering, remember that the width of the two end pieces is equal to the width of the base *minus* twice the thickness of the glass being used, and note that if water is to be contained certain recommended thicknesses of glass should be used depending upon its depth (*see* Table 1). Apart from the glass, all that is required is a small amount of bench space for twenty-four hours or less, a tube of the sealant, and a small quantity of adhesive tape.

The base is laid flat on the bench and a thin 'bead' of sealant is run along the bottom edge of what will become the back pane. This is now placed in position on the base and held approxima-tely upright by means of a pile of books or a convenient wall.

Table 1: Minimum recommended thicknesses for sides of aquaria (mm)

Depth of water	Length of tank						
	300	400	500	600	750	900	1000
200	3	3	3	3			
250	3	3	3	3			
300	3	4	4	4	5	5	
400		5	5	6	7	7	7
500			6	7	7	8	8
600				8	9	10	10

Then each end piece in turn has a bead of sealant applied to two adjacent edges and these are also placed on the base, the back being brought up into contact with them and taped in position. Finally, the front pane is similarly treated with sealant, but at either end of this pane the sealant is not applied to the edges but to the areas which will come into contact with the end panes. When this has been offered into position and taped, a 'fillet' of sealant is applied to the inside angles of all joints and the tank is left to cure for twenty-four hours. The cage is then ready for use unless further modification is required, for instance the fixing of lips or lugs on which a lid is to rest, or the installation of a glass divider to create land and water areas.

With a little ingenuity many attractive cages can be constructed in this way, such as the sloping-fronted cage in Fig. 3, which has a removable front providing easy access for feeding, spraying, photography and so on, and the tall, narrow cage designed to accommodate arboreal frogs, lizards or snakes on a single plant or bough. The sealant may also be used to attach equipment or furnishings to the cages or to each other.

Where appropriate, lids for vivaria may be constructed from glass, perspex, wood or metal, the exact design and method of construction varying according to the animal(s) contained, whether or not electrical fittings need to be incorporated into it, and the appearance preferred. Although some ventilation, in the form of a panel of metal or plastic mesh, will almost certainly be necessary, the lid must nevertheless be completely escape-proof, not only for the reptiles and amphibians, but also for their food, especially in the cases where this includes species of rodents and insects which would become potential household pests should they escape. It may be a good idea to incorporate a small aperture, fitted with a flap or bung, for the introduction of food without the necessity of removing the whole lid every time. It is also an advantage to have a catch of some description to hold the lid firmly in place, and in certain cases there should be provision for this to be fitted with a lock.

Having discussed the use of glass in the construction of vivaria, it should be borne in mind that this is a somewhat fragile material and can be costly when required in larger and thicker sizes. In addition, it is not a good insulator. Therefore, for the accommodation of larger species, or in situations where insulation is particularly important but all-round viewing is not

29

(a)

(b)

Fig. 3   All-glass vivaria set up for (a) semi-aquatic, (b) temperate forest, (c) desert and (d) tropical forest environments.

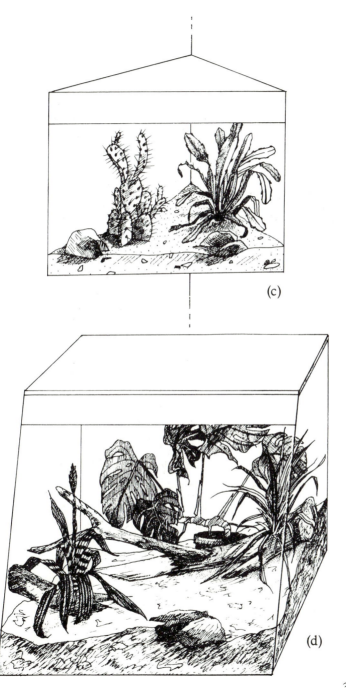

(c)

(d)

essential, the use of some other material is a more realistic proposition, perhaps using glass only for the front. Again, flexibility is at its greatest when the construction is tackled as a do-it-yourself project, and when the requirements of the eventual occupants can be borne in mind throughout the work. Plastic-faced chipboard is well suited to cages of this type, being cheap, easily worked with, readily available in a variety of widths and lengths, and above all easy to wipe clean. The most useful shape is rectangular, possibly with the facility of removable dividing walls, which add to the flexibility of the cage unit. A sliding glass front may open to the side, or slide upwards, or, if the cage is of sufficient length and the occupants are not too slender, two panes can be arranged to slide back on each other by using double track plastic channel fixed to the top and bottom (*see* Fig. 4). Upward sliding glass may create a problem if the cages are to be stacked on top of one another. One solution is to fix the channelling at each side with a slight tilt, so that as the glass is raised it also moves slightly outwards and clears the bottom of the cage above.

Care must be taken that a wooden floor does not sag in the middle, since this will prevent the front from fitting properly and may leave a gap into which a snake or lizard will be able to wedge its snout and widen sufficiently to escape. If this is a problem (it occurs mainly when objects such as rocks and logs are placed in

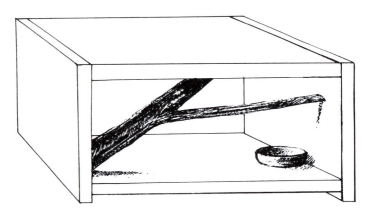

Fig. 4   A wooden cage with sliding glass front for housing snakes and other large terrestrial reptiles.

the centre of the cage), an extra leg or two may be necessary. A ventilation panel may be situated in the sides, top or back, but in such a position that the adjacent cages will not block the air-flow.

Metal vivaria are available in certain shapes and sizes, and these have the advantage of being strong, and capable of being scrubbed out if necessary. Most examples have a sliding glass front, and some have an additional 'door' in the top for feeding, etc. There may be provision for installing a light-bulb or heating element under the floor, as well as a light fitting near the top of the cage. Their biggest drawback, as mentioned above, is that they are not always perfectly suited to one's requirements, and being of metal construction they require special techniques if they have to be extensively modified, and are therefore somewhat inflexible.

Having covered the most popular types of vivaria, both commercially produced and home-built, a word or two should be said about improvised containers which are often pressed into service, and which in many cases are well suited to the keeping of reptiles and amphibians. For many years I have been using plastic seed propagators which have a shallow tray (make sure that you get the type without drainage holes), to which is added a tall transparent 'lid', thus creating a miniature greenhouse. These come in a variety of sizes, and may be usefully employed in the housing of small varieties of frogs, salamanders, lizards, and even snakes, provided that the top part rests snugly on the tray. The better types have adjustable ventilation slots in the top, and these may be used for this purpose, and also for the introduction of food and water, but when used with certain species, notably tree-frogs, geckos and snakes, mesh will have to be fixed beneath the openings.

Sweet-jars, large jam-jars, lunch boxes and ice-cream containers may all be used to provide temporary homes for surplus animals, or for rearing young, although environmental control is limited to placing the container in a room of suitable temperature, and ensuring adequate ventilation.

Outdoor accommodation, i.e. the building and use of an outdoor vivarium or reptiliary, is really beyond the scope of this book, but a few guidelines will not come amiss. A well-drained site is essential, preferably on a south-facing slope to make maximum use of the sun for both light and heat, and a rockery for basking on and hiding in, as well as a small pond, are beneficial

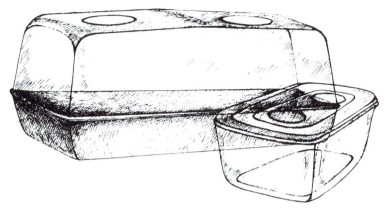

Fig. 5 A plant propagator and lunch box adapted for housing small reptiles or amphibians.

to most species. Construction of the outer wall may be of brick, timber, plastic sheeting or glass, but some escapes should be anticipated during the first few months as the new inhabitants investigate every means of climbing, leaping, or burrowing out of the 'utopia' you have created for their enjoyment. An overhanging row of glazed tiles or a barrier of plastic drainpipe will deter many of the climbers, and deep foundations will foil all but the most determined of burrowers. Leapers can be handicapped by ensuring that no plants or rock structures provide good jumping-off points. However, in spite of all these precautions, escapes are almost inevitable, although the truants will often stay in the vicinity of the reptiliary, some even returning to it either periodically or permanently. The desire to escape will be strongest in animals whose territorial instincts are being tested by overcrowding, and careful attention to sex ratios and the relative sizes of the inhabitants will go a long way towards creating a settled community.

Somewhere in the enclosure there should be some means of getting well below the surface during inclement weather. If this is achieved by an arrangement of pipes leading to the nether regions, great care must be taken to ensure that the entrances to them are sheltered, or they will otherwise provide a means for the water to enter and accumulate below. The pipes should lead to a chamber containing some insulating material, such as chopped straw or vermiculite, and in temperate regions it should be below the frost level if the animals are to use it for hibernation. It is an advantage if the chamber is accessible so that its contents may be checked occasionally, preferably during the summer when it is not occupied.

One advantage of the reptiliary, apart from the relative freedom it offers its occupants, is that a certain amount of natural food such as flies, spiders, grubs, etc, will be available (it goes without saying that pesticides, which may be harmful to reptiles and amphibians, should not be used in the vicinity of the reptiliary, if at all); but it also possesses the disadvantage that any food which you introduce will also be fair game to the local bird population. This may of course be looked upon as a bonus — a reptiliary and a bird-table combined is a definite asset to the all-round naturalist — but if the 'poaching' becomes unacceptable the only answer is to stretch black netting across the enclosure. (This may be necessary in any case as cats in particular, and possibly also rats and large birds, can play havoc with a colony of small reptiles or amphibians.) For species requiring a little more protection from the weather, an adapted garden frame, either heated or not, according to the species to be kept, or a greenhouse or conservatory, will give the animals relative freedom as well as security.

Rather less ambitious than a full-blooded reptiliary, but useful none-the-less, is a garden pond. This will accommodate several types of small amphibians and reptiles (turtles) during the summer and, if a small rockery is built around it, it may also be used to keep a semi-captive population, of amphibians at least, throughout the year – these may breed quite readily and so form the basis of a self-perpetuating colony which will be of immense interest while demanding little attention, providing that the pond is well planned and managed. An additional bonus may be the utilisation of the pond by local species, so transforming it into a miniature nature reserve.

If the pond is large enough, it should have a deep area which will not freeze to the bottom in the winter (24–30in, 60–75cm, is usually sufficient) and a shallow area where the water will warm up quickly during sunny weather and so provide suitable conditions, not only for the inmates, but also for their food, in the form of aquatic invertebrates. It is a mistake to position it underneath trees, as, apart from excluding sunlight, leaves will fall into the water and quickly transform the pond into a quagmire.

Ponds may be constructed of concrete or fibre-glass, but a butyl rubber liner provides the best means of creating a long-lasting pond quickly and conveniently. The method of construction is quite simple: a hole is dug to the required shape and lined with sand to prevent sharp stones etc. from penetrating the rubber. The liner is laid loosely across the hole, anchored around the edges with paving slabs or similar, and water is run in to weigh down the rubber into the contours of the pond. A handful of beech leaves may be placed on the bottom in order to get the biological cycle under way, but soil should be avoided. If submerged plants are considered necessary, they should be planted in individual containers which are then topped off with pebbles to prevent the compost from leaching into the water. In any case, it is important to keep such plants in check as, although one or two clumps will help to oxygenate the water and encourage small invertebrates, they must not be allowed to choke the pond to the extent that there is little or no open water available for the animals. Marginal plants, however, are important if it is hoped to breed amphibians: they provide vital cover for the young frogs and toads which are metamorphosing and so act as a dispersal corridor between the aquatic and terrestrial environments. (Suitable species are listed on page 56.)

In Britain, Northern Europe and the temperate parts of North America, such a pond and its surroundings would provide a permanent home for cold-tolerant species such as fire-bellied toads, *Bombina bombina,* and *B. variegata,* marsh frogs, *Rana ridibunda,* crested newt, *Triturus cristatus,* alpine newt, *T. alpestris* and the red-spotted newt, *Notopthalmus viridescens.* If suitable surroundings, i.e. a rockery, are also provided, a number of terrestrial species may also be persuaded to stay around the pond and use it for breeding, the most interesting of these probably being the midwife toad, *Alytes obstetricans,* although many other possibilities exist. It should be borne in mind that if there are neighbouring ponds the animals may prefer these and emigrate: apart from the disappointment of such disloyalty on the part of the animals, this could be construed as unneighbourly should the owners not share your enthusiasm for animals which, it must be admitted, are not everybody's cup of tea.

When the pond has matured, which may take several years, newt and frog tadpoles will be able to find enough naturally-occurring food for at least a proportion of them to develop without help, but in the early days, any larvae which arrive, or are introducd, will require feeding: frog tadpoles with pond pellets as sold for fish, and newt tadpoles with living food such as *Daphnia*. It should be noted that adult newts relish frog and toad tadpoles – in fact, they probably constitute their main predator in the wild – and so if a mixed community is created it would be prudent to remove some of the frog spawn or larvae to be raised elsewhere in safety.

Finally, even if space is limited, a small shallow pond (perhaps a stone sink buried to its rim in the lawn), can house one or two pairs of interesting animals and be a source of pleasure – animals living under natural conditions can form the basis of many fascinating and original observations of their behaviour.

EQUIPMENT

Having decided either exactly or approximately which species of reptiles or amphibians you intend to keep, and having therefore formulated a rough idea of what options are available regarding accommodation, the next step is to examine the various ways in which the conditions inside the cage can be manipulated in order to produce the best possible environment for your choice. The exact specifications of the equipment will vary with the type of cage and the nature of its occupants.

Heating Equipment

Heating of aquatic set-ups is well catered for by several excellent models of aquarium heater. The majority of these are combined with thermostats to give a good degree of temperature control, and they can be obtained in a variety of sizes to suit most tank capacities. For very large aquaria, two heaters and thermostats are recommended to overcome local temperature differences, although with some species this may be considered an advantage. A thermometer will be necessary to keep check on the water temperature, but this is rarely critical in the case of reptiles and amphibians (compared with some tropical fish, for instance), and

37

a rise or fall of a few degrees will have little or no effect on them, although it may mean that the heater and/or thermostat are faulty and should be checked. Species requiring a daily temperature fluctuation can be provided with an arrangement of a heater and a thermostat with a high setting which is switched off by a time-switch, allowing another unit with a lower setting to take over for a time.

Heating a terrestrial cage is likely to prove more of a problem than heating an aquarium, because in most cases purpose-built equipment is just not available. The ideal situation is that in which cages are kept in a room where the required temperature is constantly maintained, but this is rarely possible except in the case of large collections. In any case, the temperature require-ments of the various species may differ greatly. This leaves us with the alternative of heating each cage individually, the most common methods involving the use of heat-tape, heating pads or heating cables, for 'bottom' heat, and incandescent light-bulbs or infra-red lamps for 'top' heat. The heat-tapes are produced primarily for industrial uses, such as the prevention of freezing in pipes containing water or chemicals, and may be attached to a wall up to which the cages are pushed, or one may be placed along the shelf on which they stand. Advice from the makers should be sought, however, especially where the tape is to be in contact with inflammable materials such as wood or plastic. The lengths and power ratings vary, and the whole apparatus may be control-led by a thermostat, making this a first-class method of heating a number of cages grouped together; but eventually a safe method of control needs to be properly worked out.

Two pieces of apparatus from the horticultural world are adap-table to vivarium heating: these are soil-warming cables and the heat-pads designed for propagating frames. Both give out a fairly gentle heat, although the performance of the cables can be varied according to the pattern in which they are coiled; instructions to this effect are usually supplied and should be strictly adhered to. The heat-pads may simply consist of heating wire held between two pieces of foil, or this may be sandwiched between layers of silicon rubber. The power ratings of these units are fairly low, and they are therefore unsuitable for cages in which the tempera-ture must rise a great deal above that of their surroundings. If, on the other hand, the ambient temperature is likely to rise from time to time, a thermostat may be necessary to prevent overheating, but usually, after some initial experimentation to find which size pad (or pads) gives the required temperature, this is a good system.

In all methods of bottom heating, a layer of sand, soil, or gravel on the floor of the cage will help to distribute the heat more evenly, and some products can only be used if they are covered to a certain depth with some ground material, thus limiting their usefulness. Problems also arise if burrowing species are to be accommodated in such cages, unless some barrier is present to prevent them from unearthing the equipment. Heat-tapes, cables, and pads are all relatively new additions to the list of equipment available to owners of vivaria, although none of them has been designed with this use in mind. The best type of heat-pad which I have seen recently is a German model available in four sizes to suit tanks 1–4 feet (30–120cm) in length, and rated at 8 watts for the smallest, up to 35 watts for the largest. Although these pieces of equipment are not particularly cheap, they have the great advantage of being completely waterproof and can therefore be buried in a wet substrate or even used in an aquatic set-up. They are also well-made and should last indefinitely, even when used in cages containing boisterous species. As usual, they are designed and marketed with the indoor gardener in mind – with luck, purpose-built equipment along these lines will become available soon to make life more controllable and less improvised.

The use of light-bulbs for heating vivaria is a well-tried and tested method, and in spite of one or two drawbacks is still the most popular method in use. Its main advantages are its cheapness, the availability of bulbs in a wide range of power ratings, and their dual role as a source of light as well as a source of heat (but only where this is acceptable — see 'Lighting Equipment'). Other forms of radiant heat, such as the infra-red lamps used in chick brooders, are more efficient than the normal household light-bulb, and last longer, and are therefore invaluable for heating large cages, although an alternative means of lighting them then has to be found. Forced air heating is really only applicable to large collections such as those in zoological gardens, although one rather novel idea which was described some years ago involved the use of an electric hair dryer which was wired to a thermostat and used for heating a large cage. This system would also aid in the ventilation of the cage if the dryer was arranged in such a way as to draw air from outside it, but the noise generated would create problems in most instances.

Finally, on the subject of heating, sunlight is the most natural, efficient, and economical form of heating energy available. It is also the most unpredictable. Few people are in the position of being able constantly to monitor the temperature inside their animals' cages, and to move them or draw blinds accordingly, and a glass cage placed in the sun will rapidly heat up and exceed the lethal temperature limits of even desert species. Indirect sunlight, however, is of great value, but more as a source of light than of heat.

Lighting Equipment

Because lighting and heating are often provided together, by means of light-bulbs, the psychological effects of lighting are often overlooked. Many species are by nature secretive, nocturnal, or crepuscular, and are therefore used to little or no direct sunlight, and these may be kept with the minimum of illumination, but others require light of a certain intensity and quality, and in this connection the use of 'natural daylight' fluorescent tubes has become more widespread recently, and its effects studied with no small degree of interest by the reptile-keeping fraternity. It seems that lighting of this kind offers definite advantages to certain species previously regarded as 'difficult', possibly by acting as a substitute for sunlight in the production of vitamin D_3, especially in those species which are normally exposed to a great deal of sun through the activity of basking, e.g. the majority of diurnal lizards, some snakes, and many turtles. Potentially even more beneficial is the use of 'black-lights' – fluorescent tubes which produce only a small amount of visible light but a large proportion of ultra-violet. When turned on, they glow a deep blue colour, and as a means of lighting they must be supplemented by conventional tubes or lamps, but results seem to prove that with black-lights many species which were once regarded as impossible can not only be kept alive but also encouraged to breed. More significantly, the young animals can be raised to maturity without deformities and in a surprisingly short period of time (assuming that plenty of food is provided). Species which have responded well to this treatment include several of the agamid and iguanid lizards — species which were ignored by experienced reptile-keepers for many years because of their abysmal record.

Having proved its worth, the black-light is now in need of controlled investigation in order to assess its optimum use, especially with regard to duration, and distance from the animals' basking positions. At present, this information can only be guesswork, but a regime of 8–10 hours each day at about 12in (30cm) above the substrate has been used successfully to rear a group of young lizards without any detrimental effects so far. It would also be of considerable interest to know if the usefulness of this piece of equipment would solve the problems associated with the raising of other animals, such as young frogs, which seem to be plagued with a ricket-like syndrome in nine cases out of every ten. The use of black-light could revolutionise the keeping and breeding of reptiles and amphibians once more data becomes available. Certainly, the deprivation of sunlight, or an acceptable substitute, necessitates supplementary feeding of D_3 if problems associated with its deficiencies are to be avoided in species of this type.

Fluorescent lighting of any kind produces relatively more light and less heat per watt than do incandescent lights, and is therefore more efficient for this purpose. More importantly, however, it gives the option of providing light without heat, and so lighting and heating may be controlled independently if required, i.e. it is not necessary to keep the light on for an unnaturally long period in order to heat animals, nor is it necessary to keep them abnormally warm because they require light.

The intensity of light should be studied, and an approximation of the animals' natural conditions should be aimed at in this respect. Note that light from artificial sources falls off rapidly over relatively short distances — for instance, the floor of a cage that is 60 cm tall will receive only one quarter of the amount of light reaching the floor of a cage 30 cm tall, if the same light source is used. A small photographic light-meter can be used to compare light intensities in various natural situations with the conditions in the cages. The actual amount of light produced by a fluorescent tube depends to some extent on its age and colour, and there is a direct relationship between length and wattage, so that for a given size of vivarium a certain maximum output prevails, the only variables being the number of tubes placed side by side and the height of the cage.

If a cage can be positioned so that it receives as much daylight as possible this is obviously an advantage, especially if plants are to be used, provided that there is no possibility of overheating. The best position (in the northern hemisphere) is near an east-facing window where it will catch the sun's rays early in the day, but become shaded later as the temperature rises. In a south-facing room, the vivarium must be placed well away from the window.

Humidity

Assuming that water is always present in a cage, either in a container or as a result of spraying, the degree of humidity is a direct relationship between temperature and the amount of ventilation. It follows, therefore, that if the temperature is more or less constant for a given set-up, the humidity may be controlled simply by arranging for an appropriate amount of ventilation, always bearing in mind that a certain minimum amount is required to enable air to circulate and not become stagnant within the cage. Sensors which monitor the humidity and maintain it at preselected levels by means of mist sprayers are at present widely used in horticulture. Their adoption, and possible adaptation, for vivarium installation would be a worthwhile project if accurate control of the humidity were considered essential (as for example in experimental procedures).

In this chapter, examples of the various possibilities have been discussed without reference to specific animals, whereas more detailed requirements are given where appropriate in the descriptions of families, genera and species in Part II.

4
Creating
the Right Environment

Having discussed the means by which an artificial environment is created, it is now necessary to see why, and in which ways, these various parameters affect the animals, and to decide to what extent we should try to duplicate nature.

Although some areas, notably certain tropical regions, have a richer herpetofauna than others, both in terms of number of species and number of individuals, reptiles and amphibians have colonised practically every kind of existing habitat by adapting, through successive generations, to prevailing conditions. Every environment is formed by a number of factors acting upon it, and these may be divided into two groups: physical factors, consisting mainly of heat, light and humidity; and biological factors, which are the influences brought to bear by other animals sharing the same environment, and which may be potential predators or prey in some cases, mates or rivals in others, or they may act indirectly by altering some other aspect of the environment. In addition, some species are closely associated with plants, which are themselves dependent upon the same physical factors, and also upon substrate.

To complicate matters yet further, some or all of these factors may vary on a daily or seasonal scale. Therefore, although it is often possible to disregard one or perhaps more of them in captivity, the interplay of several others has to be taken into account if conditions are to approach the optimum. In this respect, some species are easier to cater for than others.

TEMPERATURE CONTROL

Because they are ectotherms, all reptiles and amphibians are particularly sensitive to temperature changes, and all species have a preferred range which they will seek out and maintain given the chance (see Chapter 1). Since exact temperatures have not been established for many species, and since, furthermore, they may vary slightly according to activity (e.g. the optimum temperature for egg formation may vary from that for digestion), it is good practice to arrange for a temperature gradient by concentrating the heat source at one end of the cage, so that each animal can thermoregulate by visiting that part of the cage best suited to it at any given time. It should also be ensured that other pressures do not exist which would tend to force it away from a preferred area — for instance, hiding places should not all be at one end of the cage (see Fig. 1).

For the species which habitually bask in nature, a light-bulb, infra-red heater or spotlight, preferably with reflectors, should be directed on to one part of the cage, forming a 'hot-spot'. This will be used by the animals to raise their body temperatures rapidly so that other activities, such as foraging, feeding, mating and so on, can be pursued for a while until another spell of basking is necessary. Temperatures directly under the light source should be in excess of the preferred range, as long as adequate space for cooling off is available, and sufficient basking sites, in the form of boughs and rocks, should be provided for all the animals of this type.

A drop in temperature at night is a natural phenomenon in most parts of the world, and an attempt should be made to simulate it; although extremes, such as those prevailing in some desert regions, are to be avoided, as the animals are unlikely to have the same facilities for counteracting them as they would under natural conditions. In practice, if the room temperature is likely to drop below the lethal limit of the species concerned, a background temperature may be provided during the night by a low-powered 'bottom-heater' of some description. This recreates a fairly natural phenomenon, as the top few inches of the Earth's surface act as a giant storage radiator by absorbing the sun's warmth throughout the day and slowly releasing it during the night. Most ectotherms make use of this by spending the night under some object such as a stone or log, or in a crevice, where warmth is retained.

Controls may be made automatic by means of a time-switch, and a small thermostat may be incorporated to avoid the possibility of overheating, but where possible the correct temperature should be achieved by using a heating unit of the appropriate power, the whole principle of the gradient system being to allow the occupants to control their own temperature.

Of course, many species do not habitually bask, and, if they hail from an environment where they are protected from severe temperature fluctuations, a more or less constant temperature may suit them better, provided it is within their preferred range, and little or no drop during the night is called for. In particular, totally aquatic species and fossorial (burrowing) species fall into this category.

A seasonal fluctuation in temperature is experienced by many species, but particularly those from temperate regions, many of which hibernate during the winter. These may be grouped into induced hibernators (those which hibernate as and when conditions dictate, and which may therefore be kept active throughout the year without any detrimental effects) and spontaneous hibernators (those which cease feeding in the autumn and become inactive even if temperatures are kept at an artificially high level). Between these two groupings are a number of species which remain fairly active throughout the winter but display a diminished appetite. This may be because they have instinctively built up food reserves throughout the summer in anticipation of a lean period which does not come. The implications of these behaviour patterns are not yet well enough understood, with regard to reproductive cycles, etc, to give cut-and-dried advice; but, in general, spontaneous hibernators should be kept at a low temperature for at least part of the winter so that their metabolism slows down sufficiently for their food reserves to last them until they begin feeding again (usually with renewed voracity) in the spring. Other temperate species may be encouraged to become slightly less active by reducing or withdrawing the main source of heat, but by providing food and water if required. This simulates conditions experienced in, for instance, the Mediterranean region, where reptiles are active throughout the winter, but only on particularly mild days.

If it is intended to hibernate the animals artificially, a refrigerator may be used, provided it can be reliably controlled to remain at approximately 5°C for temperate species, and slightly higher (approximately 8°C) for subtropical ones. Such hibernation need not be for as long as that experienced in nature, a period of two or three months being sufficient. Animals to be hibernated should be in first-class condition, and should not be fed for at least one week prior to the temperature drop, which should be gradual, as should the warming-up period. The box in which the animals are kept should have a layer of very slightly damp sphagnum moss or foam in it, and it should be inspected at least once every week to check on the condition of the animals.

Apart from anything else, a dormant period may be necessary to synchronise reproductive activity, as it is usual for some species, which congregate in communal hibernacula during the winter, to mate as soon as they emerge in the spring, before they have dispersed throughout the surrounding countryside.

It is interesting to note that animals bred and raised in captivity are often not as 'tuned in' to seasonal changes as are their wild-caught ancestors, and so adapt better to life within artificial parameters. This contributes towards the desirability of obtaining and perpetuating captive bred stock.

LIGHTING CONTROL

Since in nature the sun is the main source of light as well as heat, these two factors go hand in hand where daily and seasonal fluctuations are concerned. Therefore, in situations where it is thought necessary or advisable to alter the temperature regularly, the light cycle should be adjusted accordingly. As a guideline, species from equatorial regions require a constant light regime of 12 hours light:12 hours dark, but species from temperate regions are used to a cycle which swings from 16 hours light in summer to 8 hours light in winter. It is preferable to make the adjustments at the rate of one hour at a time, as the year progresses. Of course, if light-bulbs are being used to fulfil both roles, this will happen anyway. A time-switch may be used as with temperature control – indeed, as the reduction in temperature and light occurs at more or less the same time, a preferred arrangement is to use the same switch for both functions. The light switch may be of the type which gradually dims the light, preventing the animals from being plunged suddenly into total darkness, and a further refinement is to link both heating and lighting systems to an electronic device which senses light values outside and operates the switches accordingly, thus automatically duplicating daily and seasonal cycles (but those of your locality, not necessarily the natural range of the animals).

In an aquatic environment, temperature will not diminish noticeably during the night, owing to the heat-retaining properties of water, although light will. Therefore only the latter needs to be regulated. Semi-aquatic species which bask, such as turtles, should have their main heat source, or 'hot-spot', removed during the night.

HUMIDITY CONTROL

Our understanding of how reptiles and amphibians react to humidity or barometric changes is very limited. Some species (mainly tropical amphibians), breed during, or immediately after, rain, irrespective of the time of year. This is obviously an important consideration if an attempt is to be made to breed these species. Members of at least one family of aquatic amphibians are also stimulated to breed at the advent of the rainy season, but whether they are reacting to an increase in the water level or a sudden drop in temperature, or even to variations in the chemistry of the water, is unknown. Manipulations which vary the degree of humidity from time to time are therefore bound to be of a somewhat experimental nature, but periods of 'drought' followed by a thorough spraying or raising of the water level are worth considering if it is intended to breed species which would normally experience these conditions. Fluctuations in humidity throughout the day will automatically be brought about by temperature changes, in captivity as in nature.

Notwithstanding the above, the importance of adequate ventilation should not be overlooked: a beautifully set-up and maintained vivarium can lose much of its appeal as soon as the lid is removed, releasing a build-up of stagnant and decidedly unsavoury vapour. The problem is most likely to arise where aquaria are used as accommodation because ventilation is restricted to the lid – carbon dioxide and the other gaseous products of metabolism are heavier than air and so accumulate in the bottom few inches of the container – exactly where the animals are living and breathing (or trying to breathe). A side-effect is that it becomes very difficult to grow plants in such an atmosphere.

Where a hot, dry environment is required, e.g. in cages housing many lizards and snakes, ventilation is easily provided:

Fig. 6   A snake cage set up in the 'hygienic' style.

much of the lid can be covered with mesh and, if a spotlight or similar heat source is used, a convection current will be set up as the stale air in the tank warms up, rises and exits through the top. In cages with one or more sides made of wood it is relatively easy to incorporate a panel of perforated metal or plastic near the bottom to increase further the rate of air exchange.

This leaves us with cages containing animals which require a moist or humid environment, such as amphibians and some of the small lizards and snakes (especially those coming from rainforest habitats). Very often these cages are provided with almost no ventilation in order to maintain a high humidity, resulting in the conditions described above. It is important to realise, however, that even in areas of high humidity air is constantly moving, and that in nature stagnant air rarely accumulates. Several ways of creating a high humidity without sacrificing ventilation are available.

The simplest is to spray the tank frequently with tepid water in order to replace the moisture lost through evaporation: the disadvantage here is that the surface will dry out rapidly unless spraying is carried out very frequently indeed. An alternative method is to arrange for a portion of the cage to contain standing water, either by dividing it into two parts or by placing a container of water in it. This will only need topping up occasionally and also has the advantage of creating a humidity gradient where the animals will find the part of the cage which suits them best – in fact, quite a large number of amphibians prefer an environment which is quite dry – many toads and a number of tree-frogs fall into this category. In either of the above arrangements air circulation can be improved still further by introducing air from outside the cage using a small diaphragm pump, with tubing leading either into the water or into a corner of the land area.

The best way around the problem, however, is to circulate water around the cage in one of the ways described on page 52, which will maintain a high overall humidity, even when the cage is well ventilated.

CONTROL OF BIOLOGICAL FACTORS

The biological factors bearing on a reptile or amphibian are those about which we know least of all; therefore their control is the most difficult, and subject to widely divergent opinions. Naturally, there are certain 'undesirable' pressures on wild populations which we, as vivarium-keepers, will strive to eliminate, such as predation, disease, parasitism, competition from other species and so on; but what of other factors, such as intra-specific competition (the process by which a group of young, which may number thousands of individuals, is reduced to a manageable number comprising only the fittest) or territorial rivalry, which may produce rare glimpses of spectacular displays or unique vocalisations? How far we want to go towards the 'domestication' of any particular species is a compromise between a desire to see the animals behaving naturally in surroundings in which they are unmistakably 'at home', and the equally strong desire to give them the best possible chance of survival by nurturing them in conditions which, though hygienic, are incongruous. In addition to our own inclinations, the adaptability of the species in question and the feasibility of providing it with a semi-natural environment, there may be limiting factors — it would be impractical to provide a natural set-up for a large python, for instance, but quite possible, and perhaps essential, to do so for a small tropical frog.

Plants in particular play a large part in forming the environment: they may act as food, or they may attract and support it in the form of insects or other invertebrates; they provide shelter, shade, and in some cases egg-laying sites; they contribute indirectly to the micro-climate of an area, and when dead may accumulate and rot to form the substrate. Under captive conditions, most or all of these functions can be performed adequately by artificial substitutes which are cleaner, more easily obtained, and do not require the same amount of attention as do living plants. Many people feel, however, that plants do have their uses in certain vivaria — they serve as indicators that conditions are as they should be, they add to the general effect of a well-conceived and designed set-up, and as living things closely associated with the animals in which we invest our time and resources they are worthy of our interest.

Since, as a practical proposition, the choice of 'natural' or 'artificial' vivaria will depend to a very large extent on the type of animal to be accommodated, advice to this effect is given in the family and species accounts, and so the following notes have only

Fig. 7 Part of a planted vivarium containing bromeliads and tropical ferns.

a limited application. Bear in mind though that soil and plants provide refuges for pests and parasites, so it is particularly important to quarantine any animals destined for cages of this type.

THE PLANTED VIVARIUM

If the arrangement is to remain attractive for as long as possible, planting a vivarium or aquarium requires a certain amount of knowledge of plants' requirements, coupled with elementary horticultural technique and some artistic flair in setting the plants in such a way that they will not only find conditions to their liking but will also complement each other and the animal population of the cage.

The first decision to make is whether the plants are to be planted directly into the substrate or are to remain in their pots. The latter method is preferable if the vivarium is to contain burrowing species, as these will otherwise disturb the root systems of the plants. The pots should be of the short 'half pot' type so that they can be plunged up to their rims in a suitable substrate (leaf-mould, gravel, sand etc), and a layer of stones around the plant will discourage burrowing *inside* the pot. If the occupants are not inclined to burrow, it is possible to plant directly into the substrate. By doing this it is usually easier to group the plants attractively, and they will not require periodic removal for re-potting, although if conditions suit them they will almost certainly need cutting back from time to time.

If the habitat is appropriate, dead branches may be festooned with epiphytic plants, such as orchids and bromeliads, by using fine wire or nylon thread, and winding in a small amount of moss around their roots in order to retain some moisture. This arrangement is very suitable for the display of small arboreal frogs and lizards.

The selection of plant species will depend on the amount of heat, light and humidity required by the animals. Having obtained the plants, preferably as young specimens, cuttings or seedings, the actual method of planting is similar to that employed in bottle-gardens, terraria etc, briefly as follows.

Since there will be no drainage holes in the bottom of the cage, a good layer (4–8 cm) of broken crocks should be placed on the floor before the soil is added. The latter should contain about 10–25 per cent activated charcoal (obtainable from aquarists' suppliers) to prevent it from going 'sour'. The other constituents depend upon which species of plants are to be used, but loam-based composts are preferred because their nutrients are longer-lasting than those of the artificial peat-based varieties, and therefore the addition of artificial fertilisers, which may be hazardous, is unnecessary.

A good general-purpose mixture is loam, leaf-mould and sharp sand in roughly equal proportions, but these may be adjusted according to circumstances. Aquatic plants will usually root in a substrate of medium grade gravel, but may be difficult to grow successfully unless some nutrients, in the form of a small quantity of loam, are available. Waste products from the animals will supplement this once the tank is established. Aquatic, or emergent (marsh), plants may be grown in submerged pots if required — for instance if the bottom is to be kept free of substrate for ease of cleaning.

Whatever the environment, the aim is to achieve a biological equilibrium: a state of affairs where conditions suit both plant and animal occupants, and where neither thrives at the expense of the other. This can only happen if the cage is stocked in moderation and food is added sparingly. Naturally, watering or spraying will be necessary, and many species of reptiles prefer to drink by licking drops of water from foliage, but a dish of clean water should be available at all times.

A short list of suitable plants is given below. The ones chosen represent a very small section of those available, and are included for their interest as well as for their suitability. They require a variable amount of care and attention.

Circulating Water

Several species, especially frogs, benefit from a system in which water runs over rocks or bark, or is made to trickle across the substrate. Apart from simulating the natural micro-habitat in which some of these species live and breed, this system helps to maintain a high humidity and a certain amount of air movement, and I suspect that many other rain-forest reptiles and amphibians, for instance the smaller arboreal lizards and snakes, would also benefit. Tropical plants such as epiphytes also thrive under these conditions (assuming that sufficient light is provided). There are two basic ways of creating such a system (see Fig. 8).

(i) A small circulation pump (obtainable from tropical fish dealers) is installed inside the tank and connected to plastic tubing which takes the water to a higher level where it is discharged over a pile of rocks, logs, etc, to trickle back into the aquatic section of the tank, where the pump is situated. Unless the water is made to flow through a water-tight channel (a difficult thing to arrange), the land area must be filled with crocks up to the level of the water and the tank divider must be perforated to allow the water to get back into the section housing the pump. It is not advisable to put soil or leaf-litter into the land area because it will be washed down and fill the spaces between the crocks, restrict the flow of water back to the pump and may eventually make its way into the aquatic section and block the pump. Therefore, plants should be grown only in pots which are buried up to their rims in the crocks or, better still, grown attached to branches, logs or stones.

This arrangement is fairly straightforward and makes each cage essentially self-contained. Note that a minimum water depth of about 4in (10cm) will be required for the pump to operate efficiently, and will require changing from time to time.

(ii) Alternatively, water can drain from the tank into a 'reservoir' from which it is pumped back to its starting point, possibly through a power filter. This arrangement is more complex (it involves drilling a hole into the bottom of the tank and creating an aperture through which the pipe-work can return the water), and requires more space. Its advantages are that the water can be filtered; it is not necessary to have an area for 'standing' water inside the tank; and more than one tank can be served by a single pump/filter and reservoir.

An alternative refinement to either arrangement could be the return of the water through a sprinkler, with the pump linked to a time-switch, creating a shower of 'rain' once or twice each day — a very close simulation of rainforest conditions.

Maintenance of the system consists of topping up the water regularly, either in the tank (i) or the reservoir (ii). Failure to do this will eventually result in the pump running dry and being rendered useless.

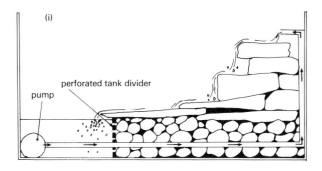

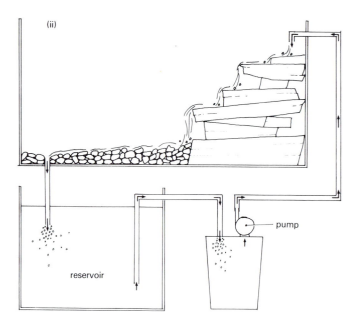

Fig. 8   Two methods of circulating water around a vivarium. (i) A closed
system – the water is pumped around by a small circulation pump
situated inside the tank. In (ii) the water drains from the tank to a
reservoir, and is returned by an externally-positioned pump, possibly
incorporating a filter.

Aquatic vivaria — tropical

Floating: *Salvinia auricularia, Riccia fluitans, Pistia stratoides* (Water Lettuce).
Submerged: *Vesicularia dubyana* (Java Moss — this does not root and may be removed and rinsed under a tap, and therefore is particularly useful), *Vallisneria spiralis, Ceratopteris thalictroides* (Indian Fern — may also be grown floating or as a marsh plant), *Cryptocoryne* species (very tough when established, prefers partial shade), *Echinodorus* species (Sword Plants — fine specimen plants for large tanks).

Aquatic vivaria — cool

Floating: *Azolla filiculoides, Limnobium spongia* (Frogbit), *Lemna minor* (Duckweed), *Lemna trisulca* (Ivy Duckweed).
Submerged: *Elodea canadensis* (Canadian Pondweed — will grow rooted or free, indispensable for breeding newts which wrap their eggs in its leaves), *Sagittaria* species.

Marsh vivaria — tropical

Cyperus species (Umbrella Plants and others — easy, attractive and recommended), *Microsorium pteropus* (an aquatic fern which will grow attached to pieces of damp wood), *Cryptocoryne* species (see above). In addition to these, many species of 'aquarium' plants are actually marsh plants, and grow particularly well in shallow water.

Marsh vivaria — cool

Acorus gramineus, Lysynachia nummularia (Creeping Jenny — very easy and fast-growing), *Sagittaria* species, *Eleocharis* species (Spikerushes).

Forest vivaria — tropical

This is the main 'houseplant' category, and suitable species abound. Especially recommended are: bromeliads, or Urn Plants, e.g. *Vriesia* species, *Tillandsia* species (mostly epiphytes including *T. usneoides* — Spanish Moss), *Cryptanthus* species (Earth Stars — mainly small terrestrial plants), and *Guzmania* species (also epiphytes, some having a number of bright red leaves). Also recommended are *Philodendron* species, *Pteris cretica* (Ribbon Fern), *Asplenium nidus* (Bird's-nest Fern), *Peperomia* species, *Maranta leuconeura* (Prayer Plant), *Selaginella* species, and for the enthusiast, several small orchids, including *Coelogyne, Dendrobium* and *Cymbedium*, the species being generally better for use in the vivarium than the hybrids.

Forest vivaria — temperate

Adiantum capillus-venerus (Maidenhair Fern), *Chlorophytum elatum* (Spider Plant), *Hedera helix* (Ivy — many varieties are available to suit almost any size or type of cage), *Pellea rotundifolia* (Cane-brake Fern). Many of the smaller native ferns are also recommended, e.g. *Asplenium* species (the Spleenworts).

Semi-desert vivaria

Crassula species, *Euphorbia millii, Kalanchoe* species, *Sanseveria trifasciata, Aloe* species, *Haworthia* species, and many other succulents.

Desert vivaria

Echinocactus, Echinopsis, Mammilaria, Opuntia and many other true cacti will stand dry conditions but need some water occasionally.

The reptiliary

The pond: *Nymphaea* and *Nuphar* (Water-lilies), *Hydrocharis morsus-ranae* (European Frogbit — this dies down in the winter), *Elodea canadensis, Lemna minor* (Duckweed — may become troublesome).
Damp areas: *Iris kaempferi, Iris pseudacorus, Primula denticulata, Mimulus moschatus* (Common Musk), various rushes and sedges. Ground cover: various grasses, such as *Festuca ovina* (Sheep's Fescue), *Erica* and *Calluna* (Heathers — but note that some species only grow if the soil is lime-free), *Hosta* species,

Dryopteris filix-mas (Male Fern) and other ferns.

The rockery: *Hebe pinguifolia, Dianthus* species, *Armeria maritima* (Thrift), *Sempervivum* species (Houseleeks), *Sedum* species.

For more information regarding available species and their preferences, the reader is referred to one or more of the reference works listed in the bibliography. These give far more comprehensive lists than there is room for here.

Other 'props' such as rock and stonework, dead branches, driftwood, bark etc, whether used in conjunction with plants or on their own, are helpful in creating a natural effect. As these objects are inert, except possibly in aquaria, their selection is based on personal taste, but rocks should consist of a single type, e.g. limestone, slate, in order to look natural, as should pieces of dead wood. A hotch-potch of different shapes, colours and textures completely spoils the appearance of an otherwise well-stocked vivarium.

Where certain delicate aquatic animals are involved, great care must be taken to avoid the introduction of objects that will seriously alter the chemical properties of the water. Pieces of wood should be well scrubbed beforehand, and then frequently inspected for signs of decomposition. Softwood types are more prone to rot than others, and these should be avoided. Pieces of roots often make particularly attractive decorations, and are usually quite hard. Most rocks merely require a thorough washing; even soluble types such as limestone dissolve so slowly as to be of little or no concern, although very crumbly varieties are best avoided.

5
Foods and Feeding

As almost everyone in these days of calorie-counting knows, food consists of different components, each required by the body for its various functions, and therefore an essential part of the diet. These components, basically proteins, carbohydrates, fats, vitamins and minerals, are not always present in the right amounts or proportions; so whereas some species of animals may have to eat several varieties of insects and possibly some plant material before their bodies can extract and assimilate their quota of essential ingredients, other species, which feed on higher animals, for instance rodents, may take in a full complement of their requirements in one meal, and may therefore thrive indefinitely on a single prey species.

For healthy animals, especially those from which it is hoped to breed, it is essential that acceptable and nutritious food is available at the right time and in the right amounts. Some species are very adaptable in their feeding habits whereas others are remarkably specialised, but if doubt exists about a species' exact requirements, the choice of a variety of food items may enable each animal selectively to 'balance' its intake and thereby minimise the chance of a deficiency in one or more components.

VEGETABLE FOOD

Herbivores, consisting mainly of the terrestrial chelonians (tortoises), and certain lizards, for instance the Green Iguana, are relatively easily catered for. Their most important requirement is a variety of foodstuffs, including lettuce and other greens, soft fruit (including tinned varieties), and, for some species, a certain amount of roughage in the form of hay or coarse grass etc. The food intake of these species is high compared with that of carnivorous species, and they should be fed at least once every other day, and preferably every day. No special preparation of the food is necessary except to wash it and otherwise ensure that it is completely free from toxic chemicals such as insecticides.

Supplementary vitamins and minerals (see below) are especially beneficial to animals in this category, and are easily mixed with the food, which is chopped up and presented in a dish or tray. Many herbivorous species are found to have small amounts of insect remains in their stomachs, presumed to have been eaten accidentally along with grass and foliage, and it may be useful to add a certain amount of animal protein to the food in the form of crushed insects, minced meat, or tinned pet-food.

ANIMAL FOOD

Carnivores, taken collectively, eat food ranging from microscopic aquatic life to fairly large mammals. The food may be bred, purchased or collected, each method having its advantages and disadvantages.

Breeding Food

Several species of insects and other invertebrates are suitable for culture and a home-grown supply can be useful, firstly to avoid the possibility of commercial supplies drying up, and secondly because by producing one's own, all stages, from minute nymphs or larvae to adults, are then available, thus providing suitable food for a wide range of species and ages. On the other hand, it is usually less time-consuming to buy or collect food items, and time spent breeding food is time which may be better spent observing or maintaining one's reptiles and amphibians, not to mention the extra space, cages and electricity required. Therefore, a system of buying and/or collecting the majority of food while maintaining a small breeding colony of one or two invertebrate species is recommended.

The breeding of larger items of animal food, such as mice, rats, fish and so on, is generally so onerous a task that most collectors are happy to leave this to specialist breeders and dealers and to buy in as required, unless of course these animals form a separate, but complementary, interest.

The most commonly cultured invertebrates are Brine-shrimp (*Artemia*), Water Fleas (*Daphnia*), White-worm (*Enchytreus* species), mealworms, and crickets. Flies may be hatched from shop-bought maggots but are far from suitable for home culture. Some other kinds of insects, such as stick insects, are not prolific enough for most purposes, excellent food though they are. The production of some of these species is described briefly; culture methods for other species may be sought in books and magazines catering for the entomologically-minded. At all times, the jars, boxes or cages containing the cultures must be kept scrupulously clean, and food and water must be uncontaminated by chemicals or pests such as mites.

BRINE-SHRIMPS

Artemia salina, Brine-shrimps, are small marine crustaceans whose eggs can withstand long periods of desiccation. These eggs may be purchased in small tubes containing several thousand eggs from tropical fish dealers. In order to hatch them and produce the very small larvae (known as nauplii), which are an invaluable food for newly hatched newt and salamander larvae, it is necessary to sprinkle some of them on to the surface of a strong salt solution (30–40 g per litre) in a jar or beaker, and if possible to aerate it. At 25°C most will have hatched in 24 hours, and if a light is placed near the container the nauplii will be drawn towards it and will be seen as a shimmering cloud of moving orange specks. They may then be siphoned off and caught in a very fine net, and washed in fresh water before being fed to the tadpoles. As they do not live for long in fresh water small numbers should be added frequently, and a new bottle or jar set up every day will provide a constant supply of shrimps.

WATER FLEAS

Daphnia, or Water Fleas, of which there are several species, are also crustaceans, and are found in most bodies of permanent or semi-permanent fresh water. They are an excellent food for large newt and salamander larvae and also for several other small aquatic amphibians. Unlike Brine-shrimps, they will live for quite a long time in the aquarium if they are not eaten straight away. Culturing them is not too reliable, but may be attempted if a regular supply is required.

Their container should have as large a surface area as possible, and be filled with rain or pond water. Before the *Daphnia* are added the water should be allowed to stand for a few days and be seeded with food, consisting of algae, yeast suspension, homo-genised spinach, or peas. As the *Daphnia* eat the food particles the water will become clear, showing that more food is required, and, although large quantities will be required once the culture gets going, care should be taken not to overfeed. The *Daphnia* should be harvested and used regularly to prevent overcrowding, but even if every precaution is taken cultures have a habit of dying out for no apparent reason, so it is wise to have more than one going at a time.

WHITE-WORMS

Enchytreus species, White-worms, grow to about 2 cm in length and live among decaying vegetation, but may be purchased as a starter culture from tropical fish dealers or by mail order. They may be cultured in covered plastic or wooden seed-trays filled with damp soil containing plenty of humus or leaf-mould. The worms are introduced into a small depression and food is placed on top of them. This may consist of damp rolled oats (porridge oats), wheat-flakes, chick-mash, brown bread or similar, and should be added sparingly to ensure that it is eaten before it can decompose. Small fragments of glass or slate are placed over the feeding sites and worms may reliably be found beneath these whenever required, but a proportion of the worms should always be left or the culture will soon die out.

MEALWORMS

Mealworms are the larvae of the Flour Beetle, *Tenebrio molitor*. They may be bred in containers having well-fitting but ventilated lids, and require a medium of chicken meal or similar. Breeding them is simply a matter of introducing a number of the adult beetles into a container which has an inch or two of the food covering the bottom. A layer of sacking or cottonwool is placed over the food, and if scraps of vegetables are placed on this occasionally there is no need to provide drinking water. After about one month the adults will have laid their eggs, and at a temperature of 25–30°C these will develop into large mealworms 12–16 weeks later, more food having been added in the meantime if necessary.

A new culture started every month with about 100 adults will yield about 100–200 g of larvae (approximately 2,000). If fewer worms are required it is possible to supply these from a single

Fig. 9 Larvae, pupae and adult of the mealworm beetle, *Tenebrio molitor*.

culture by introducing adults at intervals to start with, then ensuring that a certain number of larvae are allowed to pupate and start another generation. In this way, all stages from egg to adult will be present at any given time, but food will need to be added as necessary. Eventually, the top inch or two of the culture will have to be scooped off for sub-culturing, and the rest, consisting mainly of the dust-like droppings, disposed of.

Note that mealworms contain very little usable calcium, and animals fed entirely upon them may develop dietary deficiencies. In addition, their hard exo-skeletons make them rather indigestible to many animals, although this problem may be overcome by using only those which have recently moulted, recognisable by their soft, white appearance.

WAXWORMS

Waxworms are the larvae of the greater wax moth, *Galleria mellonella*, which is a pest of beehives. In appearance they are white and plump, and burrow quickly into their food if exposed to light. Waxworms are sometimes available commercially, but cultures take up little space and have the advantage of providing food in a range of sizes. They are relished by all insectivorous lizards and frogs and are a highly recommended food.

Culture methods vary, some being quite elaborate, but the following has been found to be satisfactory. The larvae, when purchased, will be living in a mass of culture medium, held loosely together by the webs which they spin. There will usually be sufficient uneaten food to maintain them until they pupate. The whole mass is placed in a plastic lunch-box which has two or three 1-inch (2.5-cm) diameter holes cut in the lid, each covered with very fine metal gauze (similar to that illustrated in Fig. 5). The moths will emerge after a few weeks and mate almost immediately − the box must be opened with care at this time! They lay their eggs around the edge of the box lid in a narrow strip containing many hundreds of eggs. This strip can be lifted off of the plastic with a fingernail and placed in a similar box containing about 2 inches (5 cm) of fresh medium (a strip about 2 inches long will contain enough eggs for a single culture). The medium consists of wholemeal flour and powdered yeast in the proportion of 20:1. To this is added a mixture of equal parts liquid (clear) honey and glycerol until the medium holds together reasonably well if squeezed. When the eggs hatch

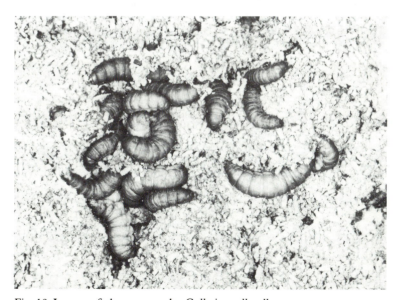

Fig. 10 Larvae of the wax moth, *Galleria mellonella*.

the larvae will burrow down into this and nothing will be seen for a few weeks, but they grow rapidly and may require sub-dividing into fresh cultures as they run out of food. Young waxworms can be harvested at any time, ensuring that enough are left to start the next generation (20–50 will be more than enough to satisfy even a large collection of reptiles and amphibians, potentially producing over 6,000 larvae). At 30°C the life-cycle from egg to egg takes about 6 weeks: two or three cultures started at intervals will ensure a regular and adequate supply and, if a surplus is generated, they will keep for several weeks if kept cool (10–15°C).

Note that the newly-hatched larvae are so small that they can pass through the gap between the box and its lid. In my experience, if the box is kept somewhere light they prefer to burrow into their food rather than do this; but, if necessary, the boxes can be stood in trays of water in order to prevent stray larvae from 'migrating'. They are only likely to become a pest if potential food is left lying around.

CRICKETS
Crickets of several species are suitable for culture, and most are acceptable food to reptiles and amphibians. The adults are

Fig. 11 House crickets, *Acheta domestica*.

winged, and the females may be recognised by a long spike, the ovipositor, projecting from the end of their abdomens. An old aquarium is a suitable container for breeding these; if it is deeper than 30 cm and has smooth sides there is no need to use a lid. The bottom should be covered with a thin layer of sawdust or vermiculite, and plenty of crumpled newspaper put in one end for the crickets to hide in. They can be fed on chicken meal, crushed dog biscuit or similar food, and slices of vegetable may be added occasionally.

A pad of cotton wool is thoroughly moistened and put in a shallow dish (petri-dish) for the crickets' water supply. The adults will also lay their eggs in this, and two or three times each week the dish and pad should be removed and covered, and a fresh pad substituted. At 25°C the eggs will hatch in about 3 weeks, and unless the small nymphs are to be fed immediately to very small animals they should be transferred to a fresh cage and treated in the same way as the adults. The complete life-cycle takes about 3 months at 25°C, and by careful planning a small colony can provide a constant supply of crickets at any stage of development.

When required, they are shaken from the newspaper into plastic beakers or other suitable containers, and may then be placed in a refrigerator for 5 or 10 minutes in order to slow them down before being added to the vivarium. This makes them easier for slow species to deal with, and reduces the risk of them escaping to set up home in an inaccessible corner of the vivarium.

A word of warning. Crickets, especially the brown species, *Acheta domestica*, are partly carnivorous. It is by no means unheard of for them to destroy a clutch of reptile eggs before it has been found, or even to kill or mutilate newly-born lizards or animals which are weak and relatively helpless, e.g. when torpid at night or when having difficulty in sloughing. Even if only small crickets are introduced, any that are not eaten immediately may thrive unnoticed in the favourable environment of a vivarium and eventually grow big enough to cause damage. A further hazard exists in planted tanks where they may set up home amongst the roots of plants and eventually kill them. The answer to all of these problems is to use only crickets of appropriate size, and in numbers which can be 'mopped up' almost immediately by the animals, and to avoid creating too many nooks and crannies in the vivarium.

FLIES

Flies are not recommended for home breeding for obvious reasons, but their larvae (maggots) may be purchased from fishing bait suppliers and allowed to pupate and subsequently emerge. The adult flies, or imagos, may then be fed to small amphibians, lizards etc, preferably after having been given one or two meals to increase their nutritional value. In this way, various species may be produced cheaply and in large numbers without the obnoxious side-effects usually associated with culturing flies. The most commonly available species are, in order of size, *Musca domestica*, the House-fly, *Lucilia* species, the Greenbottle, and *Calliphora* species, the Bluebottle or Blow-fly. All of these may be dealt with in much the same way.

The larvae are mixed with a handful of bran or sawdust and placed in shallow dishes or trays, in which they will pupate in a day or two. The dishes are then placed inside a fly-bag where they will eventually emerge. This consists of a square net or muslin bag measuring approximately 50 × 25 × 25 cm with a tube, or sleeve, sewn into one end. The bag is suspended inside a purpose-built wooden frame by means of loops at each

Fig. 12 Larva, pupa and adult of a fly, *Lucilia* sp.

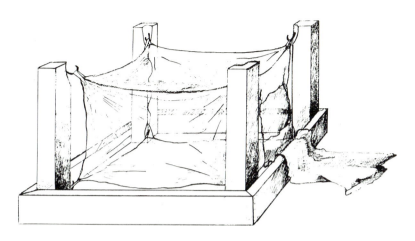

Fig. 13 Nylon mesh bag and stand for rearing flies.

corner (*see* Fig. 13). The sleeve is kept closed with a knot except when catching flies (best achieved in a plastic beaker with a snap-on lid) or when adding food, which consists of strips of liver for the two largest species, and a mash of bran and milk for the House-fly. Small dishes containing the food must be changed daily, as the flies will lay their eggs on it and these must be prevented from hatching. A pad of cotton wool placed on top of the bag and kept permanently moist will supply drinking water, or the bag may be sprayed daily. Large numbers of flies may be hatched at one time and stored for several weeks in plastic cups in a refrigerator.

The somewhat elaborate measures necessary to produce flies in this way are compensated for by the huge numbers produced in a small amount of space at very little cost, and by the high nutritional value of this food.

Purchasing Food

Most of the species mentioned above may be purchased through aquarium suppliers or reptile and amphibian dealers, and for most people this will be the most convenient method of obtaining them, although slightly more expensive.

Additional 'live' food available through suppliers are *Tubifex* worms, which are small, red, mud-dwelling worms, collected commercially and marketed as tropical fish food, and which are a favoured food of newts and small turtles. They may be chopped up by repeatedly cutting into a clump with a pair of scissors for feeding to newt and salamander larvae. Owing to their rather unsavoury origins, *Tubifex* worms can be a source of infection, but this may be avoided if they are well washed in fresh water. They may be kept alive for quite a long time in cool running water, for instance in a beaker into which water is dribbled slowly and allowed to overflow.

Fish-eating snakes should be persuaded to eat small dead fish (whitebait, for instance), which may be stocked for this purpose by dealers, or obtained from fishmongers. Alternatively, many species will accept fish which has been cut into strips of a convenient size and shape. Wherever possible, each strip should contain some bone, and this may be achieved by using flatfish and slicing them transversely.

Biological suppliers may be able to supply frozen frogs if necessary, and frozen mice, rats and chicks are usually available from specialist reptile dealers.

The moral question of whether or not to feed live vertebrates to snakes is very controversial. In Britain and Eire, and possibly elsewhere, prosecutions have been brought against people known to have done so, yet virtually every zoo, dealer and private collector will have resorted to this method of feeding at some time or other if it has been found to be necessary. A responsible attitude would seem to be to feed only dead prey unless a captive was in real danger of starving to death through want of live food. Every live food-animal should be removed from a cage immediately if a snake shows no interest in it, and provided with adequate accommodation, food, water, bedding and warmth until it is to be used. Of hundreds of rodent-eating snakes kept over the years, I cannot remember one which could not eventually be persuaded to accept dead prey. If keepers of snakes are in doubt as to the legal position of feeding live mice, rats, fish etc to their animals, they are strongly advised to seek expert advice pertaining to their particular country and circumstance.

Apart from the moral issue, the feeding of dead prey has several advantages: live rats etc have been known to injure or kill snakes with which they have been left; dead prey may be purchased in bulk and stored frozen until required (but must be properly thawed before feeding or enteritis may ensure); and the task of maintaining furry (and often smelly) animals is eliminated, leaving more time to enjoy reptiles and amphibians.

Collecting Food

Although not often resorted to these days, the collection of at least some food is recommended because a far greater variety of food thus becomes available, and in addition it encourages an interest in, and an understanding of, other groups of animals associated with reptiles and amphibians. Its disadvantages are unreliability of supply, the amount of time involved, and the risk of introducing food which has been contaminated with pesticide, herbicide or other toxic substances. As a rule, only the smaller food items will be collected, but small birds and mammals freshly killed by traffic may also be used provided that the possibility of poisoning can be ruled out, and the bodies are frozen for a few days to eliminate ecto- and endoparasites. Small species of fish may be collected, using a pond net, but make sure that there are no laws regarding the catching and taking of such animals. Frogs, newts, lizards etc, although figuring in the diets of some species (mainly snakes), are not likely to be collected for feeding purposes except in very exceptional circumstances, when conservation laws and regulations should again be checked.

When collecting smaller items, always collect well away from grass verges, hedges and other areas which may have been recently sprayed or contaminated by traffic fumes.

A variety of aquatic invertebrates, including *Daphnia, Cyclops,* and midge, mosquito and other insect larvae, may be collected by using a fine-mesh pond or dip net, preferably one tapering to a point at the apex. The net is simply swished around a few times then emptied into a bucket containing clean water from the pond or stream. Animals living in fairly fast flowing waters, such as the freshwater shrimp, *Gammarus,* which is an excellent food for many species, are usually adapted for living beneath rocks and stones where they are not liable to get swept away by the current. They may be collected by placing the net slightly downstream and then kicking lightly at the substrate. Any of the animals thus disturbed will end up in the net.

Fig. 14 Coffee jar with mesh lids of varying sizes to sort insect food.

Before using any of the invertebrates or fish collected from ponds or streams, ensure that none of them is a potential secondary host to parasites of the amphibians or reptiles to which they are to be fed. This is more likely if food is collected in areas where the latter are found, because most parasitic worms etc are host-specific and their ranges coincide with those of their host.

Terrestrial insects may be caught or trapped by several methods. Probably the most productive is sweeping with a large butterfly net amongst long grass and other herbage, where a large number of invertebrates may be collected if conditions are right. The catch is transferred to a glass or plastic jar, and for a prolonged foray several jars will be needed. Sorting the catch according to size is easily done, as follows: place the jar(s) in a refrigerator for a few minutes to subdue the insects, then change the lid for another with an insert of mesh of the appropriate size (*see* Fig. 14). Now the insects can be shaken into the vivarium, the mesh retaining those which are too large. If several different sizes are required in a number of vivaria, a series of lids with different mesh sizes can be used, starting with the one with the smallest apertures and working up.

Smaller numbers of insects may be collected by hand and kept in small containers, or they may be sucked into a flask or tube using a 'pooter' (*see* Fig. 15). Alternatively, whole leaves which have become heavily infested with aphids etc can be plucked

Fig. 15 A 'pooter'. By sucking sharply through the short tube, small invertebrates are drawn into the flask through the long tube. The fine mesh covering the outlet prevents them from being swallowed!

and placed in the cage to be picked clean. Moths and other night-flying insects are attracted to lights and it is not difficult to devise a trap which exploits this fact. The simplest consists of a sheet hung up with a lamp behind it. Insects are attracted to the glow and settle on the sheet, from which they can be picked by hand and placed in a tin or box.

SUPPLEMENTS

Either because they lack variety in their food, or because they are deprived of sunlight, or both, many captive reptiles and amphibians show signs of deficiency of one or more of their essential food components. This may be apparent in their appearance (for instance a lack of colour, or minor deformities) or merely in reduced vigour and general debility (the animal shows loss of appetite, lethargy and abnormal behaviour).

Although these ailments are dealt with in Chapter 7, the methods of preventing them, or of correcting slight problems, consist of improved feeding. Where possible, a more natural diet should be substituted, but often it is necessary to resort to the addition of artificial supplements to compensate for an inadequate or unnatural diet. These may be liquid or powdered substances, and may be sprinkled over food, added to drinking water, or administered directly to the animal orally. Some supplements consist of one or two vitamins or minerals only, whereas others contain a whole range of these substances and are known as multi-vitamin or multi-vitamin with mineral substances. Since the exact dietary requirements of many species are not known, the latter type is usually preferred.

Examples are Vionate and Pervinal, which are powders, and Abidec which is a liquid. Other similar brands may be sought at chemists or drug-stores where they are sold primarily for children, and in pet shops where their main market is dog and cat owners. Preparations designed specifically for reptiles, e.g. 'Nekton-rep' and 'Vitalife', are now becoming available in Europe and North America. These contain vitamin D_3 which is needed by reptiles (as opposed to D_2, which is needed by mammals), and should therefore be more suitable. Some experimentation with dose-rates is still necessary, however. Dosages are extremely difficult to suggest. As a prophylactic measure, i.e. for animals which show no signs of deficiency, enough Abidec to colour the drinking water a pale straw colour once per month, or a light dusting of multi-vitamin powder on every alternate feed, is about right. If signs of deficiency are noticed, the amounts, or the frequency of dosing, may be stepped up gradually until an improvement is seen. In serious cases a vet will have to be consulted. A few guidelines for the feeding of supplements to the various orders are given below. Note also the remarks concerning the use of 'natural daylight' and black-lights in the section on lighting.

NEWTS AND SALAMANDERS

A variety of foodstuffs should be easily obtainable, therefore supplements will be unnecessary. Otherwise, powder may be dusted on the food of terrestrial species.

FROGS AND TOADS
Powder sprinkled on the food is beneficial unless they are fed largely on sweepings, in which case it will be unnecessary.

TURTLES AND TORTOISES
These easily become subject to vitamin and mineral deficiencies, especially of vitamins A and D, and a calcium : phosphorus imbalance. In growing animals this produces soft and deformed shells. Vitamin and mineral powder at the rate of 1 mg per g bodyweight may be added to the food together with extra calcium in the form of calcium carbonate, i.e. powdered chalk. Some species will take land and water snails, complete with shells, and these are obviously beneficial. Pelleted foods are available for aquatic and semi-aquatic turtles, and these contain all the vitamins and minerals necessary; they may be used without additional supplements, provided that they are palatable to the turtles.

LIZARDS
Basking species are especially prone to dietary problems unless a vitamin and mineral powder is sprinkled on to the food, or vitamin drops are added to the drinking water. Females of some species will voluntarily eat pieces of crushed egg-shell or dried and crushed cuttlefish bone, and store this material for the production of eggs.

SNAKES
Apart from a few fish-eating species which may suffer from a lack of Vitamin B (*see* p. 96), and a very few insectivorous species which may become slightly deficient in calcium, phosphorus and Vitamin A, snakes do not require any food supplements whatever.

METHODS OF FEEDING

Most small species of frogs, toads, newts, salamanders, turtles and lizards may be fed *ad lib* on a daily basis. If a day passes without food being offered, no harm will be done. Long absences, however, will require some forward planning in the form of either a large feeding of live food which will live in the vivarium for the required period, or the help of a neighbour.

The correct amounts of food required will have to be arrived at by trial and error, an appropriate amount being added initially and the occupants being left to eat it. If uneaten food is present the next day, the amount may be reduced; if on the other hand it is avidly devoured immediately it is introduced, the amount should be increased. Apart from live insects etc, any uneaten food should be removed after a few hours (less in the case of certain aquatic species whose environment would soon become fouled by rotting food).

Large species may be fed less frequently — two or three times weekly. In the case of medium to large snakes, a meal every one to two weeks is adequate, provided the animal is healthy and growing steadily. Many amphibians and reptiles are stimulated to feed by movement, and groups of animals are liable to become frenzied when food is offered, biting and grasping each other in the mêlée. This often results in wounds which may take considerable time to heal, and in extreme cases a large animal may kill or even swallow a smaller cage-mate. These animals must be carefully watched during feeding, and as a general rule animals of widely differing size should not be kept together, even if of the same species. An additional problem which arises with snakes is that two specimens will sometimes begin to swallow an item of food from opposite ends. When they meet in the middle one may engulf the other, therefore always observe snakes when they are feeding if there are two or more in a cage.

Occasionally an animal is obtained which is reluctant to feed. This may merely be due to the trauma associated with its capture, shipping and subsequent new surroundings; it is also commonly caused by too low a temperature, which is easily corrected. If the problem persists, however, several 'tricks' may be employed to start it feeding once more. The simplest method is to offer as wide a variety of food as possible in order to tempt it. If by doing so it is persuaded to eat something not easily obtainable, it will gradually have to be weaned back on to something more convenient, either by offering the two foods together and gradually reducing the proportion of the former one, or by transferring the scent of the first food on to the second. For instance, a snake which will only take lizards may be fooled into taking dead mice if a lizard is rubbed over the mouse's skin in order to make it smell like a lizard. Another method would be to feed it a lizard and as soon as it has eaten it, and while it is still in

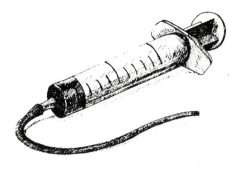

Fig. 16 A plastic syringe adapted for force-feeding snakes etc by the addition of a length of soft rubber or plastic tubing.

the right mood for eating, introduce a mouse. Snakes which only eat other snakes, of which there are a few, will sometimes take dead mice if they are wrapped in the sloughed skin of another snake.

Many species are shy feeders, and will only feed if provided with a darkened box, or a secluded corner in which the food is placed. Animals which have recently fed, and especially snakes, should not be handled or otherwise disturbed after a big meal or they may regurgitate it and be reluctant to feed again for some time.

Occasionally an animal which has been feeding well will suddenly stop. This may have several causes: it may be sick, it may have over-eaten and begun a self-imposed fast, it may have become 'bored' with a monotonous diet, or its built-in clock may have told it to stop feeding and hibernate, even though summer conditions are being artificially maintained. In addition, reptiles, especially snakes, are inclined to cease feeding if they are about to slough their skin, or if they are gravid or pregnant. If there is a natural reason for the fast, let matters run their course — cool the animal for a hibernation period if it requires it, or allow it to lose a little weight, but if the fasting still persists then a medical reason should be sought. The following are some of the many problems which can cause a loss of appetite: endoparasite infestation, mouth-rot (necrotic stomatitis), or mechanical damage. All require urgent medication before normal feeding can be expected.

Force-feeding

If all else fails, force-feeding may be resorted to. In its simplest form this entails opening the animal's mouth, inserting an item of food, then carefully returning it to its cage. This may be sufficient to stimulate feeding. If the animal continually drops the food, the next step is to hold it gently but firmly, and by using a rounded glass rod or similar implement carefully push small items of food down the throat and into the stomach, which in snakes is about one third of the way along the body. It may then be necessary to hold the mouth closed and gently massage the throat for a few seconds to prevent the food from being ejected.

If both the above methods fail, a liquid food, based on raw egg yolk with homogenised liver and vitamin and mineral additives, can be introduced by means of a syringe fitted with a length of rubber or PVC tubing, which is lubricated with egg yolk and passed down the throat and into the stomach. In this way, drugs etc can also be given, but care should be taken not to stress the animal unduly, nor to continue force-feeding longer than necessary.

WATER

Every species, even those coming from arid desert regions, should have a bowl of fresh, clean drinking water available at all times. It should be ensured that ground-dwelling forms can find it, and that it is shallow enough to allow them to drink from it, possibly by plunging it to its rim in the substrate. Certain species, notably chameleons, are loath to drink from a bowl but will lap droplets of water from foliage. These should be catered for by spraying the cage two or three times every day, or by individually offering water from a pipette, which they will soon learn to lick. Some terrestrial species require a container which they can sit in and submerge themselves completely, especially prior to sloughing their skin. It may be desirable to place a stone or twig in the bowl to prevent the animals or their prey from drowning.

OVERFEEDING

Under natural conditions, a balance exists between the amount of energy expended in catching food and the nutritional value of that food. Thus the animal maintains itself in reasonable condition and at the same time grows, reproduces and so on at a fairly steady rate. In captivity, however, food is normally available with little outlay of energy; thus there is a very real danger that the animal will eat more than is good for it. In addition, many species have a period of enforced fasting during which time they use up food which their bodies have stored during a period of plenty — this again does not often occur in captivity. Obese animals are of little use for breeding, nor do they live as long as those which are lean, so an effort should be made to regulate food so that obesity does not occur. A swollen tail can be a sign of obesity, as can fat deposits round the neck and upper limbs. If necessary, food can be withheld for several days or even weeks if an animal becomes overfed, when it will eventually return to its normal sleek and active self. Species that normally hibernate store food reserves, and if a dormant period is arranged for them they will feed with renewed vigour when they are warmed up again in the spring.

6
Breeding

More than anything else, the successful breeding and rearing of any animal species is a yardstick by which the keeper can measure his or her skill in creating the right environment, and in practising good management for that particular species. In addition, at a time of public concern over the dwindling numbers of wild animals, species which lend themselves to captive breeding, and subsequent distribution amongst other enthusiasts, have much to recommend them, and there should be no reason why a long list of amphibians and reptile species is not among these.

The last ten to fifteen years have seen an enormous advance in our knowledge of the conditions necessary for breeding amphibians and reptiles. Up until then, they were bred more by accident than design, and often in spite of rather than because of the way in which they were kept; but at the present time many species are known to be fairly easily bred if housed and fed within more or less precise guidelines. An important aspect in this relatively new approach to the hobby is the wide and speedy dissemination of data through a growing network of society newsletters and journals.

It may be encouraging to bear in mind that it is an inherent desire in all animals to reproduce, and in so doing to project their genes forward into the next generation. The task, therefore, is not one of 'making' them breed, but rather of ensuring that the prevailing conditions do not prevent them from doing so.

Where appropriate, detailed information on breeding is given under each species, genus, family or order in the second part of this book, but certain techniques are common to several or all of the orders and are described here in order to prevent repetition later on.

SEX DETERMINATION

Differences between the sexes are either primary, i.e. due directly to the presence or absence of the various sex organs, or secondary, i.e. hormone dependent, resulting in differences in body shape, colour or behaviour, and are often linked with courtship, and therefore more obvious in sexually mature animals, especially during the breeding season (see Table 2 and Figs. 17 to 22).

Table 2: Common methods for sex determination in reptiles and amphibians

Order	Males	Females
Newts and Salamanders	Enlarged cloacal margins. Crests, bright colours, and tail filaments in some species during breeding season.	More rotund body shape.
Frogs and Toads	Usually nuptial pads in breeding season, and vocal sacs (wrinkled or grey throat).	More rotund body shape.
Turtles and Tortoises	Concave plastron and longer tail. Occasionally smaller size.	Convex or flat plastron.
Lizards	Occasionally bright colours, crests, dewlaps etc. Often larger head, pre-anal pores and femoral pores.	Comparatively plain in appearance. Pre-anal and femoral pores absent or very small.
Snakes	Swelling at base of tail. Proportionately longer tail, resulting in larger number of sub-caudal scales (count on sloughed skin).	Tail tapers sharply immediately behind cloaca. Fewer sub-caudal scales.

Note: Many of the above characteristics are only apparent in mature animals.

In certain species of reptiles where there are no external clues as to the sexual identity of an individual, it is possible to establish the presence or otherwise of the male sex organs by *gently* inserting a probe into the cloaca and attempting to push it back into the base of the tail. In males, the opening caused by the inverted (i.e. inside-out) hemipenes allow the probe to be inserted

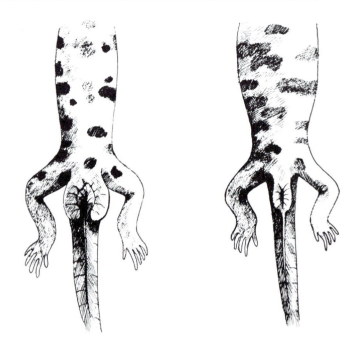

Fig. 17 Male (left) and female newt.

for several times the distance possible in females. It must be emphasised that this operation can seriously damage animals (particularly their breeding potential) if it is not carried out with the utmost care. The probe should be of a size appropriate to the species, completely smooth and lubricated with water, liquid paraffin etc before use.

A more sophisticated technique, the use of steroid analysis to investigate hormone quotas, is beyond the scope of most individuals but may be of use in laboratories or zoological gardens. A reference is given in the bibliography.

CONDITIONING

Animals will only breed if their bodies can supply the necessary energy and materials. Therefore they must be well fed with the correct food. In the case of certain species which lay calcareous eggs, i.e. the turtles and tortoises, the crocodilians and some lizards, either the food must contain a high proportion of calcium or this must be given as a supplement. Deformed eggs, deformed young or embryos which die before hatching are often indications of vitamin or mineral deficiency in breeding females.

An important thing to realise is that the material for egg and sperm production is not obtained directly from food but via fat-bodies which swell gradually during the non-productive season and then allow their stored nutrients to become available prior to the breeding season. In temperate species it can take a year or more for these to develop sufficiently, at least under natural conditions, and so it is unreasonable to expect an animal which was previously neglected to suddenly start producing sex cells after a couple of weeks of intensive feeding − the rule is to ensure a steady supply of food throughout the year (unless the animal hibernates for part of it), and in this way sex cells will start to form as soon as the environmental cues trigger the system.

STIMULI

It is likely that the appearance of certain prey species is a seasonal cue for breeding in some species, especially those coming from regions where other environmental factors are constant throughout the year. Persuading such species to breed will therefore depend largely on luck.

Hibernation (*see* page 45) plays a very important part in the conditioning of some temperate species. Temperature, light and

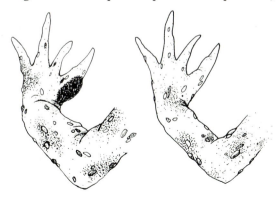

Fig. 18 Fore-arms of male (left) and female frog.

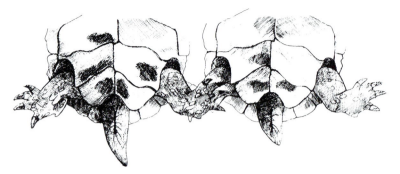

Fig. 19 Male (left) and female tortoises showing differing tail lengths and position of cloacae.

humidity levels are probably the most important factors connected with the reproductive drive in amphibians and reptiles. Species from temperate regions usually breed in the spring, those from sub-tropical regions may breed during autumn or winter, and those from equatorial regions may breed at any time of the year. Breeding may be dependent on rainfall, barometric pressure and so on. Many of these conditions can be duplicated in captivity.

Certain species are more likely to mate if the sexes are kept separate prior to the breeding season, then introduced to each other at what is judged to be the optimum time. The presence of extra males may stimulate rivalry and sexual activity in some species, and in snakes (and possibly other groups) the females appear to be more attractive to the males immediately after they have sloughed.

MATING

The actual process of mating may be over in a few minutes, or it may take hours. Some species mate repeatedly for a period of several days or even weeks. There may be a period of courtship leading up to the actual mating, or the male may pursue and mate with the female with no preliminary behaviour. Female lizards which have mated often have small scars on their necks where they have been bitten by their mates. Male snakes crawl over their mates and often both individuals will glide around the cage together, the male's head just behind that of the female.

This may be accompanied by jerks or twitches by both snakes. Two males sometimes engage each other in combat by rearing up with the fore-parts of their bodies intertwined — this should not be mistaken for courtship. Male tortoises chase and butt females throughout the breeding season.

Many, and possibly all, species of reptiles have the facility for storing sperm from a previous mating, and using it to fertilise subsequent clutches of eggs. In this way, a female may lay eggs for four or five years following a single mating, but fertility diminishes after the first year, and females will normally mate every year if given the chance, with the exceptions of a few temperate species which, due to a short season of activity, produce eggs or young only every second or third year, using the non-productive years in between to regain fitness. In captivity, it may be possible to overcome this by optimum feeding and a slightly extended season. (Species which normally breed once annually may be encouraged to do so two or more times under artificial conditions, but the size and quality of the young should not be compromised for the sake of quantity.)

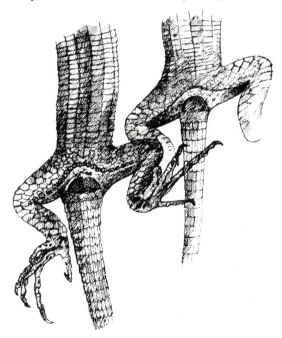

Fig. 20 Male (left) and female lizard, showing femoral and pre-anal pores.

As a rule, matings between individuals of different subspecies should be avoided; the animals so produced are rarely as attractive as either parent, and may cause confusion in future generations. An exception may be made where the mate of a particular subspecies is unobtainable because it is rare, legally protected, etc. Any offspring resulting from such matings must be identified as hybrids, or intergrades, when disposing of them to other collectors. Where a mate is required, it is often worth advertising for the loan of one through the medium of a society newsletter or similar circular. Progeny-sharing schemes of this nature may be the only hope of producing young of the more rarely-kept species, but bear in mind the precautions regarding quarantine, etc.

PREGNANCY

When a female amphibian or reptile of a live-bearing (or 'viviparous') species is carrying young, it is said to be 'pregnant'; when a female of an egg-laying (or 'oviparous') species is carrying eggs,

Fig. 21 Male (upper) and female lizards (*Gonatodes vittatus*) showing sexually dimorphic marking (see also male and female *Chamaeleo jacksoni*, pp. 227–8).

the equivalent term is 'gravid'. Pregnant or gravid females often seek out additional warmth to speed the development of their embryos or (unlaid) eggs. Many species bask for longer periods and flatten their bodies beneath the heat source. As the eggs or young take up an increasing amount of space in the female's body, she may cease feeding until birth or egg-laying has occurred. Most female snakes slough their skin a few days before they lay their eggs, whereas egg-laying in lizards and chelonians can often be predicted by scratching or digging activities as the search for a suitable nest-site takes place. Heavily gravid or pregnant amphibians seem to swell to the point of bursting just before they produce their eggs or young. Animals which are heavily gravid or pregnant should be handled as little as possible.

PARTURITION

Viviparous species (and the term viviparous is used throughout this book to refer to all those species which bring forth living young, although strictly speaking many of them should be known as 'ovo-viviparous') usually give birth without problems. Small species of reptiles appreciate an area of slightly moist sphagnum or similar material, because the young are usually wet and sticky when born; otherwise they may adhere to newspaper or become covered with pieces of sand or gravel. They may cluster round the female for a while, but there is no evidence of maternal care in any species of viviparous amphibian or reptile.

EGG-LAYING

All chelonians and crocodilians, and some lizards, lay hard-shelled, calcareous eggs. These may be buried or hidden, or attached to a piece of rock, wood or the side of the vivarium. Chelonians and crocodilians, which normally bury their eggs, require an area of friable soil in which to carry this out. Certain crocodilians also use vegetation (dead leaves etc) to build a dome-shaped nest over their eggs. In a large cage or an outdoor enclosure these materials can form part of the substrate, and in smaller vivaria they can be contained in suitably deep vessels.

Most oviparous lizards and all oviparous snakes lay eggs which are encased in a soft, parchment-like shell, which allows water to

85

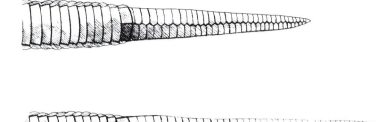

Fig. 22 Male (lower) and female snake. Note the longer tail and slight swelling immediately behind the cloaca of the male.

be drawn into the egg throughout incubation, and these species require a damp substrate in which to bury their clutches. Several alternatives may be used, but the most popular is free-running sand (i.e. horticultural sand rather than builder's sand), which may be used on its own or mixed with an equal volume of granulated peat. In vivaria, this may be contained in plastic lunchboxes or similar, and provided it is always kept moist, and the rest of the cage is kept dry, the gravid female(s) will almost always use this. Signs of egg-laying are disturbance of the medium and females that become much thinner overnight, and if a transparent box is used for the medium all or part of the clutch may be visible through the base or the sides. In outdoor enclosures, a similar system may be used, or an area of sandy soil kept damp by regular spraying. This must be inspected once or twice daily during the laying season so that eggs buried in it do not become cold, or disturbed by the egg-laying activities of other females.

Even more importantly, eggs must be removed quickly from cages in which crickets have been used for feeding. If this is not done, insects which have not been consumed will quickly find the eggs and begin to eat them. The best arrangement by far is to remove the gravid female(s) and house them in a separate cage into which less destructive food species (e.g. flies, caterpillars) can be substituted, or food may be withheld altogether.

INCUBATION

In practically every instance, it is better to remove the eggs rather than to let them remain in the vivarium where they are laid. The exceptions are certain geckos, which may attach their eggs to the side of the vivarium where they must be protected by taping a small container over them until they hatch, and several species of pythons, in which the female coils around the clutch throughout incubation.

Normally, hard-shelled eggs may be removed and partially buried in dry sand or, in the case of small gecko eggs, merely placed on a dry surface in a suitable container. If they are spherical, they can be prevented from rolling around by first placing a layer of clean pea-gravel over the base of the container.

Soft-shelled eggs can be incubated *in situ* if they have been laid in a lunch-box, or they can be moved to a clean box containing a similar mixture of sand and peat, moistened until it retains its shape when squeezed in the hand, and, if possible, rendered

Fig. 23 A clutch of incubating snake eggs (*Elaphe obsoleta*) in a plastic box containing a layer of moist peat and sand.

sterile by heating over steam in a pressure cooker for 20–30 minutes. Alternatively, vermiculite, preferably of a fairly fine grade, may be used, mixed with approximately its own weight of water; this is cheap, light, easily stored when dry, and does not require sterilisation (provided it is used once only and then discarded). Whatever the medium, the eggs should be partially buried by making a small depression for each and then gently drawing the medium up to their midline. In this way, each egg can be easily inspected without disturbing it. In many clutches, the eggs are sticky when laid and adhere to each other in a clump. If possible, it is preferable to separate them by gently pulling them apart, but if they are not found for several hours this may be difficult to do without risk of damage, in which case the clump should be arranged in the substrate in such a way that each egg comes into contact with the medium without being completely buried.

The container should be closed, although small air holes may be made. A polythene bag, part filled with the incubating medium and tied at the top, makes a cheap alternative to lunchboxes. If the container is kept closed throughout the incubation, additional water should be unnecessary, but if the eggs begin to shrivel the medium surrounding them may be lightly sprayed.

If the reptile collection is kept in a room which is heated to 25–30°C, it is necessary only to place the container, complete with eggs, on a shelf where it will not be disturbed, and to check occasionally for signs of fungus, drying-up, hatching, etc. If such a room is not available, an incubator may be necessary. This can be adapted from a plant propagator, built from scratch, or an unused vivarium can be pressed into use. Efficient insulation will enable a small unit to be heated adequately with a small light-bulb, heat-pad or heat-tape, but a certain amount of ventilation at the top and near the bottom is helpful in maintaining an even temperature throughout the incubator. It is important to incorporate some means of control to keep the temperature within certain limits. A range of 25–30°C gives good results, and the temperature may be allowed to fluctuate between these extremes (for instance, by using a fairly crude thermostat or by setting different temperatures during the day and night). Alternatively, it may be set precisely at one value with an accurate thermostat, such as one of the electronic units available commercially for aquaria (or a similar instrument may be built quite easily and cheaply, using one of several published circuits). Known temperature values are especially important if methods are to be repeatable, or if published data are to be of value to others.

During incubation, the eggs swell as they absorb water and the embryo develops. Eggs which do not do this may be infertile, or the medium may be too dry. In some cases, the embryo can be seen as a pink area within the shell, gradually becoming darker as the incubation progresses. Towards the end of incubation, the shell may partially collapse around the young reptile as it uses up all of the available fluid. Shortly after this, one or more slits will appear in the shell and the young animal will emerge, although occasionally the hatchling remains in the shell for several hours or even days, poking its head out from time to time and pulling it back in if disturbed (*see* Plate 40). There is no need to help the young animals out of their shells (neither is there any harm in it provided they are ready to emerge). In containers housing several eggs it may be advantageous to remove the young as soon as possible in order to prevent them from trampling on, or otherwise disturbing, their future brothers and sisters, as there may be several days between the first and last emergence, even within a single clutch.

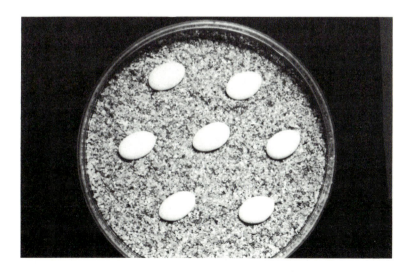

Fig. 24 Lizard eggs (*Agama atricollis*) incubating in vermiculite.

If reasonable precautions are taken, it is unlikely that fertile eggs will become seriously affected by mould, although infertile ones often are after a short period. Reptile eggs possess a degree of protection against mould, and a slight discolouring of the surface is nothing to worry about. If an egg becomes badly affected, it should be isolated from the others if possible, and incubated separately or discarded. A pad of cotton wool, moistened with a weak solution of domestic bleach (1% sodium hypochlorite), can be used gently to wipe the mould away, and this may control the problem until the egg(s) hatch.

INCUBATION TEMPERATURE AND SEX

Recent research has shown that, in many reptiles, the sex of the offspring is not fixed by the time the eggs are laid, but depends on the temperature at a critical point during their incubation, usually quite early on. The fancy term for this is 'temperature-dependent sex determination' (TSD).

This effect has been observed in nearly all of the crocodilians and turtles so far studied and in many of the lizards, but with an important difference: in crocodilians and turtles, low temperatures produce males and high temperatures produce females; in lizards the reverse is true — low temperatures produce females and high temperatures produce males.

The exact values vary according to species, but if it is found that only one sex is obtained at a certain incubation temperature, raising or lowering it for subsequent clutches should prove to be beneficial. Alternatively, each clutch may be divided into two or more groups, each group being kept at slightly different temperatures. They will, of course, hatch at different times, but a better sex ratio will probably be obtained as a result. (It may, however, be considered an advantage to produce far more females than males in order to optimise breeding potential, or more males than females if these are more attractive or colourful, for instance.)

REARING YOUNG

The young animals, whether they arise from pregnancy, the gravid process or metamorphosis, may require treatment which is rather different from that of their parents, due mainly to their size. Hatchling snakes rarely feed until they have sloughed their skin for the first time, usually 4–10 days after birth or hatching, and other young reptiles and amphibians may hide away and refuse food until they have adjusted to their surroundings.

It is often helpful to keep the young of small species in lunchboxes or similar small containers, where their progress can be observed more easily. In such containers, they are able to find their food with little trouble, which is not always the case in large vivaria. Growing animals require ample feeding and, with some species, meals should be supplemented with vitamin and mineral preparations (*see* Chapter 5).

It may be of use to others, and also for one's own future reference, if, for each animal, a record is kept of parentage, date of birth or hatching, meals, growth-rate, dates of sloughing, and the first signs of any sexual behaviour. This may necessitate the identification of individuals, which, for many species, can be achieved by roughly sketching their markings on the back of their record cards.

BREEDING PROGRAMMES

Although it is always gratifying to obtain breeding successes of any kind, as our knowledge of life-cycles and captive techniques grows, it should be possible to breed selectively from individuals which are of particular interest or value. Any selection should, however, be based on fitness rather than on freak mutations or abnormalities, although it is, of course, quite permissible to breed for bright colour and vivid markings, provided other factors, such as size and general physical vigour, are not sacrificed.

Where two definite colour phases of a species exist, e.g. black and white axolotls, the relative frequency of each will probably be controlled by a single pair of genes, one dominant, the other recessive. Where both types occur in the same animal, the dominant gene will control the appearance of the animal, although it may produce offspring of the other phase, depending on the gene complement, or genotype, of its mate. However, if individuals of two subspecies having slightly different colours or markings are mated, the offspring will usually be intermediate in appearance. They may be known as 'intergrades', although,

Fig. 25 A young gecko (*Phelsuma laticauda*) immediately after hatching from its calcareous egg. Its twin is yet to hatch.

strictly speaking, this term is reserved for individuals which occur naturally in the area where the ranges of the two sub-species merge.

In general, these very simple mechanisms hold true throughout the animal kingdom, although in some cases abnormalities are caused by different types of gene interaction, and predictions about the colour and markings of offspring are not easily made. In practice, well-marked parents usually produce well-marked offspring, but if only one parent is well-marked it may be necessary to breed for two generations before there is any noticeable improvement in the colony.

At the other extreme, as breeding of reptiles becomes more regularly achieved, the danger of inbreeding begins to loom on the horizon. Except for a few scientific purposes, colonies of amphibians and reptiles should be encouraged to maintain as much variability as possible in order to prevent a loss of vigour, or a so-called 'inbreeding depression' after a few generations. This is achieved by avoiding matings between close relatives, such as brothers and sisters (full sib) and mothers and sons or fathers and daughters (half sib), as far as possible. The rate of inbreeding is dependent on the size of the breeding colony and the method of choosing the breeders for the next generation. The larger the colony, the lower the rate of inbreeding for any given system. For rare animals in small colonies, a maximum avoidance system is recommended. This involves keeping a record of the parentage (or pedigree) of each animal in the colony, and matching pairs in such a way as to maintain the largest possible gene-pool. Take, for instance, a colony of lizards with 8 pairs. Each pair is numbered 1–8, and in the following generation the matings are made up as follows:

New pair no.	female from	male from
1	1	2
2	3	4
3	5	6
4	7	8
5	2	1
6	4	3
7	6	5
8	8	7

If this is done for each generation, the rate of inbreeding would be just over 1.5% per generation, and using this system the colony could survive for many generations without requiring fresh blood. Of course, the 8 pairs need not be in one collection, but could be an aggregate of several collections, each 'contributing' one or two pairs, and with an agreement to exchange a few young each generation. Since most species have a reproductive life of several years, a relatively small original breeding nucleus could provide an enormous number of descendants before more wild stock would be required.

7
Diseases

As a rule, reptiles and amphibians are remarkably free from disease; nevertheless, newly acquired specimens should, whatever their source, be isolated for a period of at least two weeks (preferably more). During this period, rigid precautions must be taken to avoid any risk of cross-infection since the newcomer may be suffering from an infectious disease (*see also* page 26). If any disease is suspected, veterinary advice should be sought *as soon as possible.*

Do-it-yourself veterinary treatment is most strongly opposed, and for this reason only the most common and easily dealt-with problems are described, with emphasis on prevention and recognition rather than on cure. Similarly, prophylactic treatment (i.e. preventive medication), is not recommended, except where this can be carried out easily and without risk of any side-effects. Examples are the use of vitamin and mineral supplements on food, in drinking water or directly into the mouth, and the administering of a worming substance, for instance piperazine citrate, for those species, such as tortoises, which are often found to be infested with roundworms (nematodes).

CONTROLLING DISEASES

In the case of most hobbyists' collections, where all or most of the animals are of necessity kept in one room, the control of an outbreak of infectious disease can be difficult. However, certain elementary measures can be taken.

1) Isolate infected animals immediately, but resist the temptation to start shuffling other animals around in order to remove the most valuable ones from the vicinity — this may

94

only help to spread the infection.

2) Never transfer water-bowls, furniture, uneaten food, etc, from the contaminated cage to another.

3) Service the infected cage last — feeding, watering and cleaning should be carried out after all other jobs in the animal room are done.

4) Wash your hands, and use a disinfectant 'dip' for all tools and equipment after cleaning *every* cage in the room. Formalin, 70% alcohol or neat domestic bleach (sodium hypochlorite) are satisfactory disinfectants for this purpose. Remember to rinse equipment in clean water after using Formalin or bleach; both chemicals can be injurious to the skin.

5) Disinfect every cage each time it is cleaned out. For reptiles, a solution of 3–5% sodium hypochlorite, or a quaternary ammonium compound, e.g. Cetrimide (diluted as indicated), or, in emergencies, a strong solution of ordinary washing soda (sodium carbonate), may be used. Phenols and Coal-tar derivatives (e.g. 'Dettol' and the so-called 'pine' disinfectants), are toxic to reptiles and should not be used. Amphibians are particularly vulnerable to toxic chemicals, although a weak solution of sodium hypochlorite (1–3%) will not be harmful, provided the vivaria are thoroughly rinsed afterwards.

6) Remove soiled bedding and dead animals from the room immediately by placing them straight into a polythene bag which can be tied at the top and disposed of. Do not leave such materials lying around in a refuse bin in the animal room.

ENVIRONMENTAL DISEASES

The great majority of diseases affecting captive reptiles and amphibians are caused by incorrect husbandry. Temperature, humidity and spatial requirements must be met to within certain limits or the animal(s) will become sick and eventually die. Animals suffering from poor management may show loss of appetite and subsequent emaciation, lethargy, poor colour, dull skin, sunken eyes, surface wounds and sores, and in some cases extreme nervousness. With these, the cure consists of adjusting conditions until a more favourable environment is created. The guidelines offered throughout this book should help to achieve this.

NUTRITIONAL DISEASES

The next most common problem is that of incorrect or inadequate nutrition. This is more likely to affect some species than others, especially where dietary requirements are unusual or poorly known. Assuming that ample food is available, nutritional diseases consist primarily of vitamin or mineral deficiencies, the most important of which are the following.

Calcium : phosphorus Imbalance

Most common in turtles and lizards, this may be recognised by soft shells (in turtles) or bones, and resulting deformities. It is caused by offering food which is low in usable calcium (mainly meat, plant material and mealworms), and can be avoided by using a better diet, e.g. whole animals in place of meat, crickets in place of mealworms, etc, and by adding calcium to the food in the form of a mineral and vitamin supplement, ground cuttlefish shell, or as a chemical such as calcium lactate. In each case, the food is lightly dusted immediately before being offered.

Avitaminosis A

This is characterised by swollen eyelids and loss of appetite (mainly in turtles). It is avoided by regularly placing a drop or two of cod-liver oil on favoured food items and by including liver, green vegetables and fish in the diet. Badly affected animals may require injections of vitamin A by a vet.

Avitaminosis B

This may take several forms, depending on which one of the B-complex substances is lacking. B_1 (thiamine) deficiency affects the nervous system in snakes which are fed exclusively on fish, giving rise to convulsions and, eventually, death. The culprit is an enzyme in the fish which digests the thiamine, thus depriving the snake of it. If the dead fish is warmed up to about 80°C for five minutes, immediately before feeding, the enzyme is destroyed and the problem eliminated. Vitamin B_2 (riboflavin) deficiency causes paralysis of the hind legs in certain lizards (particularly iguanids, agamids and similar families). It can best be avoided by the use of a multi-vitamin supplement.

Avitaminosis D

This is particularly common in basking lizards and turtles. Vitamin D_3 (not D_2 as in mammals) is necessary for the uptake of calcium and phosphorus, and is therefore essential for correct bone and shell formation. In diurnal reptiles, it is probably synthesised under the influence of ultra-violet radiation, i.e. sunlight, and absence of this may result in a deficiency with the same symptoms as a calcium:phosphorus imbalance. Vitamin D_3 is obtainable commercially and can be mixed with a calcium supplement and sprinkled over the food, or a proprietary vitamin and mineral supplement may be provided. It should not be used without calcium or the calcium in the animal's skeleton may almost natural type of light, e.g. True-lite and Vita-lite, may also be beneficial to basking animals, but should not always be relied on to take the place of Vitamin D supplementation.

BACTERIAL INFECTIONS

Salmonellosis

Infection with *Salmonella* bacteria does not necessarily cause signs of disease in reptiles. When it does, the infection is characterised by fluid faeces, sometimes greenish. Its main importance is as a zoonosis, i.e. it can be transmitted from animals to man. It is for this reason that the keeping of certain species, notably the red-eared terrapin, has been disallowed by some authorities. The risk is not very great, provided that normal hygienic measures are taken after handling the animals or cleaning their quarters. It is important to remember that even apparently healthy animals may be excreting *Salmonella* bacteria. Cure of Salmonellosis may require the use of an antibiotic, administered (in the case of the animals!) by a vet, and even then there is no guarantee that the causal organisms have been eliminated.

Mouth-rot, Mouth Canker or Necrotic Stomatitis

This is quite common in snakes and may also be encountered in other reptiles. It can be recognised as a yellowish area inside the mouth, which may produce a 'cheesy' matter which builds up along the rows of teeth and, in extreme cases, prevents the mouth from closing completely. By this time the animal will be refusing food. Since the bacteria involved are common in the environment, mouth-rot would appear to result from wounds inside the mouth, and is most commonly found in animals under stress, i.e. the newly imported or poorly maintained. Vitamin C (ascorbic acid) may be given daily, and the infected area irrigated with 25% aqueous sulphadimidine, or with hydrogen peroxide, but veterinary advice is recommended.

Respiratory Infections

These can be recognised by gaping, wheezing and bubbling from the mouth of infected animals. The nostrils may become completely blocked, and breathing laboured and clearly audible. These infections are quite common, and mild attacks may be cured by movement to warm, dry and well-ventilated accommodation. Serious cases require veterinary treatment with antibiotics such as tylosin.

'Red-leg' (in Frogs)

This may be caused by a variety of bacteria and can be fatal unless treated. Chlorinated water is a good means of control, and copper sulphate (1.2% solution for 1–2 hours) may be effective as a cure. Various antibiotics, such as Terramycin, may be useful, depending on the identity of the bacterium involved, and veterinary advice may be necessary. Newly acquired frogs may have red areas on their thighs and hands, though these are frequently caused by the abrasive nature of their transport boxes or packing materials, and will disappear in one or two days.

PROTOZOAN INFECTIONS

Amoebiasis (Entamoebiasis)

This causes a form of enteritis and can spread rapidly through a collection of reptiles with dire results. The faeces of infected animals are fluid and slimy, and food may be regurgitated. Drugs obtained through a vet, e.g. Flagyl, are effective if given in time.

ENDOPARASITES

Roundworms (Nematodes)

These are often visible as small, white, threadlike objects in the faeces of infested animals. Piperazine citrate may be obtained from pet-shops (where it is sold as worming powder or as tablets for cats and dogs) and is effective against certain species of worm. It is given at the rate of 50 mg per kg body weight. It should be dissolved in a small quantity of water and squirted down the animal's throat with a syringe, and the dose should be repeated after 2–3 weeks. If roundworms continue to be passed veterinary advice should be sought as a more specific drug may be needed.

Tapeworms

These may cause emaciation in spite of a good appetite, and segments, which are small, opaque and squarish in appearance, may be found in the faeces. An anti-helminth drug such as Diphenethane may be available from pet-shops, in which case it can be given at the (scaled-down) dose rate for dogs. If effective drugs are not obtainable commercially, or if the parasites persist, a vet must be consulted.

ECTOPARASITES

Mites

Mites, especially snake-mites, *Ophionyssus natricis*, may be a problem since they can migrate from the original host and travel from cage to cage. Although they suck the blood of their host, their main danger lies in the fact that they can act as carriers of disease from one animal to another. They may be seen quite clearly on their host as small round brown or black creatures, either moving over the animal's skin, or lodged between its scales, especially round the eye. To eliminate them, a small strip of 'Vapona' (dichlorvos), or similar material (obtainable from hardware shops) is placed in a small perforated metal container or cotton bag. This is then stood or hung in the cage for three days, by which time all the mites should have been killed. One week later, repeat this treatment to kill any newly-hatched mites. It may be necessary to repeat it again after a few months if the mites return, but the Vapona should not be left permanently in the cage as it may have harmful side-effects. Good housekeeping (regular cleaning, removal of sloughed skin, quarantining new animals) will go a long way towards the prevention of serious mite infestations.

Ticks

Ticks are larger than mites and are usually brown, black or grey. They attach themselves firmly to the skin of their host, especially land tortoises, by means of their hooked mouthparts. They can be killed by dabbing them with a drop of alcohol, for instance methylated spirits, then carefully removing them with forceps. They should be grasped, then slowly turned over on to their backs to unhook the mouthparts. If they are pulled off, there is a danger that the head will be left behind and infection may result.

FUNGAL INFECTIONS

Fungal infections may occur at the sites of wounds and abrasions and are particularly common in amphibians. The area can be bathed with 2% malachite green (medical grade), 2% mercurochrome, or full strength hydrogen peroxide may be applied with a small paintbrush. Aquatic species, such as axolotls, may be completely immersed in a strong solution of malachite green (1 g in 15 litres) for 10–30 seconds, then returned to their aquarium, or held in a 0.1% solution for up to 30 minutes. Amphibian eggs may be immersed in 0.025% malachite green for one hour to prevent fungus, although the daily removal of infertile eggs is to be preferred.

MISCELLANEOUS DISORDERS

Skin Blisters

Skin blisters in snakes and lizards are usually caused by keeping the animal in an environment which is too damp, and are a common condition in garter snakes (*Thamnophis* spp.) and water snakes (*Natrix* and *Nerodia* spp.), because these species are frequently kept in 'natural' vivaria containing an artificial swamp. Affected animals should be moved to warm, dry quarters where the blisters should quickly disappear. An antiseptic solution such as 'Betadine' can be applied to accelerate healing, but if a secondary bacterial infection has occurred antibiotics may be necessary.

Recently, a slightly different type of blister, or abscess, has been commonly found on the bodies of newly-imported snakes. These swellings are quite hard and do not disappear after sloughing even if the living conditions are rectified. Once again, Garter Snakes and their relatives seem to be the most frequently affected, although the condition may occur in other species. Although the lumps can be treated by incising them and cleaning out the pus, followed by topical application of a sulphonamide or antibiotic powder (e.g. 'Cicatrin'), they tend to be extremely difficult to get rid of once and for all, and snakes which look at all 'lumpy' should not be purchased no matter what assurances are given by the vendor.

Wounds

Wounds, often incurred through fighting, or through rubbing or banging the snout against the lid or sides of the vivarium, will usually heal without treatment if their cause is eliminated, for example by isolating animals that are being bullied, by providing adequate hiding places and by replacing metal mesh with plastic. Topical application of solutions such as Betadine or Pevidine, or of antibiotic powder such as Cicatrin, may speed recovery. In amphibians, Cicatrin may be helpful in the prevention of secondary bacterial infection; for the control of fungal infections, see above.

Inability to Slough Completely

This may occur in snakes and lizards. It is usually (but not always) associated with animals which are stressed, under-nourished or dehydrated, and whose skin becomes dry and wrinkled. The opaque period comes as normal, but sloughing fails to take place a few days later as it should. The simplest solution is to place the animal in a small container or cotton bag which is filled with very slightly moist sphagnum moss. In most instances, the skin will have come away within 12 hours. In the case of snakes, the newly sloughed skin should be inspected to ensure that the spectacle, or eye-shield, is present, as it is sometimes left behind and must then be removed to prevent it from becoming a source of infection or leading to further difficulties during subsequent sloughs. This may be carried out by wrapping adhesive tape round the index finger with the sticky side outwards, and then pressing gently and repeatedly against the eye until the spectacle becomes detached. In stubborn cases, a finger-nail may be used to locate and lift an edge of the spectacle, but great care must be taken. The use of forceps is not recommended.

8
Handling

There is no merit in handling reptiles and amphibians for the sake of it, and all specimens should be restrained as little as possible, but it is necessary to know the correct methods of grasping and holding the various types in order that they may be safely manipulated during cleaning operations or during close inspections for the purposes of sex determination, health checks, force-feeding and so on.

Fig. 26 Holding a salamander (*Salamandra s. terrestris*).

Fig. 27 Holding a toad (*Bombina maxima*).

Many small specimens are very delicate, and where possible these are best coaxed into small plastic containers or polythene bages for transportation or for examination. Those specimens which are held in the hand should be grasped firmly and without hesitation. For small, lively species, a short spell with their heat-source removed will slow them down appreciably and so reduce the risk of escape or injury. Aquatic amphibians are most easily caught in a small hand net and should only be held in hands which have been first dipped into water.

Frogs and Toads

Small species may be completely enclosed in the hand, larger ones grasped by the hind-legs.

Newts and Salamanders

These are most easily held in the palm of the hand with the index finger beneath the throat, and the thumb resting *lightly* on the top of the head or neck.

Turtles and Tortoises

There are usually no problems in handling these animals, except with specimens which bite (usually turtles). These should be held by the rear of the carapace and pointed away from the handler's body. Very large species, such as Snapping Turtles and Soft-

Fig. 28 Holding a frog (*Pyxicephalus adspersus*).

Fig. 29 Holding a turtle (*Sternotherus minor*).

shelled Turtles, may be lifted and carried by the tail for short periods. Turtles which are being examined for veterinary purposes and so on may be restrained in a net or a cloth bag, and any injections etc can then be performed through the mesh or cloth.

Lizards

Small species may be held in the same way as salamanders. Note that the tails of many species are readily discarded if grasped. Large specimens should be gripped firmly by the neck with one hand, while the other supports the animal's weight. If the tail is lashed about, this can be tucked under one arm. Many species can give painful scratches, which can be most easily avoided by wearing protective clothing with long sleeves and of close enough weave to ensure that the animal's claws do not become entangled. Elbow-length gauntlets are of value when restraining sharp-clawed species such as iguanas and monitors.

Crocodilians

Small specimens are handled in the same way as large lizards. If necessary, the jaws can be bound together. The handling of large specimens requires several people, and the jaws should first be held by a running noose attached to a pole. Their tails are particularly powerful.

Snakes

Small to medium-sized harmless snakes should be grasped firmly round the mid-body and the neck before lifting off the ground. Tame examples may be lifted by the mid-body only and then allowed to glide through the hands with the minimum of restraint, but nervous or aggressive specimens should continue to be held firmly until they are put down in order to prevent them from thrashing about and injuring themselves or their handler. When returned to their cage, the body should be released slightly before the neck, and at no time should the snake

Fig. 30 Holding a small lizard (*Mabuya* sp.).

Fig. 31 Holding a large lizard (*Varanus salvator*).

be allowed to coil round the wrist. Large constrictors, even if tame, should be handled carefully, and should on no account be draped round the neck. Ideally, one person should hold the neck while a second (and perhaps a third) takes the weight of the body.

Venomous snakes are best 'handled' at a distance, by means of a snake-hook for the heavy-bodied vipers, rattlesnakes etc, or a grab-stick or noose for the swifter and more active cobras, mambas etc. Goggles or eye-shields are essential during the handling of spitting cobras. Where close contact is essential, as with force-feeding, the snake must be immobilised first by means of a noose or snake-hook, and only then grasped firmly immediately behind the head with the thumb and index finger in the case of small specimens, and with the whole hand in the case of larger ones. Gloves may be used, but their suitability is dubious if they detract from the dexterity of the fingers. In practice, gloves which do not do this are usually so thin as to be useless anyway. The use of a catching box for all venomous snakes is very strongly recommended. This is a small dark box with an aperture which can be closed once the snake is inside. It can double as a retreat box and be left permanently in the cage, in which case it should be possible to close the aperture remotely, or it can be attached temporarily to the outside of the cage, in line with a trap-door which can be slid open to allow the snake through. Once the snake is inside, the box can be closed up and can then be used to transport the snake, or to accommodate it while its cage is being serviced (*see* Fig. 34).

Methods of transporting amphibians and reptiles include the use of jars and plastic lunch-boxes (for amphibians, small lizards and snakes), larger wooden or cardboard boxes (for turtles, tortoises, large lizards and amphibians in quantity), cotton bags (lizards and snakes) and polythene bags (amphibians, especially aquatic species). Where there is a danger of extremes of heat or cold, polystyrene or styrofoam boxes should be used — if necessary with smaller boxes or bags containing animals packed

Fig. 32 Holding a harmless snake (*Elaphe quatuorlineata*).

within — and if the danger of mechanical damage is also present (e.g. from crushing whilst in transit via air, rail etc), the box should be strong enough to withstand this. Small animals, especially amphibians, require a slightly dampened packing material (moss, or foam rubber 'chippings' are very satisfactory) and all animals in containers should be given something to grasp or coil around in order to prevent them from being thrown about — screwed-up newspaper or a bundle of dry grass is fine for

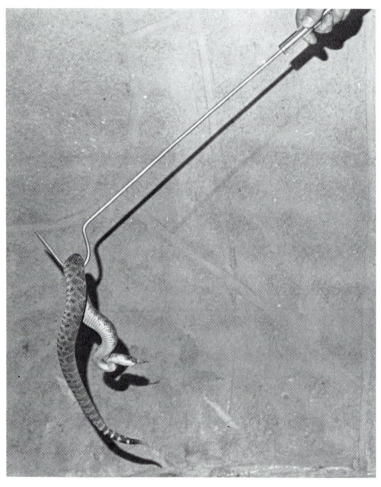

Fig. 33 Using a snake hook to lift a venomous snake (*Crotalus atrox*).

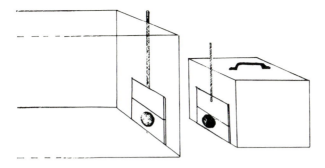

Fig. 34 A catching box for snakes.

species not requiring moisture. When collecting or transporting snakes and lizards cotton bags provide convenient temporary accommodation as they can be carried in a pocket or tucked into a belt when empty, and it is relatively easy to add animals without the existing occupants escaping. Bear in mind though that a snake-bag left in the sun rapidly becomes a death-trap for its occupants, that small species in particular are prone to dehydration if not kept in closed containers, that lizards may snag and damage claws if the material is loosely woven or frayed, and that it is possible for aggressive animals (including venomous snakes) to bite through the bag.

PART TWO

Descriptions of Species and their Maintenance

Introduction

The compilation of the list of species described in the following pages has been made particularly difficult owing to the continual appearance and disappearance of species from the hobby. This fluctuation is due on the one hand to the energies of collectors who strive to unearth new species in fresh territories, and on the other to the restrictions imposed by conservation laws, political unrest and so on.

The backbone of the list has been formed from those species which have been regularly offered for sale over the last five years or so, but in the main species that were considered to be unsuited for life in captivity through habits, size etc have been omitted. I have added several species which, though not commonly available, are of sufficient interest to warrant a place in collections, yet are relatively common in their place of origin, and easily catered for. Since it is impossible to mention more than a sample of species, I have tried to cast my net as wide as possible by including species from many parts of the world, and from as many families as is feasible, but there is an unavoidable bias towards the herpetofaunas of Europe and North America, the areas in which most hobbyists live and from which the best-known species hail. Again, certain families contain a plethora of popular species, whereas others, for a variety of reasons, do not, and the relative amount of space devoted to each reflects this. Often, relevant information on those species not listed is obtainable by turning to other species in the same genus, family and/or order.

There is good reason for dwelling longer on certain popular species than on others. The information is intended for the novice, who needs the most basic advice on the most commonly available species, as well as for the more experienced hobbyist. Since this list is by no means comprehensive, it should not be used for identification; a number of guides for this purpose are listed in the bibliography, and these should be consulted if the identity of an animal is in doubt. The brief descriptions are given only as a rough indication as to the size and appearance of animals which may be available through dealers but which may be unfamiliar to recipients of their lists. The colours and markings given are the typical ones. Many species, however, are extremely variable, and odd mutations such as non-pigmented (albino) forms occasionally occur. The sizes given are an approximate figure or range within which the majority of adult animals will fall. Exceptionally large or small individuals may occur through a variety of environmental factors, such as the abundance or scarcity of food at a certain time or place. Once again, recourse to a reliable reference work will provide more complete data.

In each case, I have tried to use the common names in most general use, but have at the same time tried to avoid names that could confuse or mislead. Neither have I attempted to invent common names where there are none.

Figures in brackets after the common name refer to colour plates.

9
Order Caudata -
Newts and Salamanders

The newts and salamanders together form the order Caudata, the tailed amphibians. In fact, the terms 'newt' and 'salamander' have no place in taxonomy; popularly, however, the word 'newt' has come to be associated with the more aquatic forms and the 'salamanders' are traditionally creatures of damp and mossy woodlands and caves.

Most tailed amphibians start life as eggs, go through an aquatic larval stage, and eventually metamorphose into small replicas of their parents, in most cases leaving the water to return one, two or three years later as breeding adults. It can be appreciated, then, that in captivity each different phase of their life must be catered for in an appropriate manner if the whole life cycle is to be observed.

Adults of the terrestrial varieties may be accommodated in vivaria furnished with damp leaf-litter and sheets of moss, liberally covered with pieces of bark, flat stones or broken clay pots, under which the animals can hide. The deeper the layer of leaf-litter, the greater the period between cleanings out, and the salamanders will prefer this arrangement. Woodland plants, such as ferns and ivy, may be used to provide additional hiding places. The substrate should not be allowed to become too wet, however, nor should it dry out; therefore good ventilation and regular spraying are necessary. Alternatively, animals may be kept in relatively sterile accommodation by using foam rubber sheeting as a substrate. In either case, the lighting should be subdued.

Their food consists of a variety of invertebrates, especially soft-bodied types such as earthworms and slugs, but most items of suitable size will usually be taken, provided they are alive and kicking, or made to appear so.

Aquatic species require an aquarium containing water of a suitable temperature and chemistry. These factors vary from species to species, but pond or rain water is preferable to tap

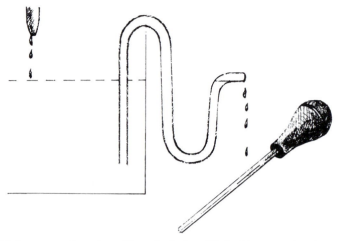

Fig. 35 An automatic syphon. The tube is first filled with water, then lowered into the water with a finger over each end. Thereafter, as water is run into the tank, it will run out of the syphon at the same rate, thus maintaining a constant level. A bulb pipette, for removing diseased eggs and uneaten food etc., is also shown.

water unless this has been allowed to stand for at least twenty-four hours before use. Artificial pond water may be made using a formula such as that given on page 134. If running or circulating water can be provided this will be of enormous benefit to those species coming from streams and rivers. An automatic siphon may be required, and a simple design is shown. If this is impractical, a small air pump can be used to operate an aquarium filter or an airstone, and this will slightly increase the number of animals it is possible to maintain in a given aquarium. Cleaning should be carried out as necessary by removing a small proportion (up to 25%) of the water by siphoning from the bottom and replacing with water of similar temperature and from the same source as that removed. If necessary, heating can be provided by a combined aquarium heater and thermostat.

Food for aquatic species consists of earthworms, *Tubifex* worms and aquatic invertebrates such as *Daphnia* and *Gammarus*. Aquatic plants add interest to the tank, and help to maintain biological equilibrium as well as some measure of security for the occupants.

Sex determination in both aquatic and terrestrial salamanders is fairly easy, provided the animals are adult. In males, the cloacal swelling is more pronounced than in females, and secondary characteristics, in the form of dorsal crests and ridges, tail filaments and enhanced colouration, are often present in males of the more aquatic species, especially during the breeding season. Ripe females of all species are more rotund if viewed from above.

Apart from a few primitive species, which do not concern us, fertilisation is internal, achieved after the female has taken up a sperm mass, or spermatophore, deposited by the male. This is sometimes preceded by an elaborate display, often involving the use of the dorsal crests in those species in which they are present. Having accepted the spermatophore, the female proceeds to lay eggs. These vary in size and number and are laid in small clusters, or singly, and attached to aquatic plants, debris or stones. Some species are particularly specific in their laying sites and carefully fold the leaf of an aquatic plant over each egg as it is laid. A few species retain the eggs in their bodies until they have hatched, and then deposit well-grown larvae into the water, and in at least one species development is entirely internal and the young animals skip the aquatic stage completely.

The time taken for the eggs to hatch varies from one to six weeks according to the species and temperature. The larvae are long and slender, with three pairs of feathery gills and sometimes with well-formed legs. They require very small live food at first, such as brine-shrimp nauplii and young *Daphnia,* and graduate to larger *Daphnia* and worm foods as they grow. The brine-shrimp should first be washed to remove excess salt, and as they will not live for long in fresh water they should be fed in moderation, ideally several times a day, and the uneaten bodies should be removed frequently by siphoning. In view of this it is an advantage to restrict the movements of the nauplii by keeping the larvae in shallow water, say 2–3 cm deep, where they are more or less bound to come into contact with, and eat, a number of the brine-shrimps while they are still alive. Plastic seed trays and glass or enamelled pie-dishes are excellent vessels for housing the very young larvae. Large larvae may be treated as aquatic adults, and will eat earthworms (chopped or whole, depending upon size), *Tubifex* worms, maggots, and a variety of other fresh-water life. They may even be trained to accept minced or chopped meat, although this should be free of fat, and should in any case be fed only occasionally.

It is not unusual among some species, notably those of the genus *Ambystoma*, for a proportion of the larvae to remain in the water instead of metamorphosing in the usual way. These animals continue to grow and eventually attain sexual maturity and breed, although they are still larvae. This is known as neoteny, and the reason for it may be physiological or genetic.

Family Ambystomidae - Mole Salamanders

This exclusively North American family comprises about twenty-five species, several of which may be kept in vivaria, and one of which may well be the most widely kept of all amphibia — the Axolotl, whose life history is rather special, as are its requirements (see below). All of the other forms can be catered for in much the same way — a damp, mossy vivarium with plenty of hiding places, and a good supply of earthworms, crickets, locusts etc. Depending upon their range, several species do very well in outside reptiliaries although owing to their secretive natures they may not be in view very often. This can be overcome to some extent by keeping them in relatively small enclosures where they may be found more easily. Shade and moisture are of course essential, and if breeding is anticipated a suitable pond will be necessary. Spawning takes place in the normal way, usually in spring, and the larvae begin to metamorphose at the end of the summer, whereupon they start feeding on small terrestrial insects etc. All species having a northerly range may be allowed to hibernate.

In all species, the males are more slender than the females, especially in spring when the latter swell with developing eggs, and the cloacal margins are more prominent in males.

Ambystoma maculatum   Spotted Salamander

EASTERN NORTH AMERICA

12–15 cm. The Spotted Salamander is aptly named, for its markings consist of a number of quite large round yellow or orange spots on a dark grey background. It is rather a slender species, and has a long tail.

Care and breeding are as in the family description, but this species is prone to skin disease if denied occasional access to open outdoor enclosures. The eggs are laid in small packets and take 4–8 weeks to hatch. By the time the young metamorphose, 10–15 weeks later, they measure about 5 cm in length.

Ambystoma mexicanum Axolotl (1)

MEXICO

15–30 cm. Although the Axolotl can be induced to metamorphose artificially (whereupon its name also metamorphoses to Mexican Salamander), its main interest lies in the fact that as a larva, albeit a rather overgrown one, it is capable of reproduction. This necessitates accommodation in an aquarium for the whole of its life, a simplification which has helped to popularise the species amongst fish-keepers as well as with amphibian aficionados. Add to this its willingness to breed under artificial conditions (compared with other amphibians), and its existence in two colour forms, black and white, and it is not difficult to see why the Axolotl provides an ideal introduction to the field of amphibian maintenance.

Despite this, in its natural haunts of Mexican mountain lakes the Axolotl has become sufficiently scarce to be listed as an endangered species, proving that the benefits of large-scale captive breeding cannot be overstated; for the availability of tank-bred animals ensures that no more Axolotls need be taken from the wild.

Much research has been and is being done on the Axolotl, and as a result information on its care is plentiful and may be regarded as a basis for the care of all aquatic newt and salamander larvae. It is tolerant of a wide range of temperatures, and may be successfully kept between 10 and 25°C, and has even been known to survive beneath ice. At lower temperatures its feathery external gills become reduced in size, because in cool, well-oxygenated water they are less necessary. As they are larvae, they should be kept in non-chlorinated water, and when they are cleaned out care should be taken to ensure that the fresh water does not differ greatly in temperature from that which they are used to. Approximately neutral water (pH 6.5–7.5) is preferred.

They will eat earthworms, maggots or pieces of raw meat or liver, although they may need training before they will take non-living items, by initially dropping each piece directly on

Fig. 36 *Ambystoma mexicanum*, the Axolotl, white phase.

CAUDATA—NEWTS AND SALAMANDERS

to their snouts. Although they can take quite large pieces of meat, they are unable to digest them properly, and pieces of about 1 cm cubed are about right for an average-sized adult, about four or five such pieces being a suitable meal if given three times weekly.

Their aquarium may be completely free from any furnishings, making it easier to keep clean, or a layer of pebbles may be added to improve its appearance. Plants, unless they are very robust, rarely thrive alongside these large, clumsy animals.

The sexes are easy to distinguish once the animals become sexually mature (usually at 18–24 months of age), the females being much plumper when viewed from above, whereas the male's cloaca forms an obvious swelling. At 21°C or more the females will come into breeding condition at any time of the year provided that adequate and suitable food is given. Mating may be induced by a sudden lowering of the temperature, or it may take place spontaneously if the sexes are kept together. It takes the form of a rather weak display by the male following which he deposits one or more spermatophores, which are picked up almost immediately by the female. During this stage the animal should be disturbed as little as possible. The females will begin to lay eggs 1–2 days after courtship has been observed, as many as 500 being laid, mainly attached to stones, twigs or aquatic plants, if present. These eggs should be removed and incubated in

Fig. 37 *Ambystoma mexicanum* – black phase.

123

shallow trays or pans. Care and development of the young follow the usual course, except that metamorphosis does not occur. Overcrowding is the biggest cause of death in growing animals, since they frequently snap at each other, inflicting serious injury, and often biting off whole limbs (these will in fact regenerate, provided infection does not set in).

The black and white forms are merely colour variations, and will readily breed with each other, the colours of the resulting offspring following the typical predictions for mendelian gene interaction (*see* page 91).

Ambystoma opacum   Marbled Salamander

EASTERN NORTH AMERICA

8–10 cm. This is a small but attractive and interesting species. The markings consist of about twelve silver transverse bands across its body, which is otherwise dark grey or black. It may seem less common than other ambystomids, because it rarely appears on dealers' lists, but perhaps this is because it does not form the large breeding congregations that make the other species vulnerable to collectors. Instead, the Marbled Salamander lays its eggs, of which there are 50–100, on the land, in soil or leaves in a damp place. This occurs in the autumn, and the female then curls around the egg-cluster until it is covered with water following the autumn rains, whereupon the eggs hatch and continue their development in pools or puddles.

Care is as in the family description. No records of captive breeding have been traced.

Ambystoma tigrinum   Tiger Salamander

NORTH AMERICA

12–17 cm. The Tiger Salamander may be regarded as the typical species of its family, being well known and with a wide distribution; at least seven subspecies are recognised. This large stocky salamander occasionally grows to 30 cm in length, and depending on subspecies its markings consist of bars and/or blotches of cream or yellow on a grey or brown background. Tiger Salamanders adapt well to captivity and will live for many years, quickly overcoming their natural timidity. Their ideal

124

temperature depends somewhat on their origin, within the range 15–25°C. Owing to their size they are able to tackle large insects and worms, and usually have rather good appetites.

Breeding takes place in the spring, but it is unlikely to occur in a small indoor vivarium. The eggs are laid in small packets, each female depositing several of these. Neoteny is quite common in this species. In the United States, the larvae of this animal are sometimes sold as fishing bait.

Family Salamandridae

This family has such a varied list of members that no one common name can be assigned to it without risk of confusion. As well as the salamanders from which the family gets its name, newts make up a large proportion of the species. Representatives of the family may be found in Europe, where it is the dominant family of tailed amphibians, and in parts of Asia, North Africa and North America.

The males of several of the aquatic species are adorned with dorsal crests and intensified markings during the breeding season. These are used in stereotyped courtship displays during which the male confronts the female and indulges in sessions of tail waving, which serve to waft scent particles towards the female's snout, preparatory to depositing his spermatophore. In these species the female deposits her eggs singly, and carefully wraps the leaf of an aquatic plant around each one — a tank planted with a suitable species, such as *Elodea* or *Sagittaria,* is therefore essential in breeding these species.

In other species courtship may be far less ritualised, and in many a form of amplexus occurs, the males grasping the females from below by using their limbs and/or tail in order to prevent her from swimming or crawling away.

The accommodation of salamandrids is obviously dependent upon their natural habits. The newts may adapt to an aquatic environment throughout the year, simplifying their care, but this is unnatural and it could well be that this can reduce or eliminate their willingness to breed. Terrestrial species, and newts during their terrestrial phase, may be kept satisfactorily in a vivarium containing a layer of leaf-mould liberally covered with bark, etc, for cover. Artificial habitats, comprising moist tissues or foam rubber in glass or plastic containers, may also serve as temporary quarters.

Cynops pyrrhogaster   Japanese Fire-bellied Newt

JAPAN

8–10 cm. The commonest and best of the Asian newts, this species is chocolate brown above and bright orange or red beneath. Owing to its prominent parotid glands and dorso-lateral ridge, it appears almost square in cross-section, particularly in the case of males.

This is a tough, undemanding newt, which may be kept in clean cool water throughout the year. Its food and general care are as in the family description, but to date captive breeding has presented difficulties. The females swell with eggs, and the males' tails take on a purplish sheen, but egg-laying rarely occurs, or at most only a few eggs are laid. It seems likely that a hibernation period is essential, and well-planted, well-aerated water appears to give the best results.

Notopthalmus viridescens   Red-spotted Newt

EASTERN NORTH AMERICA

6–10 cm. An attractive newt, similar in general appearance to the European *Triturus* species. The adults are olive above, yellowish-green below, with spots or lines of red on the flanks, the shape and extent of which depend upon subspecies. The male has no crest during the breeding season, but a broad tail fin develops, and dark rough patches appear on the insides of his hind legs — these help him to grasp the female, for in this species amplexus occurs.

The juvenile form is totally different in appearance, being a small brick-red to orange creature with a few small black markings, and it has even been given a separate name, Red Eft. The Eft is completely terrestrial in habits until it becomes of breeding size, by which time its markings have changed to the adult phase.

Care and breeding are as in the family description, the Red Eft being treated as a small salamander.

Pleurodeles waltl   Ribbed Salamander

SOUTHERN SPAIN, MOROCCO

15–30 cm. The Ribbed Salamander is a robust, rough-skinned species, distinguished by two rows of tubercules marking the ends of its ribs. In colour it is mainly olive-brown, young examples often being marked with darker blotches.

In captivity it does very well in an entirely aquatic set-up, and rarely attempts to leave the water even if given the opportunity. A layer of pebbles should cover the bottom of the tank, and a few clumps of *Elodea* or similar plants are all that is required, apart from food, which consists of earthworms and aquatic invertebrates and occasionally chopped meat. To induce breeding, the water should be changed and the aquarium moved to a brighter position, such as an east-facing window. The male grasps the female from below with his fore-limbs and they may remain in this position for twenty-four hours or more before the spermatophore is transferred. 60–100 eggs are usual, although more may be laid if the female is large. Incubation and rearing of the young are as for the Axolotl (*see* page 121). Although the young metamorphose they do not leave the water, so there is no break or change in the feeding régime, merely a gradual increase in the size and amount of food offered.

Salamandra salamandra   Fire Salamander (2)

EUROPE, PARTS OF NORTH AFRICA AND ASIA

15—30 cm. Although there is a great deal of variation within this species, giving rise to a number of subspecific forms, all Fire Salamanders are brightly marked with brilliant yellow or orange blotches or stripes on a deep glossy black background. These colours warn predators of the high toxic secretions which are produced in, and exuded from, the prominent parotid glands above the eyes. Examples from central France and the Pyrenees are especially well marked, with a pair of broad lemon yellow bands running from snout to tail.

Fire Salamanders usually occupy mossy, boulder-strewn valleys in hilly or mountainous countryside, and are nocturnal except during wet weather when they may emerge during the day. Mating takes place on the land, the male carrying the female on his back until he deposits his spermatophore on the ground and lowers her on to it. Development may take place completely within the female's body, especially in populations from high altitudes, but the more usual method is for well-developed larvae to be deposited in water, often mountain streams. The gestation period varies according to the activity pattern of the colony, which in turn depends upon its location and altitude. The larvae may be deposited in more than one batch and usually total 15–30 in number. To begin with they are grey with a few bronze blotches, but by the time they metamorphose the distinctive adult markings have appeared.

Fire Salamanders usually thrive in captivity, and may often breed. They require cool (maximum 20°C) and humid conditions, plenty of space and an abundance of hiding places. They soon become accustomed to being fed during the day, especially if their cage is lightly sprayed at the same time and the lighting is not too intense, and will emerge to capture their prey, consisting of slugs, earthworms, and other soft-bodied invertebrates. They may be kept successfully in an outside reptiliary if this is well planted and situated in a damp shady corner.

Pregnant females, recognisable by their increased girth, require shallow pools with gently sloping sides for deposition of the larvae, as they habitually give birth by lowering their tail and vent into the water while the rest of their body is on dry land. If the pond or bowl has steep sides, the adults may easily drown.

Rearing of the young is as for the Axolotl (*see* page 121). The newly metamorphosed young are 3–5 cm in length and are capable of dealing with whiteworms (Enchytraeidae) and small earthworms straight away.

Triturus alpestris   Alpine Newt

EUROPE

10–12 cm. An attractive purple to black newt with a plain orange belly. Small round black spots occur on the neck and flanks. Males are more vividly marked than females, especially during the spring, when they can be further identified by a very low crest along their back and tail, marked with black and white bars.

The Alpine Newt is one of the more aquatic species, some

individuals rarely venturing more than a few feet from the water, so its accommodation is simply arranged. All that is required is an aquarium containing 15 cm or more of water, heated to about 20°C in summer, and with a liberal helping of plants.

Breeding may occur in the aquarium, usually as a response to increased day length and/or temperature, but is more likely in an outdoor pond where it will become a regular event once the animals are established. This species goes through the elaborate display characteristic of *Triturus* species, the eggs being attached to aquatic plants. Care of the larvae is as for the Axolotl (*see* page 121), but upon metamorphosis the young will leave the water if allowed to do so and will then require small worm foods such as *Enchytraeus* species, fruit flies, baby crickets or graded sweepings. The terrestrial phase lasts until sexual maturity is achieved, usually in the second or third summer. Young animals may be prevented from leaving the water and fed on the more easily available foods such as *Tubifex* and *Daphnia*, but the effects of this procedure on their subsequent breeding behaviour are unknown.

Triturus cristatus   Crested Newt

EUROPE

10–15 cm. A dark, rough-skinned newt with an orange belly irregularly spotted with black. During the breeding season (spring) the males have a high ragged crest from which the species derives its name. At other times the crest is barely visible, but may be felt as a slight ridge. Females lack this, but individuals from some parts of the range may have a dull yellow vertebral stripe, also present in juveniles of either sex.

The Crested Newt invariably leaves the water at the end of the summer, if not before, and also attempts to do so in captivity, even if this merely means clinging to a small emergent rock. When this occurs, arrangements should be made to house it for a while in a damp, mossy vivarium following which a few weeks' hibernation at around 4–6°C (for instance in the bottom of a refrigerator) will prepare it for the next breeding season. Animals forced to remain in water throughout the year still grow crests in the spring, but their general vigour and willingness to breed are diminished.

Care of adults and larvae is as for *T. alpestris*.

Triturus helveticus Palmate Newt

EUROPE

5–9 cm. A slender newt with pale brown back and orange underside. Dark spots mark the sides and a few are found on the belly. The breeding male develops a low straight crest and a distinctive tail filament.

Care and breeding are as for *T. alpestris.*

Triturus marmoratus Marbled Newt (3)

EUROPE, NORTH AFRICA

8–12 cm. In shape and size this species is similar to *T. cristatus,* to which it is closely related, but its colouration immediately sets it apart from all other newts, being bright green and black above, with a grey belly. The females are further decorated with a bright orange vertebral stripe, and the male has a high black and white barred crest during the breeding season.

In captivity this species seems content to lead a more aquatic life than other *Triturus* spp. provided the temperature remains around 20–25°C, but in the wild it leads a terrestrial way of life once breeding is over — forced upon it in many instances because the pools in which it breeds begin to dry up rapidly. Animals kept in moist vivaria are often more brightly coloured than those kept aquatically.

Breeding in aquaria is quite possible, but these should be as large as possible and well planted. Care of the eggs and larvae is as for *T. alpestris.* This species has been known to hybridise with the Crested Newt, producing young which have the bright orange ventral markings of that species, combined with the green and black dorsal markings of the Marbled Newt. A more attractive newt would be hard to imagine.

Triturus vulgaris Smooth Newt

EUROPE

5–9 cm. Very similar in appearance to *T. helveticus,* except that the breeding males have a beautiful serrated crest and heavily spotted bodies. The females, however, are difficult to separate, but those of the present species usually have slightly deeper orange bellies, and there may also be a small amount of ventral

130

spotting. Their care and breeding are as for *T. alpestris.*

Family Plethodontidae - Woodland Salamanders

This very large family is confined to the New World save for one genus, *Hydromantes,* which is found in Italy. The family is not a popular one amongst vivarium-keepers, presumably because its members are, in the main, small secretive species, often of non-descript appearance. In addition, many species are rare or have very limited ranges.

However, several members of the genera *Plethodon* and *Pseudo-triton* are of moderate size and are attractively coloured or marked, and are occasionally available. Their care follows that of other terrestrial salamanders — cool, damp conditions, plenty of hiding places, subdued lighting, and a diet of small earthworms and other soft-bodied invertebrates.

Their life-cycle differs radically from those of other families in that development takes place inside the egg, which is almost always laid in a damp place on land, there being no aquatic larval stage. It would be of great interest to breed these species, but as far as is known this has not yet been accomplished, at least on a predictable scale.

Plethodon glutinosus　Slimy Salamander

NORTH AMERICA

8–12 cm. A sticky, slender salamander, marked with many small white flecks on a dark grey background.

The Slimy Salamander occurs beneath leaf-litter and logs etc on damp shaded hillsides. Its care is similar to that of other salamanders (*see* page 117), but this species is quite quick-moving, and may be given flies and other lively insects to eat. No records of captive breeding have been traced.

Pseudotriton ruber　Red Salamander

EASTERN NORTH AMERICA

8–12 cm. A red or orange salamander, speckled with round black dots. Old individuals sometimes become dull orange or brown.

This is a slender species which is also quite agile.

Although the Red Salamander is terrestrial, it comes from very damp habitats and this should be borne in mind when arranging its acommodation. A layer of damp moss or foam rubber with broken crocks or pieces of bark probably suit it best, and it is essential to keep it cool (maximum temperature 20°C, preferably less). Its food consists of small invertebrates, possibly including aquatic species which live in shallow streams, such as *Gammarus*. No records of captive breeding have been traced.

10
Order Anura - Frogs and Toads

As with 'newts' and 'salamanders', the two terms 'frog' and 'toad' may lead to confusion. What is the difference between a frog and a toad? Strictly speaking, toads are members of the genus *Bufo* and frogs belong to the genus *Rana*. However, as this leaves the vast majority of anuran species without labels, we arbitrarily assign one or other of these categories to each, the dry warty species usually being called toads, the smooth slippery ones frogs. Some species are variously classed as first one, then the other, depending upon the author. As frogs and toads are all anurans, i.e. tailless amphibians, as far as the herpetologist is concerned the distinction exists only in common usage.

The typical frog or toad life-history must be well known to just about everybody, the 'frog-spawn–tadpole–froglet' transition being taught, and perhaps demonstrated, in every biology class. However, not all species keep to the rules, and the varied ways of reproduction within this order are alone worthy of a book, and some of these more unusual life-cycles will be noted in the succeeding pages where they apply to species which are suitable and available for vivarium culture.

A summary of a typical frog's breeding and development is as follows. Breeding activity may be initiated by increased day length, temperature or humidity, and may or may not be preceded by a period of hibernation. In many species the male calls to attract a mate, and in large breeding aggregations there may be competition between males. Prior to egg-laying, the male grasps the female in a characteristic embrace, known as amplexus, the position of which varies slightly, depending on species. This stimulates the female to lay her eggs, which may number from a few to several thousands. As this occurs, the male sheds his sperm to fertilise them, and they swell until they form large floating masses.

In captivity the eggs may be removed at this stage to incubate; alternatively, if the aquarium has been specially prepared for breeding purposes, the adults are returned to their permanent quarters. The water should be suitable for the development of the eggs: approximately neutral (pH 6.5—7.5), free of chlorine or other contaminants, and at a temperature approximating to that in the animals' natural habitat. As a rough guide, this will be 15–20 °C for temperate species, 20–25 °C for sub-tropical species, and 25–30 °C for tropical ones. A formula for artificial pond water is given below for use if suitable water is not obtainable from natural sources.

Make two stock solutions as follows:

Stock A	*Stock B*
175 g NaCl	5 g NaHCO$_3$
35 g CaCl$_2$	2 l distilled water
2 l distilled water	

Add 20 ml of solution A, and 20 ml of solution B, to 5 l distilled water to make artificial pond water.

Note that many freshwater parasites infest frogs and toads at some stage in their life-cycle, often entering the host during its tadpole stage and maturing after it has metamorphosed. Water collected from ponds where frogs and tadpoles occur is therefore likely to contain some of these parasites and is best avoided. Rainwater from small temporary pools or, ideally, spring water, should be used whenever possible.

Care of the eggs consists of ensuring that the water is adequately aerated, if necessary by the use of an air pump, and daily inspection and removal of eggs that have been attacked by fungus. This is best achieved with a bulb pipette. A weak solution of 0.025% malachite green may be used to inhibit fungus growth if required, but normally only infertile eggs are attacked, and provided these are removed before they go bad and damage adjacent eggs there should be no serious trouble of this nature.

Upon hatching, the larvae will remain attached to the jelly mass for a day or two, then disperse and attach themselves to plants or to the sides of the aquarium. Gradually, the yolk-sac from which they derive their nourishment is absorbed, and feeding commences. Their first food is usually algae, and it may be possible to provide this by adding plants and other objects on which an algal film has formed, and if well lit the container will be colonised by soft algae on which the larvae will graze. A more reliable food source is lightly boiled lettuce, or flaked fish food. The latter is probably more nutritious, but over-feeding must be avoided at all costs, or the water will quickly become fouled, killing the larvae. Siphoning with a narrow tube should be carried out daily in order to remove uneaten food and other waste, topping up with water of similar temperature and type. Growing plants help to keep the water oxygenated and 'sweet'. The maintenance of a biologically balanced aquarium is not easy, however, especially if large numbers of larvae are present, and artificial means of aerating, and possibly filtering, the water are usually required. If a power filter is used it must draw water from a part of the container to which the tadpoles have no access, or they may get drawn up into the pump. This is most simply avoided by partitioning off a corner of the container with a perforated divider.

As the larvae grow, their food requirements escalate, and if inadequately fed they begin to devour each other — a sure sign that more food, or food with a higher protein content, should be given. Eventually their hind legs appear, followed by their front legs, and at this point their appetites diminish as their tails are absorbed and their life on land begins. Emergence may be assisted by placing rocks or flower-pot fragments in the water, which should be shallow, or the container may be tilted so that one end is left uncovered by water. This land area should be covered with rubber sheeting to help the tiny amphibians to escape from the water tension, and caves of broken flower-pots should be available for hiding under.

From now on their care and maintenance is similar to that of the adults, although their food will necessarily be smaller — baby crickets, whiteworm, small flies and graded sweepings. If food is always available the young grow rapidly, and some small species may reach sexual maturity within six months of metamorphosis. Normally, however, this is attained in one to two years.

Care of the adults consists of maintaining suitable levels of temperature and humidity, which of course depend upon the origin of the species concerned, and of offering a suitably varied diet. Most anurans are by nature shy and retiring, and the lighting, planting and arrangement of rocks, logs and other retreats should reflect this if they are to adapt successfully to captive conditions. Hibernation at 4−6°C, for those species which require it in order to breed, may be achieved by placing the animals in a container filled with moist moss or foam rubber, and keeping them in the bottom section of a domestic refrigerator for the required amount of time (*see also* page 45).

Family Pipidae - Tongueless Frogs

This primitive but very interesting family consists of three genera in Africa and one in South America. All the species are entirely aquatic and may be easily maintained in aquaria of suitable size containing water of around 23–28°C. A lid should be fitted to prevent them from leaping or climbing out.

All of the following species are well worth keeping owing to their fascinating life-cycles as well as their appearances.

Pipa pipa   Surinam Toad (4)

SOUTH AMERICA

15–20 cm. The body of this species is remarkably flattened in form. The fore-legs are small and the fingers end in strange star-shaped appendages, which are sensitive to touch and of undoubted usefulness in the murky waters which form the toads' natural habitat. The hind legs are large and powerful, with enormous webbed feet. The eyes, when they can be located, are small and appear to have been put on in the wrong place. In colour, the animal is completely mottled in various shades of grey and brown, but varies in shade depending upon its surroundings. Its upper surfaces are covered with small pointed protuberances, whereas its ventral surface appears to have two 'seams' — dark grey lines running up the midline and across the throat region.

It is an easy animal to care for, requiring an aquarium of around 100 litres per pair, filled with neutral or slightly acid water heated to about 28°C. It seems most happy if there is plenty of plant life to hide in, a useful variety being Java Moss, *Vesicularia dubyana,* which can withstand the constant buffeting it gets from the toads' movements. Live fish are the preferred prey, taken with startling rapidity as the toads lunge forward, propelled by a single kick of their flippers. However, they may also be persuaded to take strips of meat and liver if these are moved about, or dropped slowly in front of them. Contact with finger-tips appears to initiate an attack more often than visual contact.

Sexing non-breeding adults is not always easy, although the female has an extendable ovipositor which is slightly tubular at all times. Males call underwater with a clicking 'song', but it is often difficult to see which animal is involved. At the advent of the breeding season (simulated by raising the water level and dropping the temperature suddenly), the animals become quite active, milling around and often quivering if one should come into contact with another (irrespective of sex).

Egg-laying is a complicated affair, the male holding the female in front of the hind legs, and the pair of them swimming upwards and then over to complete a somersault. While they are upside down a number of eggs are laid and manoeuvred on to the female's back where, being slightly sticky, they stay. After several such sorties 60–100 eggs will have been laid, covering the female's back, although some will have fallen to the floor. Twenty-four hours later the female's back will have begun to swell around the eggs, and by Day 10 each egg will be embedded in its own individual chamber where its development right up until metamorphosis will take place. This is achieved in 12–20 weeks, when the tiny toads emerge by pushing their way through the membranes that cover each pocket.

In captivity, it seems quite common for all the eggs to fall from the back of the female after 4 or 5 days without ever having become properly embedded. The reason for this is not clear, but it is thought that infertility may be a cause.

On other occasions, the eggs develop normally but the young are weak and either die before leaving their compartments or shortly afterwards without feeding. It is possible that water quality, especially its pH value, is important.

Another species, *Pipa carvalhoi*, is occasionally available. This is smaller than *P. pipa* and less flattened in appearance. Its care is similar and it has the advantage of being much easier to breed – the young are released from the female's back as filter-feeding tadpoles, and these may be reared in the same manner as that described for *Xenopus laevis*.

Hymenochirus boettgeri   Dwarf Clawed Toad

AFRICA

2.5–3.5 cm. This very small pipid looks like a miniature version of the Surinam Toad, and is probably somewhere between it and *Xenopus* on the family tree of evolution. It may be kept in a small, dimly-lit aquarium, perhaps in company with tropical fish, but if serious attempts to breed it are planned it should be kept separately in small groups, in fairly shallow water of 20–25°C. When the females become plump, showing that they are ready to spawn, the temperature is raised slightly to stimulate breeding behaviour.

The spawning procedure is essentially similar to that of *Pipa pipa*, the pair rising to the surface then turning over on to their backs, at which stage the male 'pumps' the female slightly and 1–12 eggs are expelled. Unlike *Pipa* species, however, *Hymenochirus* do not carry their eggs; they are left to float to the surface or to sink to the bottom of the aquarium. Up to 1,000 eggs may be laid, although a proportion of these will almost certainly be infertile.

Hatching takes place after 48 hours, and after a further 4–5 days the tadpoles begin to feed on protozoa and other microscopic life, not on plant material as is usual amongst anuran larvae. They soon progress to larger fare, which in captivity may be brine-shrimp nauplii or small *Daphnia*, and after 3–4 weeks the limbs appear. Complete metamorphosis takes place after a total of 6–10 weeks, and the young toads become sexually mature within a year, by which time they can deal with *Tubifex, Enchytraeus* worms, large *Daphnia*, and adult brine-shrimp.

Xenopus laevis   Clawed Toad

AFRICA

8–15 cm. The Clawed Toad is pale to dark grey dorsally, with an off-white underside. Its skin is smooth and slippery, and its hind feet are large and well adapted for swimming. The fore-legs are much smaller, and are used to push food into the mouth. Clawed Toads spend most of their time lying motionless, just below the surface of the water.

Their care is extremely simple. They are content with an

aquarium containing 8–20 cm of warm water, and two good meals each week, consisting of worms, fish or pieces of meat. Their aquarium may be furnished with gravel and rocks, but if necessary they will live quite happily in a bare tank.

Females are much larger than males, and have small fleshy flaps (anal papillae) immediately above their cloacae. Breeding may be stimulated in the same way as for *Pipa Pipa*, or it may be induced artificially by injections of hormone, chorionic gonadotrophin, prepared specifically for this purpose, and available from biological suppliers. Detailed instructions for its use are included with each set of chemicals; but the usual régime is to give a primer injection to condition the animals, followed by a larger dose two or three days later to initiate amplexus and egg-laying. Following the injection, the pair should be left undisturbed in a dark place until mating is over. To prevent them eating their own eggs, the bottom of the container may be covered with a raised grid through which the eggs can fall out of harm's way, but this is usually superfluous. The eggs are removed and incubated in a separate aquarium or shallow dish, those affected by fungus being removed as soon as it appears. The tadpoles differ from those of most other anurans in that they feed on suspended food particles, and because of this are of unusual appearance and habits. Their typical posture is to hang head down at an angle of about 45° in mid-water, their long whip-like tail vibrating rapidly to produce a current which will bring their microscopic food to them. By regularly gulping at the water and expelling it through their gill slits, micro-organisms and edible detritus are filtered out.

When the animals are kept in captivity, this food may take the form of liquefied fish food as fed to newly hatched fish-fry, or of organic 'soup' taken from natural ponds. Food should be added only when the cloudiness produced from the previous batch has been eliminated by the feeding activities of the larvae. *Xenopus* tadpoles reach a very large size, and a large brood may have to be divided and re-accommodated several times before they metamorphose. The young toads are, like their parents, carnivorous; appropriate foods are *Tubifex*, small pieces of earthworm or finely minced liver.

Adult or larval *Xenopus* species should not be released into local ponds or rivers where they could establish colonies which become detrimental to native aquatic wildlife.

Xenopus tropicalis

WEST AFRICA

Males to about 4 cm, females 6 cm or more. *X. tropicalis* has recently become widely available through the tropical fish trade, where it is usually sold as a 'Dwarf Aquatic Frog'. It is a small replica of the better-known *X. laevis*, being dark grey dorsally, lighter beneath, and occasionally having a dirty yellow or rust-coloured patch just forward of the eyes.

Temperature 24–27°C, although lower temperatures can be withstood, at least for a while. This is a very hardy, very voracious species, ideally suited to those with a limited amount of space, but definitely *not* good company for small tropical fishes, which invariably end up as very expensive food for a creature which is perfectly content with a steady supply of earthworms, *Tubifex*, or small insects dropped onto the surface of the water. Unlike the larger species, it is not too destructive and can be given a planted aquarium provided that robust, well-rooted plants such as *Vallisneria* or *Cryptocoryne* spp. are used. A pile of rocks or a piece of driftwood will provide a refuge, and a small filter will cope adequately, enabling the set-up to be more or less permanent. Although I can find no records of captive breeding, I suspect that reproductive activity can be induced by allowing the water-level to drop over a period of weeks through evaporation and then raising it suddenly by the addition of cooler water, simulating the onset of the rainy season which is its natural stimulus. The tadpoles are typical of the family, being filter-feeders, and require similar attention to those of *X. laevis*.

Similar species: *X. mulleri* and *X. borealis*, intermediate in size between the two previous species, are sometimes available. Their care is identical to that of *X. laevis*.

Family Discoglossidae - Fire-bellied Toads, Painted Frog and Midwife Toad

Although this Old World family has few species, several of them are frequently available and make splendid subjects for the vivarium. They are characterised by a tongue which cannot be extended as in other frogs and toads, and as a result feeding takes the form of a somewhat clumsy lunge, with the fore-limbs sometimes helping to push the food into the mouth. Some species demonstrate aposematic (warning) colouration consisting of a brightly coloured underside which advertises the toxic properties of their skin, while the dorsal surface is green or grey and provides camouflage. When threatened, these species suddenly raise their limbs and arch their backs, exposing the bright colours and startling the aggressor. Captive examples, however, rarely perform. Yet another species, *Alytes obstetricans,* though being of much more sombre appearance, possesses one of the most remarkable life-histories of any frog or toad (see below).

The discoglossids require a damp or semi-aquatic vivarium which should contain plenty of hiding places in the form of bark, rocks or broken plant pots. Insects, especially crickets and flies, are avidly taken, either on land or from the surface of the water, which should be 5–10 cm deep, and may be partially covered with floating plants such as *Salvinia* species.

The sexes are distinguished by the more slender outline of the males, which also have thicker fore-limbs than the females. Their calls are limited to short single notes, repeated several times. Breeding, which usually takes place in the spring, but which may continue throughout the summer, can often be induced by increasing the duration of light, or by moving the tank to a lighter position. The tadpoles will graze on algae or boiled lettuce, or will eat artificial diets such as flaked fish food. The European species may safely be hibernated through the winter, and are amongst the best choices for the garden reptiliary and pond, where, under conditions of semi-liberty, they will breed regularly.

Alytes obstetricans   Midwife Toad

EUROPE

4–5 cm. A small grey toad, almost as broad as it is long, with large round eyes. This species is different from the rest of the family in that the males do not develop nuptial pads during the breeding season.

Alytes is the least aquatic of the discoglossids and is often found amongst rocks or in burrows some considerable distance from water. It is also amongst the shyest species, and should be given the security of a well-planted vivarium with plenty of

Fig. 38 *Alytes obstetricans*, the Midwife Toad – this male is carrying a string of eggs.

hiding places. A water area is unnecessary so long as a fair degree of humidity is maintained.

Breeding has rarely been achieved in captivity, which is a great pity as the Midwife Toad's life-history has attracted a good deal of interest over the years. Its nocturnal courtship is carried out entirely on land, the male attracting the female with his call, which is described by some authorities as bell-like. He then clasps her high up on her back while the eggs are laid and fertilised. These are few in number, 20–40 being the average, and arranged in a string. The male immediately entwines this around his hind legs, and by visiting pools and puddles when necessary he keeps them moist, at the same time giving them a high degree of protection. When they are ready to hatch, he deposits them in a small body of water, often man-made troughs and cisterns when available. Here they grow to a surprisingly large size, and characteristically hang tail down from the surface, diving rapidly to the bottom if disturbed. The newly metamorphosed young are relatively large.

Animals kept out of doors in a suitable enclosure often do breed, however, and several small but thriving colonies have survived for many years in parts of England. Although they are secretive and difficult to observe under these conditions, their calls will be heard throughout the warmer months of the year and animals can usually be found if stones, etc, are turned over occasionally.

Bombina bombina   Fire-bellied Toad

EASTERN EUROPE, WESTERN ASIA

4–5 cm. The back is grey or greenish-grey, the underside bright red or orange mottled with a roughly equal amount of black. The voice of this species has given it the common name of *Unke* in Germany.

Care is as given in the family description. This species is very aquatic, and may benefit from a vivarium containing rather more water than land. For some unknown reason, this is a difficult species to breed; newly imported animals often go into amplexus but rarely lay eggs. However, they thrive in captivity and are particularly long-lived. They will live outside throughout the year, provided that there is a suitable site for hibernation.

Bombina orientalis   Oriental Fire-bellied Toad (5)

SOUTH-EAST ASIA

6–7 cm. This almost unbelievably colourful species has a bright red and black ventral surface, and an equally bright green and black dorsum. Apart from the usual sex differences, the male's back is slightly rougher than that of the female, but his most obvious distinguishing feature is the greater thickness of his fore-arms.

Care and breeding are as in the family description, but low temperatures such as those experienced in outside reptiliaries should be avoided; however, a drop of 5–10°C in the winter is tolerated, and may be beneficial. If water is permanently available, as in a divided vivarium having roughly equal areas of water and land, and if a temperature of around 25°C is maintained, this species breeds easily and repeatedly throughout the summer. The male grasps the female in a pelvic amplexus at every opportunity, particularly during feeding sessions or other periods of activity. If not in breeding condition she will respond with a repeated rejection call until released, otherwise egg-laying commences several hours later, usually during the night. A single spawning may produce up to 300 eggs, laid singly or in small clumps, but smaller clutches (up to 100) are more usual, especially if breeding has occurred regularly. The eggs rest on the bottom, which may be covered with a layer of stones or pebbles to which they will adhere slightly. They may then be removed for rearing in the usual way.

Alternatively, the adults may be kept for most of the year in a terrestrial set-up containing damp moss or a layer of foam rubber, with the usual caves of rock, bark etc, and introduced to a separate breeding tank only when eggs are required, then subsequently returned, allowing the eggs to develop *in situ*. They hatch in 8–10 days, and if fed well the young begin to metamorphose 3 weeks later. Sexual maturity is attained during their second summer.

Captive-bred young are rarely as colourful as wild-caught animals, owing to the absence of the red pigment, canthaxanthin, in their unnatural diet of insects and so on. This can be remedied by feeding young frogs on fresh-water crustaceans such as *Daphnia* or *Gammarus,* or by adding the extracted pigment to their diet as a supplement (as with colour feeding of flamingos, certain tropical fish etc).

Bombina variegata   Yellow-bellied Toad

EUROPE

4–5 cm. Similar in appearance to *B. bombina,* except for the yellow, rather than red, underside. Where the ranges of the two overlap, they may hybridise, in which case the markings and colouration are intermediate between the two forms.

Care and breeding are as for *Bombina orientalis.* A very easy species. If kept outside they should have access to a shallow pond, well stocked with plants, particularly floating and emergent types amongst which they can hide. During warm weather they spend much time floating on, or just below, the surface.

Discoglossus pictus   **Painted Frog**

EUROPE, NORTH AFRICA

6–7 cm. A stocky, robust frog, completely lacking the warts found on the other members of the family. The colour is variable, but is usually some shade of brown with darker blotches. An attractive form has a pale vertebral line, starting at its snout. The males differ from the females in that they have webbed rear feet.

The requirements of this species are as in the family description. Breeding is easily accomplished in an outside pond. Up to 1,000 very small eggs are scattered singly over the substrate or among water plants. These are easily reared, although the tiny froglets require very small food at first.

Family Pelobatidae - Spadefoot Toads

Spadefoot Toads are found in both the New and Old Worlds, and are named for a horny protuberance on the 'heel' of each hind foot, which is used to dig rapidly into loose substrate. Those species which hail from arid regions, of which there are several, are noteworthy for their explosive breeding activity brought on by rainstorms, and for the extremely rapid development of their larvae, which takes place in evaporating pools of water.

One species is frequently available.

Megophrys nasuta   **Asiatic Horned Toad (6)**

SOUTH-EAST ASIA

6–10 cm. This species is unmistakable due to its three fleshy horns, one above each eye, and another on the end of its snout. In colouration, it is normally a mixture of brown and reddish-brown hues, which provide a good camouflage when the toad is resting amongst dead leaves.

It requires a warm (20–28°C) vivarium with a good depth of fairly loose leaf-litter, in which it will half bury itself. From this position it will ambush quite large insects such as crickets, locusts and cockroaches. No records of captive breeding have been traced.

Toads of the North American genus *Scaphiopus* (6 species), and the European *Pelobates* (3 species), are occasionally offered. They require similar treatment, but a substrate of sandy loam appears to suit them best. Conditions for captive breeding are unknown; possibly a simulation of flash-floods is required.

Family Ranidae

This large family, which includes those species that we regard as typical frogs, is widespread in distribution, being found on every continent except Antarctica. Eight subfamilies are recognised, two of which include species frequently maintained in captivity. Since the requirements of these two subfamilies differ, they are dealt with separately.

Subfamily Raninae — True Frogs

Frogs of this subfamily are too well known to require a general description. Although they are not particularly popular with hobbyists, the ranids provide the majority of frogs used in research and teaching, and as such may almost be regarded as laboratory animals. All the more surprising, then, that their reproduction in captivity is not often attempted, and correct conditions for their long-term maintenance are little-known.

Because their natural reaction to disturbance is to leap away, a large cage with plenty of cover is required if physical damage, especially to the snout, is to be avoided. Temperatures will depend on their origin, and water in which they can submerge themselves entirely should be available. The divided vivarium is therefore the most suitable accommodation in most cases. For housing great numbers, large tanks or sinks with running water are preferable, arranged in such a way that 7–15 cm of water is always present. Grid-like structures or platforms, constructed of inert materials, should be positioned at one end so that the animals can sit out of the water, and these may also serve as retreats under which they can swim. Bricks or pieces of clay plant pots provide a varied surface and prevent the animals from piling up on one another. Chlorinated water (in contrast to its ill-effects on amphibian larvae) may, in the case of adults, have the beneficial effect of reducing the bacteria population of the water, and in so doing controlling the common ailments known collectively as 'red-leg'.

Food may consist of insects, especially flies, but also crickets and locusts, and larger species may take vertebrates such as fish or young mice. In temperate species, breeding takes place in the spring, the large aggregations of breeding animals and the rafts of frog-spawn being characteristic of species in this sub-family. Hibernation is almost certainly a prerequisite of these species if breeding is to be attempted.

Pyxicephalus adspersus **African Bullfrog**

AFRICA

To 20 cm. This enormous, almost grotesque, frog is amongst the most curious of its sub-family. Its dorsal surface is dark green relieved by a series or raised longitudinal ridges. Beneath, it is creamy yellow, becoming bright yellow or orange under the fore-limbs and on the throat. Young animals are blotched in light and dark green, and have a pale vertebral stripe. Several reports of its

Fig. 39 *Pyxicephalus adspersus*, the South African Bullfrog.

147

egg-guarding habits are on record. These are rather extreme among anurans, even to the extent of its lunging at human observers.

In spite of its size, it is content with a relatively small vivarium because of its lethargic disposition. It likes to bury itself partially in moss or leaf-litter until just its eyes are above the surface, waiting for prey to come along. Large specimens will tackle full-grown mice with ease, but locusts, crickets and earthworms are equally suitable. Its appetite is prodigious, and if hungry, which is nearly always, it will lunge at prey far too large to be swallowed. In addition, it is said to have cannibalistic tendencies, especially when the newly metamorphosed young are leaving the breeding grounds *en masse*. Hobbyists are therefore warned against housing this species with other frogs, especially where there is a difference in size.

Rana catesbeiana   Bullfrog (7)

NORTH AMERICA

To 20 cm, usually smaller. This muscular species is usually green or brown with faint mottlings above, and dirty white below. The male has a larger eardrum than the female, as well as nuptial pads on his hands during the breeding season.

Bullfrogs require very large cages, preferably a greenhouse or garden frame containing a pond, and a deep layer of loose sphagnum moss or similar material in which to hide. Failure to provide adequate cover will almost certainly result in wounds to the snout. After several months the frogs become less jumpy, and once settled in they will live for many years in captivity. A temperature of 15–25°C is required during the summer, and if required the animals may be hibernated during the winter.

Adult bullfrogs have hearty appetites, requiring the equivalent of twenty or more adult locusts per week to stay in prime condition. Mice and young rats will be taken, as will fish if a suitably large water area is present, but these must be offered live, or made to appear so by being jiggled on the end of a thin blunted wire.

Breeding is unlikely except in large outdoor enclosures with extensive ponds, i.e. under semi-natural conditions. The tadpoles grow very large, and in cool climates may overwinter and metamorphose sometime during their second summer.

The large tadpoles occasionally seen in the tanks of tropical fish dealers belong to this subspecies, and are interesting to keep provided that accommodation for the metamorphosed frogs is available later. They can be kept at almost any temperature: at 20–25°C they grow quite quickly provided that their voracious appetite for softened plant material, e.g. boiled lettuce, is kept satisfied.

Rana pipiens Leopard Frog

NORTH AMERICA

6–10 cm. A frog of variable colour and markings, many forms of which are considered subspecies by some authorities. Typical markings consist of a brown or green ground colour with angular dark blotches on the back and limbs. A pale vertebral line may be

Fig. 40 *Rana pipiens*, the Leopard Frog.

present, and in many examples the markings are outlined in black.

Care is as given in the family description. This species is being bred in small numbers for research purposes, and several mutant strains exist, such as albinos. Temperature 15–25°C in summer, cooler in winter.

Rana ridibunda   Marsh Frog

EUROPE

8–12 cm. The Marsh Frog invariably has some green on its dorsal surface, a pointed snout and, in males, paired vocal sacs.

A very aquatic species, which should be provided with as large a water area as possible. It likes to crouch completely submerged, or with just its snout above the surface. Food can consist of almost any large active insect, or earthworms. Temperature 15–25°C in summer, cooler in winter.

A good choice for the outside reptiliary, it will often remain in or around any garden pool whether enclosed or not, and breed regularly, producing up to 10,000 eggs each year. However, under favourable conditions it may spread, and this could be undesirable.

Rana esculenta, the Edible Frog, and *R. lessonae*, the Pool Frog, are very similar in appearance, habits and requirements. All three species are often available, and owing to their similarity are often misidentified by dealers.

Rana temporaria   European Common Frog (8)

EUROPE, ASIA

6–10 cm. Similar to the Leopard Frog, but usually brown, yellow or greenish, and with poorly defined markings. A black mask is always present from the corner of the mouth to the eye. This is not a very aquatic species, often living in meadows and lightly wooded areas.

Care is as given in sub-family description. Temperature 15–20°C in summer, and it may be hibernated in winter.

Several other European frogs and one North American species (*Rana sylvatica,* the Wood Frog) are similar in appearance to *R. temporaria.* Their maintenance is similar to the above, but they are rarely kept.

Subfamily Mantellinae

The Mantellinae is a small sub-family of the Ranidae which is restricted to the island of Madagascar. Several of its species are brightly coloured but only one is commonly available.

Mantella aurantiaca   Golden Mantella

MADAGASCAR

2.5–3.5 cm. The Golden Mantella is a small ranid of quite astonishing appearance. Its entire surface is bright orange-gold except for a small crescent-shaped patch of bright red on the inside of each thigh. The skin has the texture, as well as the colour, of orange-peel.

Unlike several of the other brightly marked reptiles and amphibians, mantellas make good subjects for the vivarium. They are totally diurnal, active, and refreshingly bold in their manner, making them ideally suited to an attractive display tank where, despite their small size, they will be conspicuous and a constant source of interest. They come from a tropical environment and require a temperature of around 25°C, and their diet should consist of plenty of small insects, especially cricket nymphs and sweepings.

Females are rounder in shape than the males, otherwise there are no obvious sex differences. They have been bred in captivity on several occasions but this is only achieved if special arrangements are made. Their eggs are laid in small numbers in a damp and dark place on land. Upon hatching, the tadpoles make their way to water where they develop in the normal way. An appropriate set-up would therefore consist of a divided tank giving an area of water about 3 in (7.5 cm) deep, and an area of land. Pieces of flat rock, bark or cork can then be laid across the division, sloping down into the water and overlapping to provide suitable crevices for egg-laying.

151

If running water can be incorporated into the set-up, this can be arranged to run down over the layers of rock or bark and will greatly increase the chances of breeding this species as well as enhancing the appearance of the vivarium (*see* page 52).

Family Dendrobatidae – Poison Arrow Frogs

Without a doubt the Poison Arrow Frogs are like living jewels — the Neon Tetras of the amphibian kingdom. They come in a dazzling array of clashing primary colours, blues, yellows, reds and glossy black, and their bold inquisitive dispositions make them highly desirable vivarium subjects. They are exclusively South and Central American in origin, many of them limited to small areas of rain forest within this region.

They possess a virulent poison in their skin, and this is the reason for their spectacular warning colouration and presumably for their apparent boldness, and, as their name suggests, the poison of some species is extracted by certain Amerindians and used to tip their arrow-heads. The poison is not dangerous unless ingested or introduced into the bloodstream, but caution indicates that handling should be avoided wherever possible, and that if it is necessary the hands should be washed immediately afterwards.

All the species are small and rather delicate in appearance, but most do well in captivity, especially in densely planted vivaria. These should be fairly tall, as the frogs like to clamber amongst plants and branches. Although a high humidity is required, a stagnant atmosphere should be guarded against, so ventilation must be efficient. A small sunken dish of water will create an area of locally high humidity, but as the adults swim badly, or not at all, this should have plenty of pebbles or twigs in it to provide easy access and egress. Running water, provided by a small circulation pump or power filter, creates perfect conditions for them and is worth considering if a serious study is to be made.

Breeding is particularly fascinating and has been accomplished with several species. They breed repeatedly throughout the year provided that they are well fed and conditions are to their liking. The males, distinguishable upon close examination by their vocal slits, are particularly territorial and will fight amongst themselves for dominance. The territory holder calls from a log, or a low leaf or branch, a typical call being a high-pitched trill lasting from five to twenty seconds, usually performed in the evening. A female that is ready to spawn approaches the male and may pursue him. Eventually a satisfactory spawning site is chosen and the female deposits a small clump of spawn on the ground or, more commonly, on a leaf. The male then crouches over the leaf and fertilises the spawn − alternatively, the male may shed his sperm onto the site first and the eggs are laid over it. One or other of the parents remains near the eggs until they hatch and then encourages the tadpoles to wriggle on to its back and transports them to a small pool of water where they complete their development. Under vivarium conditions it would doubtless be safer to remove the eggs to a small container where they could be kept damp until they hatched, then tipped into an aquarium for rearing, but in doing this the opportunity to observe a most fascinating aspect of amphibian behaviour would be lost.

Regular breeding occurs during the spring and summer, the main stimuli being high temperature (25−30°C), high humidity and an abundance of food. A light cycle of 12 hours light:12 hours dark should be maintained throughout the year. The animals may be housed in pairs or in small groups containing more females than males. If single pairs are kept, it is probably worth allowing the parents to tend their eggs, but small dishes of water or bromeliad plants will have to be provided so that the tadpoles can be moved once they have hatched. If more than one pair is present, it will be necessary to remove the eggs as they are laid, or one of the other frogs will certainly eat them. The leaf or stone to which the eggs are attached should be removed to a small covered dish containing enough water to moisten, but not cover, the eggs. They will hatch in 1−2 weeks and wriggle off into the water.

A well-tested alternative is to provide the frogs with an artificial spawning site in the form of a clean petri-dish covered with a half coconut shell with a section removed for access (like an igloo). The frogs will invariably use this in preference to a leaf and it can then be removed, complete with eggs, and replaced with another. The eggs can be left in their dish, which is covered, until they hatch.

Because the tadpoles are carnivorous they must be housed individually and fed on flaked fish food, freeze-dried brine-shrimp or one or two drops of chicken egg-yolk. Feeding must be regulated to provide plenty of food without fouling the water, which must be changed regularly. Development is completed in about two months, when the froglets will metamorphose, already showing some signs of the bright colours of the adults. Although clutches are small – less than 20 eggs – each female should lay at regular intervals throughout the breeding season and fairly large numbers can be reared. Breeding size is attained after about twelve months and the adults may live as long as ten years.

Food for dendrobatids should be small but plentiful, as they have surprisingly large appetites. Young crickets are relished, as are ants, which form their main diet in the wild.

The most commonly available species are described briefly as follows.

Dendrobates auratus Green Poison Arrow Frog

COLOMBIA, PANAMA, COSTA RICA

2.5–4 cm. Normally a black or brown frog with spots or stripes of green or greenish-blue, often metallic in appearance.

Care and breeding as in the family description. The call is a low buzz lasting about two seconds. Clutches of 2–13 eggs have been reported from captive females. One of the easiest species to keep and breed.

Dendrobates histrionicus

COLOMBIA, ECUADOR

2.5–3.5 cm. One of the most commonly available species and also one of the most variable. Most specimens are black and red, but the marking may take the form of red spots on a black background, red and black stripes, or black scribblings on a red background, with practically any intermediate pattern – in fact, no two are alike. The form with broad black transverse bands alternating with equally broad bands of red or yellow is now known as *D. lehmanni*.

Care and breeding are as in the family description. The call has been described as 'quack-like', and complex courtship movements have been noted. One of the more difficult species

— they often appear to do well at first but weaken and die a few weeks later for no apparent reason.

Dendrobates tinctorius Dyeing Poison Arrow Frog

THE GUIANAS, NORTHERN BRAZIL

3.5–5 cm. The largest dendrobatid and one of the gaudiest, being black with a yellow snout, two yellow dorsal stripes and yellow spots or blotches on the sides. The lower flanks, throat, thighs and ventral surfaces are heavily patterned with blue.

Care and breeding are as in the family description. A tough and relatively easy species.

Dendrobates leucomelas Yellow-banded Poison Arrow Frog (9)

VENEZUELA

3–3.7 cm. This brilliant yellow and black species is rather 'chunky' in shape, females being on average slightly larger than males. The call is high-pitched and lasts for about six seconds.

Care and breeding are as in the sub-family description. Quite easy.

Phyllobates lugubris Lovely Poison Arrow Frog

COSTA RICA, PANAMA

2–3 cm. A small, glossy black frog marked with two gold or yellow stripes from the tip of the snout, through each eye, and right down the back.

Care and breeding are as in the subfamily description, but in the case of *Phyllobates* species the eggs may be hidden beneath a leaf, log or stone.

P. vittatus is similar — it lays about a dozen eggs which hatch and metamorphose in about one month.

Forty-four other species of *Dendrobates* and three of *Phyllobates* have been described, and several of these may be available from time to time. The remaining dendrobatid genus, *Colostethus*, differs from the others in that its members are not brightly coloured: neither are they poisonous. Their life-histories, and therefore their requirements, are probably similar to those of the other members of the family, although they are rarely kept.

Family Rhacophoridae

The Rhacophorids, for which there is no convenient common name, are exclusively Old World in distribution. They are small to medium in size, and many species are remarkable for the construction of foam nests. These are formed by beating a small quantity of specially produced fluid with the hind legs. Their eggs are then laid into this frothy mass which protects them from desiccation until they hatch, at which time they wriggle out of the nest and drop into water.

Many forms are arboreal and have adhesive pads on their digits to improve their agility, thus paralleling the better-known Hylid Tree-frogs described later. Arboreal Rhacophorids require tall, spacious vivaria with plenty of boughs and broad-leaved plants to climb and rest on. The terrestrial species may be treated as typical frogs, i.e. damp vivaria with hiding places, and a small area of water. Food should consist of flies, small crickets, locust-hoppers and sweepings.

Chiromantis xerampelina   African Grey Tree-frog

AFRICA

5–6 cm. This arboreal species is marked in various shades of grey, providing good camouflage when it is at rest on bark.

Care is as in the family description, but possibly slightly drier than other species. It is a foam-nest builder, about 200 eggs being laid, but no records of captive breeding have been traced.

Polypedates (Rhacophorus) leucomystax   Asian, or Yellow, Tree-frog

SOUTH-EAST ASIA

5–8 cm, the females being very much bigger than the males. A variable species which may be brown, buff or yellowish above, sometimes with four darker longitudinal bands. Individuals are subject to colour changes, often becoming much paler during the night. The digits have expanded tips like most other arboreal frogs, and the snout is pointed.

In captivity, this species requires a large vivarium which should be at least 45 cm high. A temperature of around 27°C is satisfactory, and the air should be humid but not stagnant. Branches and, if possible, living plants should be included, although the sides of the vivarium are most likely to be used as resting places; and a diet of crickets, flies and sweepings should be provided.

The females may be twice the length of the males and about four times their weight: their throats are white in colour, whereas those of the males are grey. A large cage or, better still, a heated greenhouse is probably necessary to breed this species, but would be well worth the effort owing to its fascinating life history. The pair go into amplexus after dark and climb into a position above the water, usually on vegetation, a log or a vertical surface. Egg-laying is accompanied by the formation of a frothy mass of bubbles, produced from mucous secreted with the eggs and whipped up by the pair's hind legs. The eggs, numbering about 250, are distributed throughout this foam nest and remain here until they hatch. At this point the foam begins to liquify and the mass of tadpoles slides down into the water, where they complete their development in the normal way.

Rhacophorus species from Asia are occasionally available, including the interesting forms which are able to glide from trees by means of their large webbed feet (e.g. *R. reinwardtii*). Their care and breeding, as far as is known, are as in the family description. All are arboreal or cliff-dwelling, and most build foam nests, but details of captive breeding are unknown.

Family Hyperoliidae – Reed-frogs or Sedge-frogs

AFRICA

The Reed-frogs form a group of species which are not always easy to identify, but which are similar in habits and requirements, and are therefore treated together.

They are small frogs (up to about 4 cm) with adhesive pads on their toes for climbing. Their colours vary tremendously even within species, but some of the most attractive are bright green, yellow or striped. The males have a chirping call, and the large

Temperatures are not too critical, although 20–28°C is preferred, and food should consist of flies (e.g. *Musca*), small crickets and graded sweepings.

Hyperolius marmoratus Marbled Reed-frog

SOUTHERN AFRICA

2–4 cm. This pretty species occurs in several 'phases' – the two most common are: 'marbled' (sometimes known as *H. marmoratus marmoratus*) in which the cream background is speckled all over with black; and 'striped' (sometimes known as *H. marmoratus taeniatus*) in which the same basic colours are arranged as longitudinal stripes, like a humbug. Juveniles of either phase are plain brown.

This species, which is not always available, is one of the easiest to care for. It requires a temperature which is in keeping with its sub-tropical origins, about 23–25°C and a diet of small insects – flies and cricket nymphs are good standbys. Although they may be housed in small containers such as lunch-boxes and plant propagators, they require slightly larger accommodation if they are to breed. A successful arrangement consists of a 25-litre aquarium half-filled with water. A polystyrene platform is wedged across one end of the tank, onto which food can be dropped – the frogs will invariably spend most of their time resting on the vertical glass surfaces. A small clump of Java Moss is placed in the water and the female will attach her eggs to this. It can then be removed to another container, complete with eggs, and replaced with a fresh clump.

In this way, several batches of spawn, each numbering 200–300 eggs, may be obtained every 10–14 days from each female! The tadpoles are fed on fish-flake and/or boiled lettuce and metamorphose in approximately 60 days. The juveniles require plenty of hatchling crickets or small sweepings if they are to be raised to maturity.

Similar species: frogs of the genus *Afrixalus* are imported occasionally. Typically, these are brown with a broad cream stripe along each side of the back. They are characterised by numerous small black-tipped spines over the head, body and

Fig. 41 Juvenile Reed-frog *Hyperolius marmoratus.*

limbs. Care is as for *Hyperolius* spp., but all *Afrixalus* lay their eggs out of the water, attached to emergent vegetation. In some cases leaves may be wrapped around the clutch. No records of captive breeding have been found.

Kassina senegalensis Running Frog

AFRICA

3–4 cm. This species is beautifully marked with buff and black stripes. It is plumper than *Hyperolius* species, and is much less arboreal, therefore it is without toe-pads.

Family Microhylidae

This family is represented in the New and Old Worlds, but no members occur in Europe or Australia. Although many species are very interesting biologically, for instance the bizarre bur-rowing forms of *Breviceps*, there is only one species which is commonly available for vivarium culture.

159

Kaloula pulchra   Asian Bullfrog or Painted Frog (10)

7–8 cm. This is a strikingly marked species, its back being a rich mahogany brown, with a dark-edged, irregular cream band down each side. It is rotund, and it has no distinct neck, giving it an almost spherical shape.

This is among the easiest of tropical frogs to keep, being remarkably placid in disposition and not at all fastidious in the matter of diet. It likes to dig itself into a layer of leaf-mould or moss, but will emerge in the evening to look for food, which consists mainly of insects. Its preferred temperature is 23–30°C.

Apparently, it can survive dry conditions by burrowing, and emerges to breed with the onset of heavy rain, but unfortunately captive breeding has not been reported.

Other Microhylids may occasionally be available, most of them being burrowing species, and may be treated much the same as *Kaloula*.

Family Bufonidae - True Toads

The toad family is a very large one, absent only from Antarctica, Australia (but introduced there) and Madagascar. The majority of species belong to the genus *Bufo,* the typical squat, short-legged, warty toad, its ungainly appearance off-set by beautiful eyes and podgy, human-like hands.

Broadly speaking, the toad's development is similar to that of the frog's, genus *Rana* (*see* page 148), differing only in the arrangement of the spawn which is laid in long strings rather than in clumps. The actual number of eggs laid is staggering — as many as 35,000 have been estimated for one of the larger species.

A poisonous secretion is produced in glands behind the head (parotids), and sometimes in other parts of the body. The fluid is milky in appearance, and although it can be harmful if swallowed, it is unlikely to be of any danger under normal circumstances. Captive animals very rarely use the facility of secreting the venom.

1 *Ambystoma mexicanum*, the Axolotl (white phase). Note the external gills, present throughout the animal's life.

2 *Salamandra salamandra*, the brightly-marked European Fire Salamander.

3 *Triturus marmoratus*, the Marbled Newt — a juvenile specimen.

4 *Pipa pipa*, the Surinam Toad –
recently-spawned female with eggs stuck
to her back.

5 *Bombina orientalis*, the well-named Oriental Fire-
bellied Toad.

6 *Megophrys nasuta*, the Asian Horned Toad.

Rana catesbeiana, the familiar North American Bullfrog.

Rana temporaria, the European Common Frog – part of a spawning aggregation.

Dendrobates leucomelas, one of several brilliantly-marked Poison Arrow Frogs.

10 *Kaloula pulchra*, the Asian Bullfrog o
Painted Frog.

11 *Bufo marinus*, the Giant Toad c
South and Central America.

12 *Bufo viridis*, the Green Toad.

3 *Litoria caerulea*, White's Tree-frog, a large species from Australia and New Guinea.

14 *Hyla cinerea*, a green tree-frog from south-eastern North America.

15 *Hyla meridionalis*, another green tree-frog, this time from Europe and North America.

16 *Sternotherus minor*, the Loggerhead Musk Turtle.

17 A juvenile *Chrysemys scripta elegans* the popular Red-eared Turtle.

18 *Cuora amboinensis*, the Amboina Box Turtle, an Asian species.

19 *Terrapene carolina triunguis*, the Three-toed Box Turtle, a colourful North American species.

20 *Testudo graeca*, the Spur-thighed Tortoise – a popular pet in Europe.

21 *Geochelone denticulata*, one of two forest tortoises from South America.

22 *Coleonyx variegatus*, the Banded Gecko, a desert species from North America.

23 *Gonatodes humeralis*, a diurnal gecko from Trinidad.

24 *Geckonia chazalae*, a North African desert species.

25 *Phelsuma laticauda*, the Flat-tailed
Day Gecko.

26 *Anolis carolinensis*, the Green or
Common Anole.

27 *Basiliscus plumifrons*, the Plumed
Basilisk – a colourful semi-aquatic species
from South America.

28 *Iguana iguana*, the Common or Green Iguana – a large and spectacular species.

29 *Physignathus cocincinus*, the Thai Water Dragon – an agamid with obvious similarities to *Basiliscus* and *Iguana* species.

30 *Chamaeleo jacksoni*, Jackson's Chameleon – female.

31 *Tiliqua gigas*, the Blue-tongued Skink –
one of the largest species in the family,
hailing from New Guinea.

32 *Gerrhosaurus major*, a large species of
plated lizard.

33 *Lacerta viridis*, the Green Lizard.

34 *Podarcis lilfordi lilfordi*, Lilford's Wall Lizard – a totally black (melanistic) sub-species.

35 *Podarcis pityusensis vedrae*, Vedrà Wall Lizard – a particularly colourful island subspecies.

36 *Anguis fragilis*, the Slow-worm – one of several legless lizards.

37 *Leptotyphlops humilis*, the strange Slender Worm Snake from North America.

38 *Boa constrictor*, surely amongst the best-known species of snake.

39 *Liasis albertisi*, d'Alberti's Python – a colourful species from New Guinea found in only a few collections.

40 *Elaphe obsoleta obsoleta*, the North American Black Rat Snake – a hatchling emerging from its egg.

41 *Elaphe obsoleta lindheimeri*, the Texas Rat Snake – a young example with opaque eyes, showing that it will shortly slough its skin.

42 *Elaphe guttata*, the Corn Snake or Red Rat Snake – a deservedly popular species which breeds readily in captivity.

43 *Lampropeltis zonata*, the strikingly marked Californian Mountain Kingsnake.

44 *Natrix tessellata*, the Dice Snake – a semi-aquatic European species.

45 *Thamnophis sirtalis concinnus*, an attractive subspecies of the Common Garter Snake.

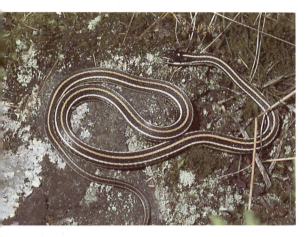

46 *Thamnophis sauritus*, a Ribbon Snake – a slender relative of the Garter Snake whose care is rather similar.

47 *Opheodryas aestivus*, the Rough Green Snake – both beautiful and easy to care for. It will eat only insects such as crickets.

48 *Vipera ammodytes*, the Sand Viper, from the dry, rocky regions of south-eastern Europe.

Most species like to burrow, or at least to retire beneath a stone or log, and their accommodation should provide for this. Toads are not particularly active creatures, and their vivarium need not be as large as for the livelier species of anurans, but it should reflect the size of the species to be kept. This can vary from 3 cm to over 20 cm in length.

The temperature should be in accordance with the species' origins, but in general not too warm. Food will consist of insects, insect larvae and other invertebrates, and some of the larger species may be capable of taking small vertebrates. Toads' appetites are enormous — they will normally sit by the food dish until it is completely empty. So in order to prevent obesity the amount offered should be rationed, unless the animal is obviously underweight.

Temperate species normally hibernate, and may be allowed to do so in captivity by withdrawing their heat source or by storing them in a cool place such as a refrigerator. Animals kept in outdoor enclosures or greenhouses will normally dig themselves in for the winter if provision is made for this. Locally occurring species soon colonise a garden pond if encouraged to do so — for instance, by introducing a string or two of spawn and providing plenty of hiding places nearby.

Males can usually be distinguished by their darker, more wrinkled throats, evidence of their vocal sacs, or by the presence of dark nuptial pads during the breeding season. In most species females are markedly larger than males. The breeding of captive examples is not common except in outdoor enclosures.

Bufo bufo   **European Common Toad**

EUROPE, ASIA, NORTH AFRICA

10–15 cm. A uniform grey, brown or olive-coloured toad with a white or cream underside. This species is unusual in having no vocal sac, and therefore no breeding call. Apart from this, its breeding behaviour is typical for northern temperate *Bufo* species. In early spring the males begin to arrive at the breeding ponds, often travelling long distances to get there. When the females arrive several days later there is intense competition between the males, the largest individuals usually being the most successful in procuring mates. In their excitement males may grasp practically anything of appropriate size, sometimes giving rise to large scrummages of males with one female (usually dead or dying) in the centre. Amplexus is axillary, and the spawn is laid in large strings, each containing a double row of eggs. The strings sink and often become entangled around aquatic vegetation through the movements of the pair. Once spawning is complete, the female leaves the pond and returns to a terrestrial lifestyle, possibly to the same home area each summer. The male may remain at the pond for several more days in the hope of mating with other females, but will eventually also leave the pond's vicinity. Development of the larvae follows the usual pattern for anurans and the small toadlets leave the water sometime during the summer, usually coinciding with wet weather, which makes their cross-country dispersal less hazardous.

The Common Toad will live in captivity for many years if cared for as in the family description. An 80–100 litre vivarium will accommodate one adult pair or four to six youngsters. Temperatures should not go above 23°C, and should ideally remain at about 12–18°C. This species is a very good choice for the outdoor reptiliary, or better still for semi-captivity in a greenhouse or conservatory.

Fig. 42 Spawn of the European Common Toad, *Bufo bufo*.

Bufo americanus   American Toad

EASTERN NORTH AMERICA

5–10 cm. This species may be regarded as the American counterpart to *B. bufo,* being similar in habits and in general appearance, although it is, on average, a little smaller. It differs also in having a vocal sac, and usually has a pale line down the centre of its back and a few dark dorsal blotches.

Care and breeding are as for *B. bufo.*

Bufo boreas   Western Toad

WESTERN NORTH AMERICA

10–12 cm. An attractive species, very plump, and green to olive in colour with a white or pale yellow vertebral stripe and a number of black blotches on its back, flanks, and limbs.

Care and breeding are as for *B. bufo.*

Bufo marinus   Giant Toad (11)

SOUTH AND CENTRAL AMERICA (INTRODUCED ELSEWHERE)

To 20 cm. Of the commonly available species of toad, this is the largest by far. Otherwise its appearance is quite ordinary, invariably being some shade of brown with few, if any, markings. It has particularly large and prominent parotid glands, the secretion from which is highly poisonous — sometimes capable of killing a dog if it should be rash enough to bite the toad. Its specific name alludes to its tolerance of brackish water, but it is by no means a marine animal in the true sense of the word.

For some reason, possibly poor treatment during transportation, some examples of this species do not adapt well to captivity, refusing to feed and eventually dying. However, those specimens which do begin to feed are very resilient and make excellent captives. Their cage must be large, with a deep layer of leaf-litter or moss, and with rocks and logs to provide cover. The temperature should be maintained at 23–30°C, and ventilation should be good to prevent a build-up of stale air. A shallow water bowl, or regular spraying, will create the required degree of humidity. A method whereby they are kept permanently in a few inches of warm water has been described, but is considered unnatural.

Food may include small vertebrates as well as large insects and worms etc, the main requirement being an ample supply. Examples which refuse to feed should be offered as large a range of food items as possible, and as a last resort force-fed with vitamin-fortified meat or insects. No records of captive breeding have been traced.

Bufo melanostictus   **Black-spined Toad**

SOUTH-EAST ASIA

To 10 cm. This is a common Asian toad which is imported from time to time. It is brown or yellowish-brown in colour with jet-black tips to the multitude of warts on its back, and black parotid glands. Young specimens may lack these black markings.

Care is as in the family description; it requires a temperature of 25–30°C.

Bufo viridis   **Green Toad (12)**

EASTERN EUROPE, ASIA, NORTH AFRICA

5–10 cm. A most attractive species, its markings consisting of green or olive blotches on a pale brown or cream background. A yellow vertebral stripe may be present.

Care and breeding are as for *B. bufo*. This species comes from fairly dry, arid regions and may therefore prefer a slightly lower humidity than most other bufonids, but moisture should always be present in at least part of the vivarium. This is another good species for reptiliaries.

Many other toads are available from time to time, some of the most frequently offered being *B. woodhousei*, *B. terrestris* and *B. quercicus* from North America, *B. mauretanicus*, *B. regularis* and *B. carens* from Africa. Care and breeding of these species are as above.

Atelopus **species**

The genus *Atelopus* is exclusively Central and Southern American and comprises about forty species. Most of them are

Fig. 43 *Bufo mauretanicus*, the Moroccan Toad.

brilliantly coloured, and are superficially similar to the dendrobatids, and like them are often referred to as Poison Arrow Frogs, although the degree of toxicity of their skin secretions is unknown. Only one species is commonly available.

Atelopus varius

CENTRAL AND SOUTH AMERICA

3–5 cm. An extremely variable species which may be yellow to green with black reticulations, or mainly black with yellow or red (or sometimes yellow and red) markings.

Care is as for *Dendrobates* species, but more difficult. Small worms, especially *Enchytreus* species, are taken as well as small crickets etc. No records of captive breeding have been traced.

165

Family Hylidae - Tree-frogs

The Hylidae is an extremely large family which provides rich pickings for the amphibian enthusiast. Although the family originated in Central America it has spread to the Old World, and Europe and Australasia are included in its range. The most obvious feature shared by most species is the disc-like modification to each digit, providing a very efficient adhesive surface and greatly enhancing their climbing ability. Most, but not all, species are arboreal, living amongst shrubs, reeds and trees, and some rarely or never descend to ground level even to breed, preferring to use small pools of water in the forks of trees or among epiphytic plants such as bromeliads.

Several species are brightly coloured, green being well represented, whereas others are brown or grey, being well camouflaged when resting on boughs or tree-trunks rather than amongst leaves.

Naturally, the arboreal species require tall cages, preferably containing living plants and boughs on which the frogs can climb and rest and from which they can launch themselves in pursuit of their favourite food, flies. Vivaria of this type lend themselves very well to planting with a selection of house-plants.

Most species, including all of the familiar North American and European ones, breed in ponds or slow-moving rivers, depositing their spawn in small clumps. Where species' ranges overlap, differences in the call may serve to prevent interbreeding. The choice of calling station may also play its part, as many species show distinct preferences in choosing the height and position from which they call. It may be important to consider this when arranging vivaria in which it is hoped to breed tree-frogs.

Some of the more specialised breeders include species that create mud bowls at the edge of pools in which to lay their eggs, or which lay them in folded leaves above water, the larvae sliding off as soon as they hatch. Females of the so-called Marsupial Frogs, genus *Gastrotheca*, have a fold in the skin of their backs in which the eggs are carried until they are ready to emerge, either as tadpoles or as froglets, according to species.

Unfortunately, some of the most interesting species are not readily available, but nevertheless the hylids are a very attractive and deservedly popular group of frogs.

Agalychnis callidryas   Red-eyed Tree-frog

CENTRAL AMERICA

A spectacularly marked tree-frog, having a green back, blue and cream banded flanks, and bright red eyes. Its toe-pads are well developed and it is exclusively arboreal in habits.

It requires a large vivarium, well planted with broad-leaved plants such as *Philodendron* species. For breeding purposes, some of these plants should hang over a large water area. Up to 100 eggs are laid on a leaf, the larvae dropping into the water as they hatch a few days later. Metamorphosis occurs after 30–50 days' development. The young feed on small insects, especially flies and crickets. Temperature 20–25°C.

Gastrotheca 'marsupiata'   Marsupial Frog

Note: Frogs of the genus *Gastrotheca* are collectively known as Marsupial Frogs, but several distinct species are included in the genus – specimens offered for sale are invariably described as *G. marsupiata* irrespective of their identity: in fact, this species has quite a small range in Peru and, as far as I know, is never imported.

Females of all the species have pouches of skin on their backs into which the fertilised eggs are manoeuvred. Some species retain the eggs until they have metamorphosed into fully-formed froglets without any free-swimming tadpole stage; the others empty the pouch when the tadpoles are in a fairly advanced stage of development. The species which is most often available (see below) falls into the latter group.

Gastrotheca riobambae   Riobamba Marsupial Frog

ANDES

To 5 cm. This species may be variable in colour but is typically bright green with a number of irregular brown markings on its back. Some individuals lack these markings altogether. It has well-developed toe-pads.

This species is very hardy, coming from high up in the Andes where it remains active at temperatures just above freezing point. It feeds on the usual variety of insects and climbs well. Up to 70 eggs are laid and carried by the female, where they can be seen as spherical lumps beneath the skin. When these have hatched she will go into the water and release the large tadpoles which then continue their development in the usual way. Under natural conditions metamorphosis may take place as much as a year later, due to low temperatures, but at 23°C it occurs after 7–10 weeks. The young frogs feed on cricket nymphs, house-flies, etc, but, as with some other species, precautions must be taken against rickets.

Considering the environmental conditions where this species is found, it should be possible to keep it outdoors for much of the year – in this way it may breed much more readily.

Other species: unfortunately, other species are rarely available. The species which produce fully-formed froglets would be amongst the most interesting to observe in captivity, but note that few species are as hardy as *G. riobambae* and require temperatures of 23–30°C.

Hyla arborea   European Tree-frog

EUROPE, ASIA

3–5 cm. A plump, robust tree-frog, being the commonest of the two European species. Usually green, with a dark stripe running from the eye, down each side to the groin, but the ground colour may change to brown or buff according to the frog's mood.

A large vivarium is necessary, at least 45 cm high, preferably more, with the usual selection of plants and branches for climbing about on. Temperature 21–27°C in summer, cooler in winter. A good subject for the greenhouse reptiliary. The preferred food of adults consists of large flies such as *Calliphora* species, but crickets, mealworms etc will be taken.

Breeding is unlikely in a vivarium but possible in a greenhouse if a fairly large pool containing plants is provided. The males have a loud rasping call and grip the females in an axillary embrace during mating. Up to 1,000 eggs are laid in small clumps of 3–4 cm diameter. The tadpoles grow quickly if kept warm (25–30°C), and are relatively large at metamorphosis (1–1.5 cm).

Hyla meridionalis (*see* Plate **15**) has a more southerly range but is very similar in appearance and requirements.

Hyla cinerea   **Green Tree-frog (14)**

SOUTH-EASTERN NORTH AMERICA

4–5.5 cm. An attractive, bright green tree-frog with a broad white or cream line down either side. In shape, it is more streamlined than the European species and has a more pointed snout.

Care is as for *Hyla arborea*, but this species is less hardy. The call is a loud 'quack', uttered repeatedly.

Hyla crucifer   **Spring Peeper**

EASTERN NORTH AMERICA

2.5–3.5 cm. A small pale brown tree-frog with a dark, cross-like marking on its back (hence *crucifer*). Like the preceding species, it may be very abundant in suitable habitats, which in this case is woodland.

Fig. 44 *Hyla regilla*, the Pacific Tree-frog, a hardy North American species.

This small species is very hardy, and does well in a greenhouse, although it is rather secretive. House flies, *Musca* species, are a convenient food. Its call consists of a short, repeated whistle.

Hyla regilla   Pacific Tree-frog

WESTERN NORTH AMERICA

3–4 cm. A variable species, the commonest phases of which are plain green, and light brown with dark markings. Some individuals change colour frequently, whereas others seem not to do so at all. A dark line through the eye is invariably present. The skin is very slightly rough, and the toe-pads are not well developed, indicating a terrestrial species, although it will climb into low vegetation.

Care is as for *H. arborea*. A hardy and resilient species, which would undoubtedly do well in greenhouses and suchlike.

Hyla (Ololygon) rubra

CARIBBEAN REGION

3–4 cm. A brown and cream striped frog with a pointed snout. This species is frequently introduced as an accidental stowaway amongst tropical fruit, especially bananas, and must be extremely numerous where they, and it, originate. This is a very fast and agile species which makes up for its dull colouration with its lively behaviour.

Fig. 45 illustrates a well-developed tadpole of this species, showing the typical tree-frog toe-pads.

Care is as for *H. arborea,* but conditions should be warmer (25–30°C throughout the year). A large vivarium is an essential requirement.

Hyla versicolor   Grey Tree-frog

NORTH AMERICA

4–5 cm. Rather unlike a typical tree-frog in appearance, being grey or grey-green with a warty back and robust form. However,

Fig. 45 Opposite: *Hyla (Ololygon) rubra* – the toe-pads can clearly be seen on this late-stage tree-frog tadpole.

the toe-pads are well developed and this species climbs well, its colouring and texture providing good camouflage when the frog is resting on the bark of trees. It has a bright orange groin, invisible when the hind legs are folded against the body but producing a flash of colour when the frog leaps.

Care is as for *H. arborea*. A tall vivarium with a rough or lichen-covered branch displays them to good effect. Their call is more musical than that of most tree-frogs, being a loud trill, quite unmistakable once heard. Certain southern populations have been renamed *Hyla chrysoscelis*, but their treatment in captivity is identical.

As mentioned above, *Hyla* species and their close relatives comprise an enormous group, many of which are sufficiently common and interesting to attract a following. Their care and maintenance will be similar to those species described above, with modifications according to size and to temperature preferences.

Litoria caerulea   White's Tree-frog (13)

AUSTRALIA, NEW GUINEA

7–10 cm. The White's Tree-frog is one of the most impressive of Australia's interesting but rarely seen herpetofauna, and captive-bred examples of this species are occasionally available. It is a large, powerfully-built, bright green tree-frog. The skin has a waxy appearance, and there is a distinctive fold immediately above the tympanum (ear-drum). The toe-pads are large and very sticky.

These attractive frogs make good captives, due mainly to their placid and undemanding dispositions. Although they are not particularly active, they should be given a large vivarium furnished with substantial branches and robust plants. Ventilation should be good, and a temperature of 25–30°C suits them well. Large examples are often capable of eating small mammals and other frogs, but locusts, crickets, and moths provide a satisfactory diet. They soon become accustomed to captivity and will even take food from the hand.

Captive breeding has been achieved on a few occasions. 200–300 eggs are laid, and these hatch within 24 hours. With good nutrition, rear legs develop in about three weeks, and metamorphosis occurs 1–2 weeks later. The young feed voraciously and within a further 2–3 months may grow to 5 cm. Females are capable of producing eggs on two or more occasions during each breeding season.

Osteopilus (= Hyla) septentrionalis   **Cuban Tree-frog**

CUBA, FLORIDA (INTRODUCED)

To 10 cm, males significantly smaller. Usually dark brown or bronze-brown, but occasionally green. A very large, very agile tree-frog which likes to climb.

A tall vivarium is essential, with plenty of food in the form of flies, crickets etc. Smaller tree-frogs will be taken if housed together. A temperature of 23–30°C is called for. No records of captive breeding have been traced.

Phyllomedusa lemur

CENTRAL AMERICA

4–6 cm. A large, bright green tree-frog, notable for its long slender limbs, and the slow deliberation of all its movements, a characteristic which is common to all members of the genus.

Care and breeding are as for *Agalychnis callidryas* (*see* page 167). *Phyllomedusa* species are all leaf breeders, but relatively few eggs are laid. The young are large (over 2 cm) at metamorphosis, which seems a critical period for them as they are, paradoxically, unable to swim, and may drown if escape from the water is not made easy for them.

Pseudacris **species**   **Chorus Frogs**

NORTH AMERICA

1.5–3 cm. The Chorus Frogs, of which there are seven species, are all small terrestrial Hylids, found in and around swamps and marshes. They have no toe-pads.

The care of these attractive species centres around a damp or semi-aquatic vivarium with plenty of cover, preferably in the form of prostrate living plants, such as *Selaginella,* and small ferns. Young crickets are the most convenient food, but graded sweepings are invaluable for providing a varied diet. Temperature 23–28°C.

The best species are probably the Ornate and Strecker's Chorus Frogs (*Pseudacris ornata* and *streckeri*), but the whole genus is undeservedly neglected by vivarium-keepers.

Fig. 46 *Ceratophrys ornata*, Bell's Horned Toad from South America. Note the similarity between this species and the unrelated *Pyxicephalus adspersus*, Fig. 39.

Family Leptodactylidae

A very large family of frogs, mostly confined to the southern hemisphere. They are found in Australia and South and Central America, with one genus in southern Africa.

The main interest in this family lies with the unusual breeding habits of several of the species. Few species are popular with vivarium-keepers, partly owing to the difficulty in obtaining animals from many of the regions in which they are found, and partly, no doubt, because of the rather dull colouration of most of them. Therefore, species from only two genera will be considered.

Ceratophrys species   Horned Toads

SOUTH AMERICA

Members of this genus, unfortunately not often available, show great similarity in appearance and habits to the unrelated African

174

species, *Pyxicephalus adspersus*, and the Asian *Megophrys* species. Like those species, the evolution of *Ceratophrys* has been arranged around the business of food gathering, and to this end they boast a disproportionately large head, necessary to accommodate their very large gape, and this they fill as often as possible with large insects and small vertebrates, mainly other frogs but also small rodents etc.

Their indiscriminating appetites make them easy captives, although solitary confinement (apart from like-sized members of the same species) is essential. A deep layer of leaf mould and moss into which they can burrow suits their ambushing tactics very well, and being tropical they require a temperature in the region of 23–30°. Captive breeding has been achieved, but only apparently by the use of hormones.

Eleutherodactylus johnstonei   **Whistling Frog**

JAMAICA

1–2 cm. This species, which is typical of its genus, is chosen to represent the dozens of species of *Eleutherodactylus*. It is a small brown or reddish-brown frog with darker chevrons on its dorsal surface. It is unremarkable in appearance, but has a rather novel call, consisting of a single high-pitched whistling note, repeated several times. Its most significant characteristic, shared with all of its congeners, is its terrestrial breeding habits. A small number of large eggs are laid on damp soil or moss, and the complete development process takes place within the unusually tough outer membrane, the fully metamorphosed froglets breaking free to continue the completely terrestrial cycle.

Care of this and similar species is quite simple. They require small, dimly-lit vivaria containing a layer of leaf-litter covered with moss and a few small pieces of bark for hiding beneath. Water is not necessary. The preferred temperature appears to be around 23°C, and small crickets and graded sweepings are eagerly taken. Provided that both sexes, which are indistinguishable apart from the male's call, are present, breeding should occur. The eggs are laid on or in the moss, where they may be left to develop or preferably removed to incubate in small containers of damp moss.

175

11
Order Crocodilia - Crocodiles and Alligators

The crocodiles and alligators provide some of the most spectacular and awesome exhibits for well-equipped zoological gardens, and some have even been bred in these establishments; but, in the main, private collections are unsuitable for housing adult specimens, and the keeping of young animals which are sooner or later going to outgrow their accommodation is considered rather pointless.

In Britain, all species come within the scope of the Dangerous Wild Animals Act 1976, and in both Britain and the United States the importation of most species is restricted, owing to their endangered status. In view of these restrictions, I have devoted only a small amount of space to their care.

Large containers are the most obvious necessity, and the water and air in them should be heated to at least 25°C at all times. Furnishings must be kept to a minimum for ease of cleaning, and equipment must be sturdy and fixed firmly in position. Basking is very necessary to crocodilians, and so a spotlight, heat-lamp or

Fig. 17 *Osteolaemus tetraspis*, the West African Dwarf Crocodile.

powerful light bulb should be installed above a convenient platform, and turned on for 8–12 hours each day.

Food should consist of a variety of items, including large insects (mainly for young specimens), dead rodents, birds and fish. Vitamin and mineral supplements are useful, possibly essential, especially where the diet contains a large proportion of fish or animal flesh as opposed to whole animals. Loss of appetite can often be blamed on too cool conditions.

A few species remain quite small (if 1–1.5 m can be regarded as small), and these are obviously the easiest to house and handle, but some of the best species, such as *Osteolaemus* species, are rare and no longer obtainable.

12
Order Chelonia - Turtles and Tortoises

The chelonians, or shelled reptiles, are an unmistakable and familiar group to everyone, and to the layman are probably the least sinister form of reptile. Their most obvious features are their bony shells, comprising an upper portion, called the carapace, and a lower portion, called the plastron, and their beak-like mouths, which have no teeth.

Chelonians live in the sea, in fresh water or on land, and they are popularly known as turtles, terrapins and tortoises respectively. Like the terms 'frogs', 'toads', 'newts' and 'salamanders', however, these names have no biological significance, and in some cases may cause confusion, as in the anomalies 'European Pond Tortoise' and 'Box Turtle', which is actually terrestrial and has the generic name *Terrapene*! In Australia, all species are often referred to as tortoises regardless of their way of life; in America, however, 'turtle' is the favoured expression, except in the case of the completely terrestrial members of the subfamily Testudininae, the familiar land tortoises.

The care of the various species of chelonians obviously depends to a large extent on whether they are aquatic, semi-aquatic or terrestrial in habit. Sea turtles grow to a very large size and do not make satisfactory captives, and are therefore not considered here.

Aquatic species require as large a volume of water as possible, but the animals should be able to reach the surface while their back feet remain on the bottom. Heating, if necessary, is accomplished by means of an immersible aquarium heater with thermostat, and with large species this must be constructed of an unbreakable material or positioned so that it is beyond the reach of the animals. Lighting should be good (although shy species may require a dark corner in which to hide), and may be provided by fluorescent tubes or tungsten bulbs. Artificial daylight tubes may be beneficial, especially in instances of sick or lethargic animals, or young. Most turtles are messy feeders and produce a large amount of waste, so efficient and frequent cleanings-out are necessary. A power filter may be capable of dealing with the waste from a few young turtles, but replacement of all or most of the water is usually necessary sooner or later. In large containers this may be accomplished most easily by incorporating a drain-hole in the base, otherwise the water must be pumped or siphoned out. When refilling, water of the correct temperature must be used.

Semi-aquatic species are most simply kept in an arrangement similar to the above, but with an area of 'land' in the form of a flat rock, log or artificial platform on which to climb. Its surface should not be rough, otherwise the animals may scratch or injure their plastrons, leading to sores and infections. Most semi-aquatic turtles like to bask, and their land area should be positioned beneath a heat source. The vivarium should be well ventilated to prevent a build-up of stagnant air above the water.

Terrestrial species require considerable space and are not usually suitable for small indoor vivaria except in the case of very young animals. Newspaper forms a convenient, though admittedly unattractive, surface, and this may be covered with a layer of chopped straw, peat, or wood-shavings. Gravel, though quite attractive, is difficult to clean thoroughly and for this reason is not recommended. A hot-spot should be provided by a heat-lamp, and a suitable retreat made available.

Many terrestrial and semi-aquatic species are suitable for outdoor enclosures in Europe and North America. A low wall or fence is necessary, and this should extend beneath the ground to 30 cm or more as many species are good burrowers; whereas for the smaller and more agile species an overhang should be constructed to prevent them from climbing out. Rocks and plants give a natural appearance, and if breeding is anticipated an area of friable soil will be required for egg-laying. Semi-aquatic species will obviously require a pool with gently sloping sides, and terrestrial varieties should have access at all times to a shallow tray of water.

Most aquatic and semi-aquatic species are carnivorous, although many also eat some plant material, especially as they grow larger and their food requirements increase. In captivity, most can be trained to take floating trout pellets, which provide a convenient balanced diet, but some natural food should also be given. Because of their bony shells, growing animals have a high calcium and phosphorus requirement, and this can be met by regular use of vitamin and mineral supplements, or by offering food with a high content of these substances, such as freshwater snails. Vitamin D is also essential, to help assimilate these minerals, and this may be provided by cod-liver oil given by hand at frequent intervals. Periodic use of an ultra-violet, or artificial daylight, lamp may be beneficial. Whole or chopped mammals, such as young mice and rats, are avidly taken and are a valuable source of many essential vitamins and minerals. They may be frozen, cut into pieces while still solid, and stored until required. Turtles housed outdoors with access to sunlight are less prone to dietary deficiencies, the signs of which are soft and deformed shells, and swollen eyes. High-quality pelleted turtle foods, e.g. Reptomin (*not* dried turtle food, which is useless), provide a complete diet for most growing and adult turtles, and can be recommended for those species which will accept them; their only disadvantage is the high cost, especially where large animals are concerned.

Terrestrial species are predominantly vegetarian and require a large amount of greens and fruit, and roughage in the form of coarse grass, hay etc. Supplements are particularly necessary in these species, especially young animals housed indoors. Some terrestrial species (possibly more than it is generally supposed), like a certain amount of invertebrate food in the form of mealworms, crickets, worms and so on, and these may be killed and mixed with chopped vegetables, fruit and supplements to form a balanced diet. Many tortoises will even eat dog or cat food, much of which is liberally fortified with vitamins and minerals and therefore forms an ideal staple diet, although deficient in roughage which should be fed *ad lib*.

Sex determination in turtles may present difficulties. In general, males have concave plastrons and long tails, and females have flat or convex plastrons and relatively short tails. Males of some aquatic species have long claws on their front feet which they use in courtship display, and in many species they are smaller than the females. Unfortunately, none of these differences are easy to spot until the animals are approaching sexual maturity.

Seasonal cues for breeding are consistent with the usual pattern for reptiles, but mating may take place out of the normal breeding season and the sperm stored for future fertilisation.

With few exceptions, courtship is rather direct, the male pursuing the female until she allows him to mount her; this takes place in the water in aquatic and semi-aquatic species. All turtles lay eggs, which are buried in soil or sand and may number from one to over a hundred. With captive animals it is usual to remove them from their nest and incubate them artificially. Note that the sex of the young is determined by the incubation temperature, low temperatures producing only males in most (probably all) species (*see* page 90). The young grow rather slowly, and several years may elapse before they are sexually mature.

Because their spatial requirements are often underestimated, turtles and tortoises are bred less frequently than other kinds of reptiles, particularly in the hands of hobbyists. However, good results are possible, and more serious attempts should be made. Because of their vulnerability to the unscrupulous collector, many species of land tortoise have been exploited for food and the pet and curio trade, and some have been rendered extinct in the recent past. This has led to the legal protection of several endangered species, and strict controls on the taking of many of the commoner types. Captive breeding may soon become the only acceptable way of making these interesting animals available.

Family Pelomedusidae

This family and the next form the sub-order Pleudodira, known as the Side-necked Turtles because they withdraw their heads into their shells by bending their necks sideways; i.e. when viewed from the front the retracted head is presented in profile.

The Pelomedusidae is a small family found in South America, Africa and Madagascar, of which few species are popular with vivarium-keepers.

Pelusios subniger   African Mud Turtle

CENTRAL AFRICA AND MADAGASCAR

Shell length 20–30 cm. The carapace is dark brown or black as are the top of the head and the limbs. The chin, throat and plastron are paler, often dull yellow.

In spite of its dull colouration, this species makes a good captive because it has a bold and inquisitive nature and is easily cared for. A few inches of water are adequate, with provision for coming out to bask. The temperature should be 25–30°C, and food may include pieces of meat as well as worms and insects, all of which are greedily taken. No records of captive breeding have been traced.

Family Chelidae - Side-necked Turtles

This family has members in South America, Australia and New Guinea. Apart from one rare species, all Australian species belong to it, and like all reptiles from this region they are rarely seen in captivity. Of the South American species, only one is well known to collectors, and in spite of its rarity its remarkable appearance earns it a mention here.

Chelys fimbriata Mata-mata

NORTHERN SOUTH AMERICA

Shell length 30–45 cm. The carapace is strongly ridged and has a rough, irregular surface, and as the species is completely aquatic it soon becomes completely covered in algae. The head is triangular when viewed from above, and is adorned with frills and filaments which serve to break up its outline. As with the Surinam Toad, *Pipa pipa,* which hails from the same region, the small eyes are at first difficult to locate, and the nostrils are at the very tip of its snout. The purpose of this cryptic design is to allow the turtle to lie waiting for its prey (which consists almost entirely of fish) to swim within range of its cavernous mouth.

In captivity, Mata-matas require large aquaria with a depth of water approximately equal to their shell length. They can be trained to eat dead fish, and poor appetite may be stimulated by the use of artificial daylight tubes. Unfortunately no records of breeding in captivity have been traced.

Several other Side-necked Turtles are occasionally available, including members of the genus *Podocnemis,* which are particularly colourful, their heads and necks having a pattern of yellow spots on them. All are fairly aquatic in habit, and some never attempt to emerge except for egg-laying. Their care follows the usual pattern for aquatic turtles, given above.

Family Chelydridae - Mud, Musk and Snapping Turtles

The Chelydridae, along with the remainder of the turtles and tortoises yet to be listed, form the sub-order Cryptodira. Unlike members of the previous two families, these species bend their necks upwards into a double curve so that their heads are retracted straight back, rather than sideways.

The Chelydrids are exclusively New World species, and as far as is known they are all very aquatic in habits, leaving the water only occasionally. Their care is therefore relatively simple — large aquaria with few furnishings and water of appropriate depth and temperature. Most species are secretive by nature, so subdued lighting may suit them best.

Chelydra serpentina   Common Snapping Turtle

NORTH AMERICA

Shell length 20–35 cm. A large, deep-bodied turtle, only partially covered by its shell, it is unable to retract its head or limbs completely. It makes up for this lack of protection by sheer aggression, being a difficult animal to handle safely when aroused. The carapace is black, with three distinct ridges running along it. The small plastron and the soft parts of the turtle are off-white to brown. Not an attractive creature by any means, but a fascinating one which, apart from being quite common, has the advantage of thriving under almost any conditions.

Adults require large containers filled to a depth of 30–40 cm with warm water (20–27°C). No furnishings are necessary, and would in any case present a nuisance, because owing to their large appetites Snappers require frequent cleaning. Food may consist of almost any meat, including dead mice, chicks, fish and strips of lean meat. Babies eat insects and small pieces of meat. They are by no means dainty feeders, and fingers should be kept well clear when offering food to large individuals. As an example of their capacity, a small specimen weighing about 500 g consumed four adult mice in one sitting, bolting them down whole. (Large examples weigh in at 15–30 kg!)

Similar species: the Alligator Snapping Turtle, *Macroclemmys temmincki*, is even bigger – length to 66 cm and weight to 68 kg, making it the largest freshwater turtle in the world. It is noteworthy for its habit of luring prey (fish, etc) by opening its mouth and wriggling a pink, worm-like process growing from the floor of its mouth. Care as for *C. serpentina* – most collections can only accommodate young examples, while adults make fine exhibits for zoos and public aquaria.

Kinosternon baurii Striped Mud Turtle

NORTH AMERICA

To 12 cm. This small turtle is dark brown to black above with three cream or pale yellow longitudinal stripes along its carapace. The plastron is dirty yellowish brown. The head is pointed and often has a pair of stripes running over the eyes to meet at the snout. This is an aquatic species which rarely strays far from water. It needs an aquarium measuring about 90 × 30 × 30 cm and a temperature of 20–27°C. A wide variety of food is taken, including floating insects, strips of fish, pelleted food and some vegetable material. If breeding is to be attempted, the tank will have to be partitioned to provide an area of sand for egg-laying. Apparently, a water depth of at least 15 cm is required for mating to take place as this occurs in water (as with all turtles). 2–4 eggs are laid about 25 days after mating, and at 28°C these hatch in 70–100 days. This species may breed throughout the spring and summer, during which time each female can lay three or more clutches.

Kinosternon flavescens Yellow Mud Turtle

NORTH AMERICA

10–15 cm. Similar in appearance to the above species, but the carapace is paler in colour (yellowish-brown to olive) so that the dark edge of each scute shows up attractively.

Care is as for *K. baurii* but no records of captive breeding have been traced.

Kinosternon subrubrum   **Common Mud Turtle**

NORTH AMERICA

Shell length to 10 cm. This species has a smooth brown carapace, marked with black at the edge of each plate, or scute. In common with other members of its genus, it has a hinged plastron enabling the turtle to close up tightly after its head and limbs are retracted.

It is found in marshy areas, or the margins of lakes and ponds, and requires shallow water in captivity. Provision should be made for basking. Temperature 20–27°C. It is entirely carnivorous, and will eat insects, worms and lean meat. No records of breeding in captivity have been traced, but in the wild 2–3 eggs are laid.

Several other members of the genus *Kinosternon,* and of the closely related *Sternotherus,* the Musk Turtles or Stinkpots (*see* Plate **16**), are occasionally available. Care of all of these is similar to the above, and although they are of rather dull appearance all are easily maintained and will live many years in captivity. The Alligator Snapping Turtle, *Macroclemys temmincki,* which is the largest freshwater turtle and comes from North America, is not often seen in captivity, but its general habits and care are basically similar to those of *Chelys fimbriata,* the Mata-mata.

Family Emydidae - Freshwater Turtles

Emydids are typical freshwater turtles — shallow-bodied, of medium size, and in many cases brightly coloured. They form the largest family of turtles and are found on every continent except Australasia, but are more common in the northern hemisphere, especially in North America. They have no single common name, although various genera go under the headings of Sliders, Map Turtles, Painted Turtles and others. In Britain they are all usually referred to as terrapins.

Although some species are often found away from water, the majority are essentially semi-aquatic in habit, and the care of these species is fairly straightforward. The adults require large aquaria with 15–30 cm of water, heated to 25–35°C by means of a (protected) immersion-type heater. About one-third of the area should consist of a basking platform, which may simply be a wooden board raised slightly above the water level by resting it across two rocks or house-bricks, thus also forming an underwater retreat. A spotlight or bulb with a reflector should be mounted immediately above this to form a hot-spot during the day.

Food is nearly always taken into the water to be eaten, and consists of fish, meat, some insects and worms, and, if possible, pieces of dead rodents. Trout pellets will usually be taken, and these may form a staple food. Shellfish, such as mussels and pond-snails, are relished and are most beneficial if fed complete with shell. The method of eating large items is to grasp them in the mouth, then break off bite-sized pieces by clawing with the fore-limbs. This invariably causes fouling of the water, and cleaning out is usually necessary on the day following a feed.

Many species are suitable for outdoor culture, either in the reptiliary, in garden frames or in greenhouses, provided a pool is available. Under these conditions, breeding, which is hardly practical in indoor vivaria, may be possible, in which case an area of sandy soil at least 20 cm deep should be provided for egg-laying. It will probably be advantageous to excavate the eggs for incubation under controlled conditions, as described elsewhere.

Baby emydids, on account of their bright colours and cheeky expressions, are exceedingly popular as pets. Since their requirements are frequently not understood it is worth elaborating a little on their care.

Although not difficult to rear, these tiny hatchlings need very careful attention to their temperature and dietary requirements if they are to grow normally and without shell deformities. The set-up may be similar to that of the adults, but small aquaria are the most suitable containers, with 4–8 cm of water and a land area which slopes gently up from its surface, making access easy without risk of injury. The light bulb or spotlight may be supplemented to good effect with an artificial daylight tube, and although a lid may be necessary this should not prevent a free exchange of air into and out of the aquarium. Water temperature should not be allowed to drop below 25°C, and a box-filter or power filter may be useful in keeping the water scrupulously clean at all times.

Although under these conditions the young turtles will be keen to feed, their jaws are rather weak at first, and easily swallowed food such as *Tubifex,* chopped earthworms and liver should be offered. As they become stronger, a greater variety can, and should, be available, including small fish pellets (not flake), and some plant food in the form of cress and lettuce, and aquatic plants such as *Elodea* and *Lemna.* Commercially produced dried turtle food is almost useless as a permanent diet.

Their most important dietary requirements are vitamin D, calcium and phosphorus, which are necessary in sufficient quantity and in the correct proportions to form the bones and shell of the growing turtles, without which the shell becomes soft and deformed. These requirements are best met by dusting the food liberally with a vitamin and mineral supplement (preferably one containing a high proportion of the above ingredients, such as those formulated for puppies) or with ground cuttlefish shell.

Care of the less aquatic emydids consists of accommodation in roomy vivaria or (preferably) outdoor reptiliaries, with plenty of rocks, logs and other obstacles amongst which they can forage. A large container of water should always be present, and in addition an area of their enclosure should be kept slightly damp. In general the terrestrial species will eat relatively more fruit and vegetation than aquatic species, but insects, worms and slugs still form a large part of their diet. Many individuals will eat tinned dog meat, into which extra vitamins and minerals can easily be incorporated.

Chrysemys picta   Painted Turtle

NORTH AMERICA

Shell length 10–12 cm. The Painted Turtles, of which there are four distinct subspecies, are among the prettiest of all the turtle clan, especially when young. The typically depressed carapace is marked with vivid yellow or red blotches and stripes, especially around its margins, where they are also visible from below. The head and neck are striped brown and yellow, and the legs are frequently marked with red. As in many species of freshwater turtles, the males are considerably smaller than the females, and in *Chrysemys* the former are further distinguishable by their much longer front claws.

Care is as given for semi-aquatic emydids, but note that Painted Turtles seem rather more delicate than some other species. The young are very small, about 2.5 cm, and are mainly carnivorous, but the adults' diet includes a large proportion of plant material. Breeding is only likely in outdoor enclosures. Mating is in the spring, 4–10 eggs being laid during early summer. Hatching takes place some 80–90 days later.

Chrysemys scripta elegans   Red-eared Turtle (17)

NORTH AMERICA

Shell length to 25 cm, males much smaller. The Red-eared Turtle is the most familiar emydid to most vivarium-keepers, instantly recognisable as soon as it stretches its neck by an orange or red stripe behind its eye. This marking is particularly

Fig. 48 *Chrysemys scripta elegans*, the Red-eared Turtle – an adult.

conspicuous in hatchlings, where it contrasts strikingly with the bright green carapace and the green and yellow head, neck and limbs. Adults become darker, particularly old males, but the 'ear' marking is always present. Apart from their smaller size, the males develop long claws on their fore-limbs with which they tickle the chin of the female during courtship while swimming backwards in front of her.

Basic care is as in the family description. Enormous numbers of the hatchlings die every year at the hands of dealers and misguided pet-keepers through incorrect care. They require an ample swimming area, shallow water, and nutritious, fresh food. They like to bask by floating at the water's surface, but occasionally venture out on to land. Simple set-ups are the easiest to clean and therefore best. Breeding in captivity has been accomplished, nearly always in outdoor enclosures. 5 to 12 eggs are the usual complement.

A variety of other small turtles, often collectively known as Sliders or Cooters, occasionally occur as interlopers with shipments of baby Red-ears. *Graptemys kohni* is mentioned elsewhere, and other species in this category include *C. floridana*, *C. concinna*, and *C. scripta scripta*, the Yellow-bellied Turtle. Essentially, care of all these is similar to that given above and in the family description. Several species of *Chrysemys* were formerly placed in the genus *Pseudemys*, which is now obsolete.

Clemmys insculpta   **Wood Turtle**

NORTH AMERICA

Shell length 12–15 cm. This attractive species has a flattened, brown carapace, and deeply sculptured scutes. The chin and throat are orange or red, whereas the top of the head and neck, and the legs, are dark brown or black.

Wood turtles are largely terrestrial, but always mate in the water, and hibernate in the mud at the bottom of pools. They require very large enclosures as they are somewhat nomadic by nature, and as they are also surprisingly agile security must be good. Both plant and animal material are eaten.

Fig. 49 *Cuora amboinensis*, the Amboina Box Turtle – closed up. *See also* Plate **18**.

Cuora amboinensis   Amboina Box Turtle (18)

SOUTH-EAST ASIA

Shell length 15–20 cm. Like other Box Turtles, this species is notable for its hinged plastron which can be closed up to protect the withdrawn head and limbs. It has a high-domed, rich brown carapace, and a yellow plastron. The head is attractively marked with pale yellow stripes on a dark brown background.

It is a semi-aquatic species which apparently eats vegetable matter, including algae, as well as insects and meat. A temperature of 26–32°C is required. Captive breeding is unknown.

It is a semi-aquatic species which apparently eats vegetable matter, including algae, as well as insects and meat. A temperature of 26–32°C is required. Captive breeding has been achieved on at least one occasion: 2 eggs were laid 42 days after mating, and these hatched about 11 weeks later.

Cyclemys dentata

SOUTH-EAST ASIA

Shell length 15–20 cm. The carapace of this species has distinctive toothed marginal scutes, particularly towards the tail, and is light brown in colour. The plastron is similar in colour but has an indistinct pattern of radiating lines, and the head is mottled with black and yellow.

Cyclemys (there is no common name) is very aquatic in habit, at least in captivity. It is omnivorous in diet, and is on the whole an undemanding species. No records of captive breeding have been traced.

Geomyda spinosa Spiny Turtle

SOUTH-EAST ASIA

Shell length 10–15 cm. A very striking species. The marginal scutes are drawn out into long spines, and the young in particular have an almost spidery appearance. A pink hue may be present, but this is lost as the animal grows, and adults are brown in colour.

A very aquatic species, but not easy. No records of captive breeding have been traced.

Graptemys kohni Mississippi Map Turtle

NORTH AMERICA

Shell length 12–15 cm. The Map Turtles are characterised by a toothed ridge down the centre of the carapace, formed by a raised knob at the bottom edge of each of the four central scutes or vertebrals. Their colloquial name of 'Sawbacks' describes this feature rather well. Young of this species are sometimes present in small numbers in the large consignments of young Red-eared Turtles, and are easily distinguishable from other Map Turtles by their bright orange eyes and a yellow or orange crescent-shaped marking behind each eye. The carapace is grey or olive with light and dark reticulations.

Care is as in the family description. They are semi-aquatic, more timid, and less easily reared than some other emydids. Males are smaller than females.

Malaclemmys terrapin Diamondback Turtle

NORTH AMERICA (EASTERN COASTAL REGION)

Shell length 15–20 cm. The Diamondback was formerly considered a delicacy with the result that its numbers were considerably reduced by hunters, but in recent years they have been allowed to recover. The most obvious characteristic of this and related species is the heavily grooved and sculptured appearance of the scutes, which in some individuals become pyramidal. The soft parts are usually off-white or grey with dark spots.

Diamondbacks are only found in salt or brackish water, particularly in coastal swamps. Their food consists of molluscs, insects and fish. Plants are rarely, if ever, eaten.

Care is as in the family description. Diamondbacks will live in fresh water, but some authors maintain that a small amount of salt is beneficial. Definite information is lacking. No records of captive breeding have been traced.

Malayemys subtrijuga   Snail-eating Turtle

SOUTH-EAST ASIA

Shell length 10–15 cm. This common Asian species is easily recognised by three very distinctive keels along its dark brown carapace, and two clear yellow lines originating at its snout and running back above and below each eye. Other stripes and blotches are found on the head and neck.

An easy turtle to look after, requiring a temperature of 25–30°C and semi-aquatic accommodation. Despite its name, its diet is not restricted to snails, other invertebrates and meat being taken, but plant material is rarely, if ever, accepted.

Mauremys caspica   Spanish Terrapin

MEDITERRANEAN REGION

Shell length 10–15 cm. This species, which is extremely numerous in parts of its range, is mainly brown, olive or grey in colour, with pale stripes of yellow, grey or occasionally pink on its soft parts. The carapace is depressed and has a low indistinct keel which may almost disappear with age. It is found in or around pools, streams and irrigation ditches.

An undemanding species, the adults living happily in outside pools in most temperate regions, where they may breed, up to 10 eggs being produced. The hatchlings are more brightly coloured than the adults and are quite easily reared. Care is as in the family description. They are often sold under the older names of *Clemmys caspica* or *Clemmys leprosa.*

Pseudemys scripta elegans   Red-eared Turtle
See Chrysemys scripta elegans (page 185).

Terrapene carolina   Common Box Turtle

NORTH AMERICA

Shell length 10–15 cm. The Box Turtles are renowned for their hinged plastron which the turtle can shut tightly if it is under attack. Their high-domed shell indicates that they are more terrestrial than most emydids, although they enter shallow water occasionally and are able to swim. The present species, of which several subspecies are recognised, has an orange or yellow blotched carapace, and may have red or orange areas on its head or neck. One of the most attractively marked subspecies is *T. c. bauri* from Florida, the yellow markings of which appear as radiating streaks. Another form, *T. c. triunguis* (*see* Plate **19**), is distinguishable by the three, as opposed to four, digits on its hind feet.

Care of adult Box Turtles consists of providing a large well-planted enclosure, preferably outside under semi-wild conditions, where they can clamber and forage at will. A shallow pool is essential. Food consists of insects and other invertebrates and some vegetable material, especially soft fruit and berries. Most captives will readily eat tinned dog meat and even table scraps, although the latter cannot be recommended. Captive breeding is unknown except in large outdoor reptiliaries. 3–4 eggs form a clutch. The hatchlings are best accommodated in large vivaria where temperatures of 25–30°C can be maintained.

Terrapene ornata   Ornate Box Turtle

NORTH AMERICA

Shell length 8–12 cm. Similar in appearance to the Florida form of *T. carolina,* but the markings are more regular and the plastron is elaborately decorated. It is also slightly smaller.

Care is as for *T. carolina*, but *T. ornata* can tolerate somewhat drier conditions, in keeping with its prairie origins. 3–5 eggs are laid.

Family Testudinidae - Land Tortoises

Tortoises have been kept as pets for many years, and in Europe they are part of the domestic scene in the same way as are the cat, dog and budgerigar. For many years around a quarter of a million tortoises were shipped annually from North Africa to Britain alone, but recent restrictions have eliminated this trade. In view of their exploitation, it is perhaps surprising that tortoises are still very common in parts of the Mediterranean region, being found in fields and vineyards and on mountainsides and roadsides. Their thick shells and tough leathery skin afford good protection against the ravages of predators and desiccation, at least in the case of adults, but it seems likely that a very high proportion of young perish during the first year or two. In addition to their lack of urgency, tortoises are famed for the great age which they attain, fifty years being quite commonplace for captives, with the occasional centenarian being reported. The gigantic species from islands in the Pacific and Indian Oceans may double this age.

Their popularity as pets no doubt stems from their supposedly undemanding requirements, and their complete harmlessness.

It is a poor reflection on our attitude towards the more lowly animals that in spite of the tortoise's long association with man we persist in keeping it under unsatisfactory conditions, causing the untimely death of the vast majority of newly imported animals. Much of the blame must lie with the collectors and shippers who give the absolute minimum of space and attention to the crated animals, to the pet dealers who sell them to the public without giving correct advice on their care, and to the attitude of people who buy wild animals as novelties, only to discard them when something fresh takes their fancy.

Newly imported animals need the closest possible attention if they are to adapt to a climate which is alien to them, and if they are to survive the stress of collection, transportation and subsequent 'marketing'. Outdoor enclosures should be positioned to receive as much sunshine as possible, and sheltered from cold winds, i.e. they should be south-facing and preferably arranged on a gentle slope, with ample opportunities for basking, though some shade should also be present. Although water should be available in a shallow container which the tortoise can climb into and out of with ease, the enclosure should be well drained and essentially dry. For protection at night, a retreat in the form of a straw-filled 'hutch' or a dry rock den should be provided and new arrivals placed in here every evening until they learn to find it for themselves. As much space as possible should be made available, and areas of rockery, grass and loose soil should be incorporated. Tough prostrate shrubs can provide shade but may also provide food; so cheap, quick-growing varieties are best. Boards raised on bricks make equally effective temporary shelters.

Under these conditions, tortoises will find a certain amount of food for themselves in the form of grasses, weeds and some invertebrates, but a tray of food should be provided daily, consisting of green vegetables and soft fruit, sprinkled at least once each week with a vitamin and mineral powder. A small amount of dog-meat, crushed insects or raw egg may be added occasionally, but not at the expense of roughage, a lack of which will cause diarrhoea.

Breeding is stimulated by warm sunny weather, the males doggedly pursuing the females until they stand still long enough to be mated. Owing to the obvious difficulties in accomplishing this, male tortoises have very concave plastrons to help them to maintain their position, whereas those of the females are flat or convex. As a rule, the males are smaller than the females and have slightly longer tails. During egg-laying, a nest is dug in soft earth, and a small number of eggs, usually 4–12, are laid in it, then covered. These must be removed for incubation under reliable artificial conditions.

Hatching takes place two to three months later, the exact time depending upon temperature and species. The hatchlings must be reared indoors in cages heated by light bulbs to 25–30°C. As substrate, newspaper is to be preferred, sand and gravel invariably sticking to the food and becoming ingested, which will cause intestinal blockage. Baby tortoises should be regularly placed in shallow trays of warm water to ensure that they are drinking properly and to prevent their eyes from becoming gummed up with mucus. Their food is similar to that of the adults, but it should be more finely chopped. Grated cuttlefish, or a calcium/phosphorus/vitamin D supplement should be sprinkled liberally on the food daily. Their growth rate is slow, and sexual maturity may take 10–20 years to achieve.

Since the publication of the first edition of this book, the importation of tortoises into Britain has been stopped for conservation reasons. However, a large number of these animals must still be living in gardens (often in solitary confinement), and a number of people have successfully bred the European species. Therefore, the information is retained in the hope that in the absence of fresh imports, a more serious and responsible approach to their care and, especially, breeding, will prevail.

Testudo graeca   Spur-thighed Tortoise (20)

MEDITERRANEAN REGION

Shell length 15–20 cm. The Spur-thighed Tortoise, one of the two well-known species frequently kept as pets in suburban gardens, is variable in colour, but most specimens are pale brown or horn-coloured, with a large or small area of dark brown on each scute. Each of these is relieved by a series of raised concentric growth-rings, but those of old specimens are often worn smooth. The limbs are elephantine, and the wrinkled head and neck are suggestive of great age, even in young specimens.

Their general care and breeding are summarised in the family account given above, but mention should also be made of those little 'companions' which these tortoises often bring with them in large numbers — ticks. These attach themselves, sometimes in clusters, to the soft parts of the skin around the neck and limbs, and must obviously be removed. This must be done carefully so as not to leave the hooked mouth-parts embedded beneath the skin, causing possible infection at a later date. The easiest method is to use a pair of flat-ended forceps to grasp the tick firmly, then flip it gently over until its hold is released. A drop of antiseptic may be applied to the site, but this is not usually necessary.

Testudo marginata   Marginated Tortoise

SOUTH-EASTERN EUROPE, WESTERN ASIA

To 30 cm, with a weight of 4 kg. Europe's largest tortoise, *T.*

marginata, can be distinguished from the other two species by its overall darker colouration, almost completely black in old individuals, and the flared marginal scutes on the posterior part of its carapace.

Care and breeding are as in the family description. Two clutches each year may be laid by a single female, usually in June or July, numbering 2–12 per clutch. At 25°C these hatch in about 80 days. The young tortoises grow rapidly at first but are unlikely to attain breeding size in less than ten years.

Testudo hermanni   Hermann's Tortoise

SOUTHERN EUROPE

Shell length 15–20 cm. Hermann's Tortoise is similar to the above species, but is slightly smaller and lacks the pair of small thigh tubercles from which *T. graeca* gets its common name. Its shell often has a brighter, more yellowish appearance, and for some reason it is hardly, if ever, parasitised by ticks.

All aspects of its care are as given in the family description.

From time to time other land tortoises may be offered, including the African *Kinixys* spp (Hinge-backed Tortoises), *Geochelone pardalis* (Leopard Tortoise) and *Malacochersus tornieri* (Pancake Tortoise), or the American *Geochelone denticulata* (Forest Tortoise, see Plate **21**) and *Gopherus* spp (Desert Tortoises). However, most of these are subject to some form of protective legislation and are not generally available. Their care, and in many cases their appearance, is similar to *Testudo* spp, though tropical species are obviously less hardy where temperature is concerned.

Family Trionychidae - Soft-shelled Turtles

The Soft-shelled Turtles are a distinct group consisting of relatively few species but with a wide distribution over America, Asia and Africa. As their name suggests, they lack the typical bony appearance of most turtles, although a shell does exist in a reduced form beneath the leathery covering. They are flat and pancake-like in appearance, and very aquatic in habit, emerging only to lay eggs in some cases. A typical ploy is to shuffle into the

Fig. 50 Marginated Tortoise, *Testudo marginata.*

Fig. 51 *Kinixys belliana*, Bell's Hinge-backed Tortoise – a juvenile.

sandy or muddy pool or river bottom and remain motionless until food happens by. Then the long, sinuous neck is rapidly shot out, and the prey (a fish, frog, tadpole or insect) snapped up. They also search out and eat carrion.

Although they have a reputation for quick tempers and sharp jaws, most captives seem to become quite placid. Their

198

accommodation should consist of a large aquarium with a depth of water roughly corresponding to the length of their neck, so that they can 'snorkel' — breath through their tubular nostrils — while resting on the bottom. A temperature of 25–30°C is required, and a filter may be useful for keeping the water clean. Soft sand may be used as a substrate, although it is not necessary, but some form of underwater retreat is desirable, especially for shy individuals. Soft-shells rarely emerge to bask, but artificial daylight fluorescent tubes are recommended for lighting. A land area, if included, must be absolutely smooth, as otherwise abrasions will develop on the turtles' plastrons, invariably leading to infections — this is very important.

Food should consist of dead whole fish or small rodents for adults, whereas the hatchlings will accept insects, such as crickets and locusts, from the water's surface, or aquatic invertebrates, such as *Gammarus* and insect larvae.

Trionyx spiniferus   Spiny Soft-shelled Turtle

NORTH AMERICA

Shell length 20–40 cm, males much smaller. The carapace is olive, brown or putty-coloured, with, in the case of males and juveniles, dark circular markings. In females these marks become indistinct with age and the appearance of the carapace is more blotchy.

Care is as given in the family description. No records of captive breeding have been traced.

Trionyx ferox, the Florida Soft-shell, and a few African and Asian species may be seen occasionally. They all require similar treatment. On the whole this is an interesting but neglected family.

13
Order Squamata: Sub-order Lacertilia - Lizards

As a single order combining the lizards and snakes, the Squamata is by far the most successful group of reptiles, totalling almost 6,000 species from practically every corner of the world. They also constitute the most important group to amateur herpetologists and vivarium-keepers, attracting a greater following than all the other amphibians and reptiles together. Although certain similarities exist which result in the lizards and snakes being lumped together in one order, there are enough important differrences in their habits and vivarium care to warrant their division here into two separate groupings, or sub-orders. The first is the sub-order Lacertilia, which comprises the lizards.

Lizards display an enormous degree of variation in habitat, habit and form, providing much interest for both the professional herpetologist and the vivarium-keeper. They may be nocturnal or diurnal, herbivorous or carnivorous, bright or dull, large or small. They may dwell up trees or beneath the ground, in deserts or near water, and they may give birth or lay eggs — almost any combination of these details is possible, and even a casual study of their variations and adaptations promotes respect for the evolutionary process.

Their care and breeding will obviously reflect this variation, and generalised instructions are difficult to give. Active species, which form the majority of those kept, should be given spacious accommodation, designed with the habits of the species in mind. Particular attention should be given to the heating arrangements. As stated elsewhere, most lizards have stereotyped thermoregulatory behaviour, and this must be allowed to function properly if they are to thrive and breed. This consideration must be given preference over all other aspects of their accommodation, including display, planting and so on. As a rule, the temperature they require for normal activity is higher than that required by other reptiles, and is remarkably similar throughout the sub-order, irrespective of origins; species from cool places merely bask longer or more efficiently than those from hot places, although nocturnal and fossorial species may operate at lower temperatures than related diurnal ones.

Sexual dimorphism among lizards is usually more pronounced than with other orders, presumably because in general they have a better-developed visual communication system. It can take various forms and is listed for several families. The characteristics to look for are brighter colouration, larger size, and the possession of crests, flaps, horns or other adornments in males. In addition, males of many species have obvious pre-anal and femoral pores (*see* Fig. 20) or swellings at the base of their tail.

Lizards may be either oviparous or viviparous. With the exceptions of some geckos, the oviparous types lay soft-shelled eggs which must absorb water throughout their development (*see* page 85).

Family Gekkonidae - Geckos

As a family, the 800 or so species and subspecies of geckos have efficiently colonised the whole of the tropical world and have extended into temperate regions in several continents. The ranges of some species are still spreading, by 'rafting' amongst debris to new islands, and by accidental introduction by man. Indeed, some species are so widespread that even specialists have difficulty in establishing their origin.

They are popularly renowned for a number of features not shared by other lizards. Of these, best known are the toe-pads which form the ends of the digits in many species, enabling them to climb very smooth surfaces, such as glass, and even to walk upside-down across ceilings.

Their eyes differ from most other lizards because the eyelids have become fused and transparent as in the snakes, but this is no disadvantage because their long tongues are used to wipe dust from their surfaces. The eyes move independently from one another, and owing to the mainly nocturnal habits of geckos are usually large. When subjected to daylight, the pupils contract to form a narrow slit, but a small amount of light is allowed to enter the eye through a series of pinholes along its length so that the animal is not totally without sight.

Many lizards share with the geckos the ability to discard part of their tail if it is held, and some gecko species are so prone to do this that it is almost impossible to find an individual without a re-grown tail. In other species, however, especially those coming from arid places, the tail fulfils an even more useful function: it stores fat during times of abundant food in order to tide the gecko over periods of shortage.

Having listed some of the well-known characteristics shown by geckos, it should be emphasised that not all species share all these features — there are in fact exceptions in every case.

A cage bought or built to house geckos must be escape-proof. When it is considered that most species can rapidly run up a vertical glass surface and cling upside down to the lid, coupled to the fact that they are often small and delicate and therefore difficult to recapture without risk of damage, it is obvious that special attention should be paid to security. Apart from this, a variety of designs are suitable for these lizards, always bearing in mind the natural habitat of the species to be kept. Small species and young are especially well suited to life in well-ventilated sandwich boxes and plant propagators.

The temperature for most species should be around 25–30°C during the day, with a slight drop during the night. Furnishings will obviously depend to a large extent on the habits of the species being catered for, geckos being either rock, ground or tree dwellers.

All species are carnivorous. Crickets are probably the most useful food, and may be used regularly. Apart from these, a variety of other insects may be tried, such as flies, maggots and locusts, but best of all are the mixed insects obtained by sweeping. Vitamin and mineral supplements should be given, especially to growing young, and females of species which lay hard-shelled eggs require a source of calcium and phosphorus which they will store either side of their throats until egg-laying time and by which they can easily be distinguished from males.

It has been noticed in some species, notably *Phelsuma* species, that the animals occasionally lick nectar from flowers or the juices of fallen, over-ripe fruit, and although it is doubtful whether this is essential to their health they definitely enjoy the addition of something sweet to their diet. A solution of honey and water, or artificial nectar as fed to hummingbirds, may be used, or soft fruit may be placed in the cage (although this will have to be replaced frequently to prevent it from going bad). The favoured method is to use a sugar cube, moistened with a few drops of a multi-vitamin solution such as Abidec. The geckos will gradually lick this away, and in doing so will benefit from the vitamins.

When it comes to reproduction, there is a remarkable consistency through the whole family. Apart from a handful of species from New Zealand which retain their eggs inside their body until they have hatched and thus bring forth living young, all geckos lay a clutch consisting of two eggs, or in some cases one. These are usually hard-shelled and calcareous, more like those of birds than lizards. Some tropical species lay throughout the year, others lay several times within a definite breeding season, and a few lay just one clutch each year. Note that the sex of the young is determined by the incubation temperature, higher temperatures producing only males and vice versa (*see* page 90).

In many species, mature males are readily recognised from below by two swellings at the base of their tail, each of which may culminate in a small bony spur projecting outwards, sometimes visible from above. In order to carry out detailed investigations it is necessary merely to coax the gecko on to the glass front of its cage or put it in a transparent container, such as a plastic lunch-box, when the underside can be easily examined. Females lack this double swelling, but are sometimes identifiable by the presence of developing eggs, which just prior to laying are visible through the ventral skin, or by the calcium deposits mentioned above.

For convenience, the examples dealt with here can be divided into three distinct subfamilies.

Subfamily Eublepharinae

The eublepharids are primitive geckos of which there are only a few species, scattered over America, Africa and Asia. As they are all rock or ground dwellers their digits are not modified with toe-pads, and they are notable for their slow, stalking gait, and their prominent eyelids. They lay typical, lizard-type eggs (covered with a pliable parchment-like membrane), which are buried in a damp place where the developing embryo can absorb moisture through the shell. As captives, the few species available are interesting, attractive, easily kept and frequently bred.

Coleonyx variegatus   Banded Gecko (22)

WESTERN NORTH AMERICA

8–12 cm. As its name suggests, the Banded Gecko is decorated with a series of transverse chocolate-brown bands on a cream background. Young animals are very vividly banded, but the markings become progressively less distinct with age.

They thrive in small vivaria with a substrate of gravel or newspaper and one or two piles of large pebbles or irregularly shaped rock fragments. A temperature of 21–28°C is required, and their food should consist of small crickets, mealworms and other insects. The males are easily recognised by a pair of bony spurs which project from the base of the tail. They seem not to be very aggressive, but it is advisable to keep only one male with a group of females.

The eggs are usually laid in June or July, and require an incubation period of 30–45 days. The hatchlings, which are about half as long as the adults, look rather delicate at first, but grow quickly on a similar but scaled-down diet to the adults.

Eublepharus macularius   Leopard Gecko

WESTERN ASIA

To 25 cm. A large, robust, beautifully patterned species, with black markings over a brown or yellow background. The tail is banded in black and white, and the underside is also white. The dorsal surface is studded with small, evenly spaced tubercles. Young examples are even more strikingly marked, being banded from their heads to the tips of their tails.

The Leopard Gecko adapts remarkably well to a variety of captive environments, including conditions similar to those used for animals in laboratories. They require dry conditions, but must have access to water for drinking and to a damp place for egg-laying. They may be kept on gravel, sand or newspaper, and rocks or broken pots will provide suitable retreats. The males are highly territorial and aggressive, and should most certainly be housed separately. They are distinguished by a more robust

Fig. 52 *Eublepharus macularius*, the Leopard Gecko, the subject of several
successful breeding programmes.

shape, especially in the neck region, paired swellings at the base
of the tail, and a row of pre-anal pores. Immature animals are not
easily sexed.

A temperature of 23–30°C suits them well, with a slight drop
during the night. Cooler conditions should be provided for a few
months during the winter, coupled with a shorter day length.
Various methods of breeding have been described. At the risk of
some loss of production, a fairly natural arrangement is recommended whereby a single male is kept with a small harem of
about 2–6 females. Mating will then take place at the beginning
of the breeding season, usually February–April, and continue
right through the summer. Females must be inspected frequently
for signs of developing eggs, and containers of damp sand or
similar material must be placed in the cage when laying is judged
to be imminent. Each female may lay 6 or more clutches each
year.

The incubation time varies from 47 to 100 days with
temperature, being about 60 days at 27°C. Temperature-

dependent sex determination has been shown for this species. The young animals will feed upon small crickets or sweepings as soon as they hatch, and may reach sexual maturity in 2–4 years.

Line-breeding is possible, each female being housed individually and then placed with a male for mating. This method may be very productive, and enables accurate record-keeping, but natural behaviour is obviously restricted.

Captive-bred animals are frequently available and are to be preferred over wild-caught specimens.

Subfamily Sphaerodactylinae

Geckos of this formidably named subfamily are all small (the world's smallest lizard is a member), all hail from tropical America, and all lay a single, calcareous egg. Members of only one genus (*Sphaerodactylus*) have toe-pads, but all are agile, and most are diurnal, forest-dwelling species.

They are quite easily cared for if an ample supply of young crickets, fruit or house flies, and graded sweepings is on hand. Many species are partly arboreal, and they should be given the opportunity to climb. A planted vivarium makes an attractive setting for a small colony, but note that males of many species are territorial and quarrelsome. The single egg is laid on the ground, beneath bark, or tucked away in some other secure place. Frequently, females (including those of more than one species) lay in the same place and large caches of eggs may be found. In captivity it is normal to remove these as they are laid, and they may be stored in small closed containers until they hatch. The hatchlings are often completely different from the adults in appearance, and require a constant supply of the tiniest crickets if they are to survive.

Only limited numbers of these geckos have been available so far but they are interesting and quite easily bred, and for these reasons should attract more attention from vivarium-keepers — especially those with limited space.

Gonatodes vittatus   Striped Gonatodes

TRINIDAD

6–8 cm. This species shows a very marked sexual dimorphism. The male is chestnut brown with a paler, sometimes yellow, head. From the tip of his pointed snout to his tail, a broad, black-edged, white stripe bisects his body laterally. The female is much duller. She is pale brown with dark scattered spots (*see* Fig. 21).

Although this species may be kept in lunch-boxes or similar containers, it shows itself off to good effect in a tall vivarium furnished with dead branches and living plants, especially bromeliads and other epiphytes, over which it will climb in search of food. Females lay eggs at any time of the year, at approximately monthly intervals. Each pea-sized egg takes about 3 months to hatch at 25°C, and the babies are dark brown to black with pale ocelli, and measure 2.5–3 cm.

Gonatodes humeralis (*see* Plate **23**), *Sphaerodactylus cinereus* and others are similar in their requirements. *Gonatodes ceciliae* grows rather larger, to about 8 cm.

Subfamily Gekkoninae

The majority of geckos are in this subfamily, and these species show some variation in size, form, markings and behaviour. A large proportion have toe-pads and are naturally arboreal, but in the tropics many of these are familiar inhabitants of buildings, living by day in crevices in wood and plaster-work, and emerging by night to patrol the walls and ceilings in search of some of the more obnoxious of man's commensals — the mosquitoes, flies, cockroaches and others which often abound in these regions. This type of species requires tall vivaria with well-fitting lids.

Other forms are ground-dwelling and need more floor-space, but nearly all are nocturnal or crepuscular, and the essential requirement is plenty of nooks and crannies in which to hide.

Males are often distinguishable by pre-anal pores and double swellings at the base of their tails. Many species are territorial, and males may have to be kept singly. They are the only lizards to vocalise. This is a definite advantage in nocturnal species, which may find other means of communication difficult, and each species may have more than one call.

The eggs are calcareous, and are invariably laid in pairs, the exception being those laid by young females, whose first few clutches may consist of single eggs. They are often sticky when laid and are attached to some solid object such as a piece of bark or rock in a secluded place. In captivity, they are sometimes attached to the sides of the vivarium, making their removal difficult. One answer to this problem is to tape a plastic cup or dish over them so that neither the eggs nor the newly hatched babies can be molested by the adult occupants of the cage.

Gekko gecko   **Tokay**

ASIA

30–35 cm. Tokays are real monsters compared to the average gecko, being heavily built with a large head and powerful jaws capable of giving a painful bite. They are slate-blue in colour and evenly spotted with orange or rust, an unusual colour scheme for a reptile. Unfortunately, their attractive appearance is not matched by their disposition.

A vivarium of at least 100 x 50 x 50 cm is required for a pair, with a temperature of 23–32°C during the day, and slightly cooler at night. Food should consist of large insects such as locusts and adult crickets, and mice may be taken by some individuals (but, if offered dead, these will need to be jiggled on the end of a length of blunt wire to make them acceptable).

Once a female begins to lay eggs, clutches may be produced at approximately 40-day intervals, and the incubation period will last from 100 to 200 days at 25–30°C. Newly-hatched young measure about 10 cm in length, and can attain sexual maturity in one year.

Geckonia chazalae (24)

NORTH AFRICA

8 cm. Included as an example of a rather unusual species, *Geckonia* is not often available, although it is apparently quite common in the stony North African deserts, which are its home. Its colouration, which helps it to blend with its surroundings, is brick red with a number of black and white markings on its back and sides. Its tail consists of a rather pathetic little stump, and its head is large and bony. Although it has toe-pads, they are not very effective and it does not climb well. In captivity it is a placid and engaging species, though not particularly active. It requires a small vivarium with a covering of stones or chippings. Temperature 23–30°C. Breeding in captivity is not known, but presumably it follows the usual gecko pattern.

Hemidactylus brooki   Brook's Gecko, House Gecko

WEST AFRICA (INTRODUCED ELSEWHERE)

10–12 cm. Pale yellowish brown with dark spots dorsally, paler below. Each digit ends in an adhesive disc and this species spends much of its time resting vertically on the walls of buildings etc.

Care and breeding are as in the family description. A temperature of about 25°C is called for. As usual with geckos, two calcareous eggs are laid, usually attached to a rock, branch or the sides of the vivarium. These hatch after 90–100 days at 30°C, and the hatchlings measure 4.5–5 cm in length. They may grow to sexual maturity inside twelve months. An easy species to keep and breed.

Similar species: *Gehyra mutilata*, another 'house' gecko, from South-east Asia, is similar in size and habits. It is plain yellowish brown in colour.

Hemidactylus turcicus   Turkish Gecko

MEDITERRANEAN REGION, NORTH AMERICA (INTRODUCED)

8–10 cm. The genus *Hemidactylus* contains many similar species. This one is pale brown or pinkish in colour, but its skin seems almost translucent, and is, in fact, very delicate. Its back is covered in small tubercles, and it may have a few black markings. The tail is banded.

This species is equipped with toe-pads, and it climbs well, but is more often found amongst rocks and rubble, beneath which it hides during the day. Its cage should be arranged accordingly, and although it is rather shy it will live for years in captivity.

Homopholis wahlbergii   Velvet Gecko

SOUTHERN AFRICA

8–12 cm. The Velvet Gecko is primarily grey in colour with several dark chevrons on its back. As its name suggests, its skin is quite smooth, comprised of numerous small even scales. It is not as flattened as many geckos, and it has a large head and what appears to be a permanent grin. In common with several other species, this one likes to rest head down on vertical surfaces, and pieces of bark should be so arranged in its vivarium.

Care and breeding are as in the family and subfamily descriptions.

Phelsuma cepediana Day Gecko
MAURITIUS

10–15 cm. A fabulously colourful species. The back is brilliant turquoise blue, gradually merging to an equally bright green on the flanks. Two red lines run from the head to the base of the tail, and between these and on the snout are a number of other red bars and blotches. The females are only slightly less colourful, but are somewhat smaller, and do not have pre-anal pores. They may have calcium deposits in their throats.

This species and several other equally colourful Day Geckos, which are all found in the Indian Ocean region, are unusual amongst geckos in being diurnal. Associated with this life-style, a brilliant colouration and elaborate displays, involving head-bobbing and tail-waving, have evolved. The males, and to some extent the females, are highly territorial, and established pairs or groups will rarely tolerate newcomers of either sex. They look particularly attractive in tall vivaria planted with *Philodendron* and *Ficus* species etc, among which they will skitter, almost bird-like in their quick, darting movements. Sections of thick bamboo stems make ideal hiding places, preferably arranged vertically or at a slight angle. The temperature should be 23–30°C during the day, supplied by a bulb or spotlight beneath which they can bask, and lighting, preferably by a natural daylight fluorescent tube, should be of a good intensity (doubly essential if plants are used). Their food consists mainly of insects, especially flies of various species, crickets and sweepings. Vitamin and mineral supplements are useful, and as mentioned elsewhere Day Geckos will lick a sugar cube or sweet solution, and extra vitamins may conveniently be provided via these substances. Calcium, in the form of powdered cuttlefish or egg-shell, must not be forgotten, especially as the breeding season approaches.

Breeding usually occurs during the spring and summer. The season is long and a single female may lay six or more clutches. Gravid females show signs of developing eggs through their ventral surfaces just before laying is due, and they should be inspected as often as possible by encouraging them on to a glass side of the vivarium, so that as soon as laying has taken place the eggs can be looked for. If bamboo tubes have been installed, these will almost certainly have been used for egg-laying, and may be removed complete with eggs for incubation in a separate container; alternatively, the eggs, which are often loose in the bottom of the tube, may be carefully tipped out and placed in a small lunch-box to incubate. They may be lightly sprayed with water occasionally, although it is not clear whether this is essential to their development (it is probably not, but slightly humid conditions are certainly of benefit to the hatchlings when they appear). At 25–30°C hatching occurs in 65–80 days, although there may be slight variations from clutch to clutch. Temperature-dependent sex determination has been shown for these species.

The young, measuring about 3 cm when first hatched, are most easily reared in small vivaria or lunch-boxes where, without competition and rivalry, they grow rapidly on a diet of young crickets, progressing to house flies and graded sweepings, all liberally dusted with vitamin and mineral powder, and with the addition of a 'fortified' sugar cube. Sexual maturity is reached in one year. Animals which are sick, frightened, bullied by cage-mates or about to slough lose much of their brilliance.

Phelsuma laticauda   Flat-tailed Day Gecko (25)

COMOROS ISLANDS

10–15 cm. This species is basically bright green with three red tear-drop markings on its back. On its shoulders are scattered scales of yellow or gold, and the region around the eye is bright blue. The tail is flattened above and is pale yellow.

Care and breeding are as for *P. cepediana*, above. This species, apart from being attractive, adapts well to captivity and becomes quite bold. A male lived at liberty in my office for several months, raiding open vivaria for food and visiting a sink for water.

Phelsuma madagascariensis   Giant Day Gecko

MADAGASCAR

To 25 cm. Not quite as brilliantly coloured as some *Phelsuma*

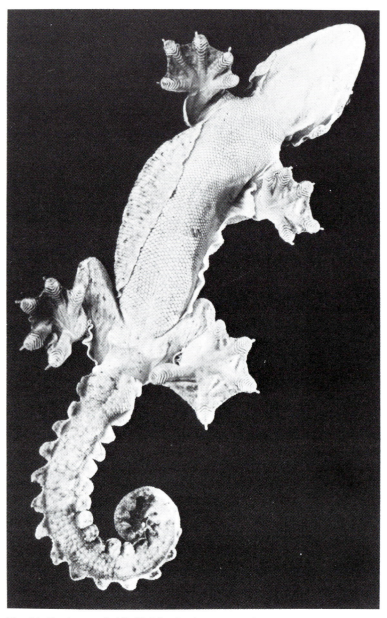

Fig. 53 *Ptychozoon kuhli*, Kuhl's Gecko, viewed from beneath to show the adhesive toe-pads and the frills and flaps along the sides of its head, body and tail.

species, this large Day Gecko is nevertheless a spectacular lizard. A number of subspecies are recognised, some of which are plain green in colour and others variously marked with stripes and blotches of orange or white.

It obviously requires a large vivarium, otherwise its care and breeding are similar to that of *P. cepediana*. Incubation of the eggs takes 45–50 days at 30°C, and the hatchlings are about 6 cm in length. They may be raised to sexual maturity in 1–2 years.

P. vinsoni, P. dubia and several other species occasionally become available. Many of these are captive-bred, since wild populations are almost all protected. Their care and breeding, as far as is known, are similar to that given above.

Ptychozoon kuhli   Kuhl's Gecko

SOUTH-EAST ASIA

15–20 cm. Although its colouration (mottled light and dark grey, with an indistinctly banded tail) is rather nondescript, Kuhl's Gecko is one of the most bizarre species. Its feet are heavily webbed, and a flap of skin grows from each side of its trunk. The wide, triangular head also has a small flap attached to each jowl, and the tail has scalloped edges and is usually coiled to one side when the gecko is at rest. The primary purpose of these frills, and the bark-like colouration, is to disguise the gecko's outline, and in particular to eliminate shadow formation. The flaps of skin may fulfil another function, that of enabling the lizard to glide or parachute out of trees and so elude pursuers, but reliable evidence that this occurs is lacking.

In captivity, Kuhl's Geckos will settle down quickly. They require a temperature of 23–28°C, and a diet of insects, with supplements. The female develops large calcium deposits if cuttlefish or similar material is supplied, and the male has a distinct two-lobed swelling at the base of his tail. Eggs may be laid every 4–6 weeks, and at 23°C they hatch after 80–100 days. The young are more brightly marked than the adults and may be reared on young crickets and flies. They can reach breeding size in one year.

Tarentola mauretanica   Moorish Gecko

MEDITERRANEAN REGION

10–15 cm. A thickset, robust gecko, with a very rough skin. Light to dark brown in colour with indistinct markings, although the tail may be banded in young individuals.

This is a tough, aggressive species, which occasionally emerges to bask during the day, but never strays far from the hole or crevice in which it lives. In the wild it is usually associated with stone walls and rubble, and will thrive in captivity if given appropriate conditions. Otherwise, care and breeding are as in the family and subfamily descriptions.

Family Xantusidae - Night Lizards

The Night Lizards form a small, rather obscure family, centred around Central America. Its members are small nocturnal lizards with fine granular scales on their backs, squarish scales beneath, and fused eyelids. They eat small insects and all appear to live in dry, stony places such as rock outcrops. They are all viviparous, although captive breeding has not been recorded for any of them. One species is sufficiently attractive to be listed occasionally by dealers.

Xantusia henshawi   Granite Night Lizard

WESTERN NORTH AMERICA

8–10 cm. A flattened lizard with a bold dorsal pattern of rich brown blotches on a yellowish background. The head is triangular in shape and the eyes are prominent. The male is said to have a pale area on the underside of each thigh, but this is by no means obvious.

A small dry vivarium, a substrate of sand and a pile of flat stones are all that is required. The temperature should be about 20–30°C. Small insects, especially graded sweepings, are eaten, usually at night. Breeding in captivity is unknown; in the wild 1–3 young are born.

Family Iguanidae - Iguanas

The Iguanidae is a New World family, although a few species occur in the Indian Ocean region. It consists mainly of small to

214

Fig. 54 *Xantusia henshawi*, the Granite Night Lizard.

medium-sized lizards, but also includes the more familiar large species found in Central and South America.

Males of many species are brightly coloured and may have crests, frills and dewlaps which can be extended during display. This is often combined with head-bobbing. Many species live in distinct colonies, each male defending a well-delineated area within it.

The majority of species lay soft-shelled eggs which are buried in damp sand or soil, but a few give birth to live young.

In captivity they require large cages or enclosures with powerful heat lamps to provide hot-spots. The smaller species are insectivorous and their dietary requirements are quite straightforward, but many larger species rely to some extent on vegetable material and their diet should consist of a limited amount of chopped fruit and as much green food as they will eat: lettuce, cress, dandelion etc. Vitamin and mineral supplements should be added two or three times each week, and a small amount of tinned dog meat can be given occasionally if acceptable. They should be fed every day, and uneaten food removed and dishes thoroughly washed a few hours after feeding.

Although gravel is a suitable substrate for most of the small species, the larger forms are more conveniently kept on newspaper, which will require frequent replacement. Arboreal species should be given tall cages and branches on which to climb and bask.

Anolis carolinensis   Green Anole (26)

NORTH AMERICA

10–15 cm. A very slender lizard with a long tail, pointed head, and small adhesive toe-pads. The males are very much larger than the females and have bright pink dewlaps, or throat fans, which are inflated when the lizard displays. The general colour of both sexes may be brown, green or grey according to the lizard's mood. The chin and underparts are white.

Green Anoles, sometimes called 'American Chameleons', live amongst shrubs, and in captivity they like tall cages with plenty of branches, and preferably some living plants, to clamber about on. They drink from drops of water rather than from a bowl, so the cage and plants should be lightly sprayed at least once each day and ventilation should be adequate to prevent excessive humidity. A light-bulb or spotlight will provide daytime heat, which should be above 23°C, and preferably approaching 30°C immediately beneath the heat source. A slight drop during the night is quite safe. Small crickets and flies are the preferred fare.

Although males will fight, a group of females with one male will make an interesting community, and mating will probably occur frequently throughout the spring and summer. Small clutches of eggs are laid at the base of plants, beneath pieces of bark, or on leaves, but they are rather delicate and difficult to hatch.

Anolis equestris   Knight Anole

CUBA, SOUTH-EASTERN NORTH AMERICA (INTRODUCED)

To 30 cm. Much more heavily built than most Anoles, this species displays a range of colours. It may be brown and white, or green, and well-marked specimens often have areas of blue on the head. The throat fan is white or pale blue.

Its care is similar to *A. carolinensis* but it obviously requires more space. Adult specimens may be persuaded to take an occasional baby mouse to supplement their normal diet of insects. No records of captive breeding have been traced.

Anolis sagrei   Brown Anole

WEST INDIES, FLORIDA (INTRODUCED)

10–15 cm. Not as slender as the Green Anole, and always brown

Fig. 55 *Crotaphytus collaris*, the Collared Lizard.

in colour, although the shade may vary and some mottling is usually present. The throat fan is deep orange with a white border, and the male may also have a low dorsal ridge from neck to tail.

This species does well in captivity (better than the commoner *A. carolinensis* which has similar requirements), but unfortunately shipments of *A. sagrei* seem to contain mainly males, and no records of captive breeding have yet been traced.

Crotaphytus collaris   Collared Lizard

NORTH AMERICA

20–30 cm. A large-headed species with long hind legs and a long tail. A pair of prominent black bands behind its head give it its common and specific names. The body is bright green, and the head may be yellow or brown. The male has a brightly coloured throat (green, blue or even orange) and may have blue patches on its belly.

Collared Lizards require very large, very hot cages. The need for a powerful heat source cannot be stressed enough, although an area for cooling off is also essential. They are desert species and a substrate of gravel and rocks will make them feel at home, and being rather nervous plenty of hiding places are called for.

217

Food, which is required in large amounts, consists of large insects, which are crushed by the lizards' powerful jaws before being swallowed. Small rodents will also be taken, as will smaller lizards, so Collared Lizards should not be housed with other, small species.

1–12 (usually 4–6) eggs are laid in the spring, which take about two months to hatch.

Iguana iguana   Green Iguana (28)

CENTRAL AND SOUTH AMERICA

100–150 cm. The Green Iguana is a frequent and spectacular exhibit in zoological gardens. A series of tooth-like scales form a crest from the nape of its neck, down its back, and on to its long, whip-like tail. A leathery flap of skin hangs beneath the jaws of the males, and this is stiffened during the characteristic head-bobbing display. Large plate-like scales adorn the head. Most Iguanas are green or grey-green in colour, but there are geographical variations. The tail is often banded with black.

These large, ferocious-looking beasts are entirely herbivorous, although many like some insect food, especially when young. Vitamin and mineral supplements are particularly important for young animals, and natural daylight fluorescent lighting is undoubtedly of some benefit.

Iguanas must be given very extensive enclosures, and young specimens of 30 cm or so should not be taken on unless this is appreciated. Even moderately-sized adults require several cubic metres of cage space, including a large water bowl or pool, and facilities for climbing. A greenhouse or similar structure is the most practical arrangement for serious attempts to keep and breed them, provided that tropical temperatures of 26–35°C can be maintained at all times. Background heating may be provided by convector heaters, but powerful heat lamps will be necessary to create basking sites during the day.

Breeding has been achieved, mainly by zoos. Clutches of 25–40 eggs are usual, buried to a depth of about 30 cm in moist sand or soil. They require a steady temperature of around 30°C to develop, and hatch in about 2 months. The hatchlings measure 25–30 cm, and grow very quickly if well fed, attaining sexual maturity at a size of about 70 cm in 2 or 3 years.

Basiliscus plumifrons   Plumed Basilisk

CENTRAL AMERICA

About 60 cm. A green or blue-green iguanid, the males of which have a distinctive crest on their heads and a raised ridge which runs from the nape of their neck, along the back and onto the upper part of the tail. The eye is bright orange.

This species has been successfully kept and bred in zoos and private collections. It requires a large cage with branches for basking, a pool or large water bowl to maintain a high humidity and a constant temperature of 25–30°C. The diet should consist of large insects such as locusts and crickets and possibly small rodents and some plant material. Calcium and mineral supplements are beneficial. From 4 to 14 eggs are buried in sand or soil and these hatch about 10 weeks later at 28°C. The young, measuring 12–15 cm in length, and showing no signs of the dorsal crest, require mealworms and cricket nymphs, supplemented as for the adults. A True-light or black-light would undoubtedly be beneficial and may be essential for rearing them successfully.

Leiocephalus barahonensis   Curly-tailed Iguana

HAITI

To about 30 cm. A well-built species, with a chunky head and thick, muscular limbs. Mainly greyish in colour, but with areas of orange, mainly on the flanks, and some blue scales, mainly on the head.

A warmth-loving species, requiring ample opportunities to bask and a stony substrate. Insectivorous. No records of captive breeding have been traced.

Phrynosoma species   Horned Lizards

NORTH AMERICA

To 15 cm. The Horned Lizards, of which there are about 12 species, are remarkably adapted to desert life. Their most noticeable feature is their discoid shape, which, during basking, is tilted towards the sun in order to maximise its warm rays. Anti-predator strategies consist of a colouration which blends well

219

with the soil type (varying from rust-red, through grey and brown, to yellow, depending upon locality), and the ability to shuffle rapidly into the sand or loose soil, leaving only the heavily armoured head exposed. In most species the back is studded with large pointed scales, often backward-pointing, and a number of very long spines project from the back of the head. They are credited with the disconcerting habit of squirting blood from their eye-sockets if molested, but few people seem to have witnessed this.

In captivity, they require large cages with a good depth of sand or rounded gravel into which they will burrow during the night, when frightened, or to escape excessive heat. A daytime temperature of 35–40°C immediately beneath the heat source is required. Their natural diet appears to consist largely of ants, but they will happily take crickets, mealworms and other small insects. Large amounts of food are required.

Captive breeding is unknown. Some species are egg-layers: large species lay around 20 eggs, smaller forms 7–15 eggs. In at least one species (*P. cornutum*), these require about 8 weeks' incubation at 30°C. A few species are viviparous, with litters numbering up to 30, but usually around 10–15.

Sceloporus malachitus   Malachite Spiny Lizard

CENTRAL AMERICA

15 cm. As their name implies, the Spiny Lizards, or Swifts, are covered with raised, pointed scales, giving them a prickly appearance. The Malachite Spiny Lizard is an especially colourful member of the genus, the male having a brilliant metallic green dorsal surface. The female is mostly grey, but with faint green markings, especially in the region around the head and neck.

Unlike most other Spiny Lizards, this species does not occur in deserts, and seems to prefer a cage with branches for climbing and a daily spraying of tepid water to raise the humidity slightly. A temperature of 25–30°C suits it, and it likes to bask. Natural daylight lighting would probably be beneficial. It is insectivorous.

Little is known of its breeding habits. One female gave birth to three young measuring about 4 cm after a long gestation.

Sceloporus occidentalis Western Fence Lizard

NORTH AMERICA

12–15 cm. Quite a slender species with a brown and grey blotched back and bright blue areas on each side of the ventral midline and a blue throat. Females and juveniles are less brilliantly marked.

These common lizards live among rocks, logs, and on walls etc. They require dry vivaria with a spotlight and plenty of hiding places. They are insectivorous. Up to 12 eggs are laid in spring or summer, and these hatch after about 8 weeks.

Sceloporus orcutti Granite Spiny Lizard

NORTH AMERICA

To 20 cm. A large species of which the males appear almost black at first, but are actually deep metallic blue on the belly and flanks, deepening to purple on the back. The female lacks the metallic colouration, and is grey, but can be distinguished from other female *Sceloporus* by a wedge of dark scales on each side of the neck.

This is a montane species and requires a dry vivarium with rocks or dead wood to bask on. A daytime temperature of 30°C or more is preferred, and food consists of insects. No records of captive breeding have been traced, an average clutch size of 11 eggs having been reported of wild females.

Family Agamidae - Agamas

The Agamas are closely related to the Iguanas, and may be thought of as their Old World counterparts, and, where similar habitats and conditions are found, several examples of parallel evolution exist. Most species occur in South-east Asia, the Middle East, and North Africa.

As may be expected, their care in captivity is similar to that of the Iguanidae, and is dictated by their diurnal basking habit and often complex social behaviour. In particular, males are highly territorial and this can cause problems where more than one is present in a cage or enclosure.

With few exceptions, the Agamas are oviparous, their soft-shelled eggs usually being buried in damp soil or amongst leaf-litter. A few of the large species make good zoo exhibits, but on the whole the family is not well represented in animal collections.

Agama stellio Agama

MEDITERRANEAN REGION

To 30 cm. A chunky, brown lizard, with a rough, spiny skin, and long back legs. There may be paler brown or yellow markings on the throat, back and tail, especially in males.

Most Agamas, including this species, come from hot, dry, scrubby regions, where they spend much of their time basking. Their vivarium should therefore be dry, and heated by a powerful heat lamp or spotlight. Because these are lively and sometimes nervous lizards, they should be given plenty of room and a jumble of rocks to hide amongst. Apart from insects, they will eat a certain amount of fruit, and should be given vitamin and mineral supplements. *Agama stellio* lay 6–8 eggs, which hatch after an incubation period of 47–52 days at 29–30°C.

Fig. 56 *Agama atricollis*, a partially arboreal Agama.

SQUAMATA: SUB-ORDER LACERTILIA—LIZARDS

Several other *Agama* species may be offered, for instance *A. agama* and *A. atricollis*. Their care is as for *A. stellio*. A female *A. atricollis* laid 7 eggs, which hatched in 75 days at 25–30°C.

Calotes versicolor   **Garden Lizard**
ASIA

To 40 cm. A slender, long-tailed species which spends most of its time in shrubs and on tree-trunks. It is mainly brown in colour, but the males have an orange or crimson head and neck during the breeding season and become strongly territorial during this time.

This species, and other members of its genus, require tall, roomy vivaria, with branches and, preferably, some living plants among which to climb and chase. They also require a high temperature and humidity, but must have good ventilation. These conditions are difficult to achieve unless a greenhouse or similar enclosure is available.

No records of captive breeding have been traced. In the wild, 10–20 eggs are buried in damp soil, and they hatch in 6–7 weeks. The young may reach sexual maturity in one year or less.

Physignathus cocincinus   **Thai Water Dragon (29)**
SOUTH-EAST ASIA

To 50 cm. A large bright green lizard with a row of enlarged dorsal scales running from the back of the head to the tail, this crest being more obvious in males. The chin is white and the throat may be white or yellow. The eye is bright amber. Superficially these lizards resemble some of the South American iguanids such as *Iguana* and *Basiliscus* spp.

In captivity they require a large cage – 1.5 metres long minimum – and a large pool in which they will bathe frequently. A strong branch or two will be necessary for basking and when first installed they will settle in more quickly if a refuge, such as a hollow log, is provided – without this they often panic when the cage is serviced, leading to damaged snouts. The substrate may be large grade gravel, or newspapers, and a temperature of 25–30°C is essential. Natural daylight tubes or black-lights are probably necessary to keep them in the best of health or if it is hoped to breed them. Unlike Iguanas, they are largely carnivorous and will eat insects such as locusts and

223

cockroaches, small rodents and a little soft fruit. Vitamin and mineral supplements are recommended, and calcium should be provided for breeding females.

This species has been bred successfully, mainly by zoos. Mating takes place during the cooler months. 9–15 eggs are laid and these hatch after about 60 days at 27°C. The hatchlings measure about 10 cm in length and require True-light or black-light, along with plenty of insect food, if they are to grow well. Sexual maturity may be attained after two or three years. Each female is capable of laying up to five clutches of eggs each year, making this one of the most prolific of lizards.

Uromastyx acanthinurus Mastigure or Dab Lizard

MIDDLE EAST

To 60 cm. This is a large heavy-bodied species with a club-like, spiny tail, with which it defends itself, and head which looks rather like that of a tortoise. The entire animal is light brown or olive in colour.

Mastigures are lizards of the desert, surviving where little else can, by spending the heat of the day at the bottom of their deep, cool burrows. Their enclosure should therefore be heated to extremely high temperatures (over 35°C beneath the heat lamp or spotlight), but should have provision for cooling off. This is best accomplished by the installation of wooden hide-boxes ('hutches'), or drainpipes, since the provision of deep layers of sand is usually impractical. They are almost entirely her-bivorous, preferring a diet of greens, including grass, fruit and the flowers of certain plants, notably dandelions. Locusts and crickets may be taken in very small quantities, and supplements are strongly recommended. They rarely if ever drink from containers but obtain their moisture from their food, and will also absorb it through the skin if lightly sprayed or placed in a shallow pan. As the skin becomes wet its colour darkens, and the body swells noticeably as it takes up water.

Family Chamaeleontidae - Chameleons

The Chameleons are perhaps the most famous lizards: their

powers of colour change are widely known and usually exaggerated; they have astonishingly long tongues which can be projected rapidly and accurately at unsuspecting prey; their clock-spring prehensile tails, and oppositely opposed digits, are adaptations to an entirely arboreal existence; and their independently-rotating, turret-like eyes are useful accessories for a hunter who may suddenly become the hunted.

In shape, Chameleons are high-sided and laterally compressed, with small tails and a bony head which is often adorned with horns, crests or flaps. Their skin is granular, and here and there a larger tuberculate scale protrudes. They climb slowly and deliberately along branches, looking for insect food and drinking droplets of water trapped on leaves. Some species are egg-layers, the females descending temporarily to the ground to dig holes in which to place their eggs, but others have solved the problem of such vulnerability by staying among the leaves and bringing forth fully-developed young.

It is a great pity that the captive requirements for Chameleons are so poorly understood, as they are undoubtedly among the most interesting of lizards, and, paradoxically, seem to take to captivity quite well at first.

The majority of them will not drink from a bowl, and must have their cage lightly misted once or twice each day, which may lead to a more humid environment than is desirable. The secret appears to be the use of well-ventilated cages placed in light, airy positions, or better still a state of semi-liberty in a greenhouse or warm room. For most species, temperature seems not to be critical. 23–30°C is probably ideal, but short periods at much lower temperatures are tolerated. This may be because many of the most frequently imported species, though tropical, live at rather high altitudes, and lowland forms may not be nearly as hardy.

A good variety of food is essential. Most individuals will refuse a type of food which has been offered exclusively for several days running, but will go back to it after a different food has been given for a while. Favoured items include locusts, crickets, flies and caterpillars, and appetites are usually hearty.

Artificial daylight tubes are of value, but natural sunlight appears to have the most stimulating effect on their appetites, and breeding is usually achieved only after some exposure to it.

Chamaeleo bitaeniatus

EAST AFRICA

To 20 cm. A small species, not particularly colourful, being brown to olive-green with paler stripes or blotches on its sides. Its powers of colour change are not great. It is, however, numerous within its range, and a fairly hardy captive.

Care is as in the family description. It is a live-bearing species, producing litters of 10–20 from April to December.

Chamaeleo dilepis   Flap-necked Chameleon

SOUTHERN AFRICA

To 30 cm. A well-built species with a bony, triangular head. Usually grass-green or blue-green in colour, but occasionally brown or buff. Spots and blotches may appear at times. If threatened, this species inflates itself with air and angles its body to present the largest surface to its aggressor. If the attack continues, it opens its mouth widely and may give a low hiss. Its bite is painless, but some time may elapse before it decides to let go.

This species makes a good captive, feeding readily on the usual insect fare. No records of captive breeding have been traced. In the wild, 20–30 eggs are laid in a damp substrate, and incubation is unusually long, several months at least.

Chamaeleo jacksoni   Jackson's Chameleon (30)

EAST AFRICA

30–40 cm, but smaller forms exist. The male Jackson's Chameleon is a modern *Triceratops* in miniature. A long curving horn projects from its snout, and two others are rooted above its eyes. These have doubtless evolved for the purpose of display, and may be used for jousting if two males meet on a branch. The body is usually bright green, but may turn pale green with brown spots, or completely brown. The area around each eye is usually turquoise, and the serrated crest running along the ridge of its back is usually yellow — a very handsome species.

In captivity it requires a large cage, or the freedom of a room, where it will confine itself to one area for most of the time. It can manage adult locusts and crickets, and may take small vertebrates, including smaller lizards.

This is a viviparous species, and breeding has been achieved in captivity, up to 30 young of 4–6 cm being born, usually in September–December.

They may be reared on young crickets, flies and sweepings, in cages furnished with plenty of thin twigs, and damp leaves from which to drink. Maturity may be reached in one year under optimum conditions.

Other Chameleons are occasionally offered, but those listed appear to be the most successfully kept to date. The Common Chameleon, *C. chamaeleon*, from the Mediterranean region, is notoriously difficult to keep alive for more than a few months. All Chameleons are delicate to some extent, and unless the rather specialised conditions outlined above are available, they should not be attempted.

The iguanid species *Anolis carolinensis* is sometimes referred to as the 'American Chameleon' in allusion to its colour-change capabilities. However, it is in no way related to the true Chameleons, which are found only in the Old World. Its care is described on page 216.

Fig. 57 *Chamaeleo jacksoni*, Jackson's Chameleon – a male with its three distinctive horns.

Fig. 58 *Chamaeleo jacksoni* – a female with only rudimentary horns.

Family Scincidae - Skinks

The Skinks are a large, indeed enormous, family, occurring just about everywhere that reptiles can live. All members of the family show remarkable similarity in appearance and habits. If the characteristics of a typical species are listed — fairly small, highly polished scales, brown in colour, pointed head, and small limbs — the vast majority of species will have been roughly described. This is not to say that Skinks make uninteresting captives or are unworthy of study; on the contrary, most species adapt well to captivity, and although brightly coloured forms are few and far between many are handsomely marked in shades varying from rich deep brown to cream. There is little difference between the sexes, but the males are often more heavily-built, especially around the head and neck, and they may be slightly more strongly marked.

In captivity they require a cage with a place for basking, and several places for hiding. A floor-covering of leaf-litter is appropriate for many species, with a scattering of bark and dead wood under which they can burrow. Some moisture seems to be essential to many species, but parts of the surface should be kept dry at all times. Some of the more specialised forms will prefer a deep layer of sand through which they will wriggle at great speed. Many such species have reduced limbs and are known as Sandfish.

A temperature gradient ranging from 20 to 30°C suits most species, and those from temperate regions may be kept cooler, or hibernated, during the winter. All species are insectivorous, although a few of the larger kinds will also take meat and a little chopped fruit. They may be either viviparous or oviparous, and females of some species are reported to coil over their soft-shelled eggs throughout the incubation — an unusual trait amongst lizards. The hatchlings or newly-born young often show brighter colouration than the adults, and in particular the tail, which is readily discarded if held, may be bright blue or red in colour, thus serving to distract the attention of a predator away from the Skink's head.

Chalcides chalcides   Seps, Lined Skink

MEDITERRANEAN REGION

20–40 cm. An example of a skink in which the limbs are reduced to almost nothing. It is smooth and shiny in texture, olive-brown in colour, and there may be a number of thin dark lines down the body. A very active species which can move rapidly through grass and undergrowth.

Care is as in the family description. The cage should be lightly sprayed occasionally, and the leaf-litter should not be allowed to dry out completely. The young, which usually number 10–20, are born live.

Chalcides ocellatus Eyed Skink

MEDITERRANEAN REGION

20–25 cm. A thick-set skink with smooth glossy scales and a pointed snout. The body is somewhat rectangular in cross-section. This species is usually buff, pale brown or yellowish brown in colour, with many small eye-spots along the back, some of which may be arranged to suggest cross-bars. It lives in sandy, arid places where it burrows into the substrate and, especially, beneath rocks and debris.

In captivity this species is hardy and long-lived. The cage should be covered with a good depth of free-running sand, scattered with small flat rocks or pieces of bark under which the skinks will hide. Daytime temperatures up to 30°C beneath the heat-source, cooler at night. In addition to their natural food of insects such as crickets and mealworms, they readily take chopped dog meat. Eyed skinks may breed in captivity, the main difficulty being the establishment of a pair as the sexes are outwardly alike – the best arrangement is to house a group of 4–6 together and let them pair up naturally. 2–6 living young are born after a gestation period lasting about two months. The babies measure about 7 cm in length and require a similar diet to that of the adults but in smaller portions. They grow quickly and without problems.

Eumeces fasciatus Five-lined Skink

NORTH AMERICA

12–15 cm. The pattern, consisting of five cream stripes on a darker background, is most obvious in the young and in females, but can usually be picked out in males, which are further identifiable by an orange or red head. Very young animals have blue tails.

Care is as in the family description. 2–18, usually about 12, eggs are laid, usually in rotting wood, and are guarded by the mother during their 4–7 week incubation.

Eumeces laticeps **Broad-headed Skink**

NORTH AMERICA

To 30 cm. A large and handsome skink, brown or bronze in colour with, in males, an orange head. The males are also easily distinguished by their much more massive jaw muscles than those of the females. The hatchlings are black with five or seven yellow or cream longitudinal lines, and a bright blue tail.

Care as in the family description. No records of captive breeding have been found, but this should not be too difficult as this species adapts very well to captivity – perhaps a short period of dormancy in the winter would produce results. Recommended.

Fig. 59 Male Broad-headed Skink, *Eumeces laticeps.*

Eumeces skiltonianus   Western Skink, Blue-tailed Skink

NORTH AMERICA

12–15 cm. In this species two broad cream stripes border the rich brown back, and the flanks are also brown. The pattern is sharply defined in adults and young, but the tails of juveniles are brilliant blue, which gradually fades with age. A very attractive species.

Care is as in the family description. No records of captive breeding have been traced, but in the wild 2–6 eggs are laid.

Mabuya multifasciata   Golden Skink

SOUTH-EAST ASIA

30 cm. A large skink which is pale yellow or buff dorsally, dirty white below. The chin and throat are yellow, turning to deep orange in front of the forelegs, the males being more intensely coloured than the females. A rainforest species.

This species is not easy. It requires a large vivarium with a substrate of dead leaves, etc, which should retain some moisture beneath the surface in order to maintain a fairly high humidity, but the vivarium must be well ventilated. Large pieces of bark will provide hiding places, and water should be available at all times. A diet of insects is required.

About 6 young are born, but this species is not bred successfully very often – possibly as a result of the dreadful condition in which they invariably arrive from their country of origin.

Mabuya quinquetaeniata   African Five-lined Skink

SOUTHERN AFRICA

15–25 cm. These are heavy-bodied species with pointed snouts. The ground colour is brown, but this is overlaid with a multicoloured iridescence. The tails of the males are orange, and a series of stripes, often rather broken and indistinct, marks both sexes.

Care is as in the family description.

Fig. 60 *Tiliqua gigas*, Blue-tongued Skinks. Several other Lizard species can be trained to accept raw minced meat.

Tiliqua gigas   Blue-tongued Skink (31)

NEW GUINEA

To 60 cm. Very large for a skink, with a broad triangular head. Pale brown or grey with about 15–20 irregular dark bands across the back and tail, and occasionally a dark stripe from neck to tail. The tongue is bright blue, and may be protruded during a show of aggression.

This species thrives in captivity, and has been bred on several occasions. It requires a large vivarium, and may be fed on dog-meat, fruit and berries as well as insects and small vertebrates. It is a viviparous species, up to 20 large young being born. These are easily reared.

Very many more Skinks are available, with varying degrees of frequency. Their care is essentially as outlined above, and generally speaking they make undemanding and interesting vivarium subjects, and are to be recommended for beginners and advanced hobbyists alike.

233

Fig. 61 *Cordylus giganteus*, the Giant Zonure or Sungazer.

Family Cordylidae - Zonures

The Zonures are all African in origin. Their most distinctive feature is their tail, which consists of a series of rings of spiny scales and may be lashed from side to side as a means of defence. In addition, the head and back may be heavily armoured with thick, plate-like scales, and occipital spines. Some species are greatly flattened in shape, an adaptation to living in narrow cracks and crevices in rock outcrops.

In captivity they all require very hot, dry conditions, a hot-spot being essential. A substrate of coarse gravel or newspaper is the most practical, and large rocks for climbing and basking on, and for hiding beneath, are important. All species are carnivorous, insects and small vertebrates figuring amongst their natural prey, but many can be trained to accept strips of raw meat and liver. Vitamin and mineral supplements seem to be very important. In general, captive breeding does not appear to be easy. All species are viviparous.

234

Cordylus giganteus Giant Zonure, Sungazer

AFRICA

30–40 cm. The largest Zonure, and an impressive animal. Its scales are very spiny, and are rust-coloured or dark brown dorsally and pale yellow ventrally. The young are faintly speckled. It lives in long burrows in arid regions.

Care is as in the family description. Very large vivaria are required. Two young are born.

Cordylus jonesi Jones' Zonure

AFRICA

10–15 cm. One of the smallest Zonures, this species is typical of the genus, having a heavily armoured head and prickly tail. It is overall reddish-brown in colour.

Care is as in the family description. 2–4 young are born.

C. cordylus, C. warreni, C. vittifer and others may be available occasionally. All are intermediate in size between the above species, and their appearance, habits, and care are similar.

Platysaurus guttatus Flat Rock Lizard

SOUTHERN AFRICA

20–25 cm. The Rock Lizards are dorsally flattened in the extreme. They live among rocks, hiding in narrow crevices, sometimes closing the entrance with their armoured tails. Males of this species are exceedingly colourful. The head and body are brilliant blue and green, the tail is orange, whereas the underparts are metallic blue and glossy black. The female is drab by comparison, being mostly brown with a cream or yellow vertebral stripe.

Care is as in the family description. These are shy and nervous lizards and spend most of their time hiding, unless they are undisturbed. Two young are born.

P. intermedius and *P. capensis,* which are sometimes offered, are similar in all respects.

235

Pseudocordylus subviridis

SOUTHERN AFRICA

25–30 cm. This species, which has no accepted common name, is somewhere between the Zonures and the Rock Lizards in appearance, being neither as spiny as the former nor as flattened as the latter. It has large, powerful jaws with which it does not hesitate to defend itself. In colour it has orange flanks, dark brown back with some yellow markings, and a pale green underside. The females are smaller than the males, and rather less colourful.

Care is as in the family description. This species is easier and less nervous than most Cordylids. Four young are born.

Family Gerrhosauridae - Plated Lizards

The Plated Lizards are closely related to the Zonures, and like them are exclusively African. Their scales are heavy, and regular in arrangement, providing a high degree of protection. They are all terrestrial in habit, many being associated with dry, rocky areas, and all are insectivorous. Their care is similar to that of the Zonures, but all of these species lay eggs. Most can be maintained for long periods, but captive breeding is uncommon.

Gerrhosaurus flavigularis   Yellow-throated Plated Lizard

SOUTHERN AFRICA

30–45 cm. Much more slender than most Plated Lizards, and rather more colourful. The back is dark brown and has two clear yellow stripes down it, and the throat is bright orange.

Care is as for the Cordylidae (*see* page 234). An attractive and easy species.

Gerrhosaurus validus

SOUTHERN AFRICA

To 60 cm. This large Plated Lizard varies from dark chocolate-brown to pale brown, and it may be marked with yellowish stripes. Although very strong, it soon becomes tame and easily handled.

Care is as for the Cordylidae (*see* page 234). Obviously, a spacious vivarium is essential for this large lizard. Four eggs are laid.

Several other species exist and may sometimes be offered for sale, including the handsome *G. major* (*see* Plate **32**). The care of all these is as above.

Family Lacertidae

The Lacertidae consists of a large number of small to medium 'general purpose' lizards restricted to the Old World. It is an important one to European vivarium-keepers, as many of its members are attractive, interesting and commonly available. Its colonisation of the numerous large and small Mediterranean islands has given rise to a multitude of species and subspecies, of which only a small proportion can be mentioned here.

All are active, basking species, and require large vivaria with thermal gradients if natural behaviour is to take place. Furnishings, in the form of rocks, logs or branches, will be used for climbing and foraging over, and for hiding under. Substrate may be of newspaper for the larger species, gravel for the smaller species; sand is not recommended. Although a small number of species are associated with damp or semi-aquatic habitats, vivaria should be dry apart from an occasional light spraying, and plants, if included, will therefore consist of succulent species such as *Agave, Aloe* and *Haworthia* species which can tolerate such conditions.

All species are insectivorous, crickets, flies and sweepings being a good basic diet, with additional vitamins and minerals as supplements. A few, particularly some of the larger ones, may be partially herbivorous, eating fruit and berries and, in some cases, the leaves of succulent plants, but, in captivity, most appear to revert to an exclusively insectivorous diet unless they are underfed. Large species will often accept small rodents, and will readily eat small lizards, making them unsuitable for mixed communities.

With the exception of *Lacerta vivipara,* lacertids lay clutches of eggs which number from 2 to 25, larger species usually producing the largest numbers of eggs. In the temperate part of their range the Lacertidae have a breeding season which lasts throughout the spring and summer and during which two or more clutches may be laid. At this time, the males, and in some cases the females, are strongly territorial, and vivarium populations must be adjusted if fighting breaks out, as victimised animals usually die from lack of food or warmth, even if they are not killed outright by the dominant animal(s). Males have prominent femoral pores, may be more brightly coloured, and have broader heads and necks.

Lacerta lepida   Eyed Lizard

MEDITERRANEAN REGION

To 90 cm, usually smaller. The largest and most spectacular lacertid. The Eyed Lizard is predominantly green or olive with small black markings on its back and prominent blue ocelli on its flanks. Young animals are pale green with a number of black-edged white spots.

Eyed Lizards do well in captivity if they are given sufficient space. They thrive in outside accommodation such as large, south-facing garden frames, and greenhouses, but they must be protected from extremes of cold. They eat large insects, such as locusts, and small vertebrates, and may be persuaded to take some tinned meat and vegetable material.

Breeding is possible, especially outside. 10–18 eggs are laid in damp sand or soil. Hatching take place about 2 months later, the hatchlings measuring some 10–15 cm in length. They can be reared to maturity in one year, although 2–3 years is probably more natural.

Lacerta viridis   Green Lizard (33)

MEDITERRANEAN REGION

30–40 cm. A handsome, bright emerald green lizard with a yellow or (in breeding males) bright blue throat. Most females have 2 or 4 thin white stripes along the body, usually edged with black, but others are uniformly coloured, like the male. Juveniles are duller, with brown or olive flanks and green backs.

Care is as in the family description. Like the Eyed Lizard, this species requires a large area, preferably outside. Small verte-brates may be taken, but vegetable material is rarely accepted in captivity. Breeding often occurs under favourable conditions, and

Fig. 62 *Podarcis muralis brueggmanni*, an Italian form of the Wall Lizard.

two or more clutches may be produced each year. 6–20, usually about 12, eggs are laid. Incubation takes about 45 days at 25–30°C, and the young, measuring 8–10 cm at first, grow rapidly and can attain sexual maturity in one year.

The Balkan Green Lizard, *Lacerta trilineata*, is very closely related, but larger. Its care is as above.

Podarcis muralis   Wall Lizard

EUROPE, WESTERN ASIA

To 20 cm. *Podarcis muralis*, of which several subspecies are recognised, is predominantly brown or green, and is patterned with a network of black markings. These may merge into a vertebral stripe in some form. The underside is pale yellow or orange, being brighter in males than females. An extremely variable species, the most attractive examples coming from northern Italy (subspecies *brueggmanni*).

This is the commonest member of a group of small lacertids which may all be loosely termed Wall Lizards. Many species are familiar to visitors to Mediterranean coasts and islands, climbing over rocks and ruined buildings where they can occur in enormous numbers. All are excellent vivarium or reptiliary subjects, provided that their requirements are fully understood. Like all lacertids, they are basking animals and must have an area of relative warmth in which to attain their optimum body temperature. They are social animals, occurring in colonies, but males are territorial, so groups of compatible individuals must be carefully built up and continually monitored for signs of aggressive behaviour. As with many species of lizard, the temptation to choose the brightest individuals must be resisted since these will invariably be males.

A variety of small insects should be offered, sweepings being a valuable source of food. A small quantity of vitamin and mineral powder should be added regularly unless the lizards live outside and have access to direct sunlight. Breeding begins in the spring, but continues throughout the summer, 3–8 eggs being laid in a damp place, often beneath a stone. These hatch after about 42 days at 23–26°C, and the hatchlings, which are small and speckled, require young crickets and graded sweepings at first. Maturity may be attained by the following spring.

Podarcis sicula Ruin Lizard, Italian Wall Lizard

SOUTHERN EUROPE (INTRODUCED ELSEWHERE)

To 25 cm. Usually a bright grass-green lizard with rows of black markings along the back and flanks. There is often a blue spot at the base of the fore-limb. It is, however, highly variable, animals from northern Italy and Yugoslavia (subspecies *campestris*) being especially attractive.

It is a lizard of rocky places and, notably, the ancient ruins which abound within its natural range; but it adapts well to a variety of habitats, and in several places where it has been introduced, including North America, it appears to be thriving.

Care and breeding are as for *P. muralis,* but this species is possibly slightly more warmth-loving.

Several other Wall Lizards are commonly available, including species from the Balearics, *P. lilfordi* (*see* Plate **34**) and *P.*

pityusensis (*see* Plate **35**), some forms of which are totally black (melanistic), *P. hispanicus* from Spain, and *P. erhardii* from Greece. Their care and breeding are similar to that of *P. muralis*. *Lacerta vivipara*, the Common or Viviparous Lizard, is not often kept, owing to its dull colouration, but it is extremely hardy (its range extends into the Arctic circle), and is noteworthy for being the only viviparous lacertid, 4–10 small dark young being born in late summer.

In addition, lizards belonging to the genera *Acanthodactylus* and *Algyroides* and *Psammodromus* may be encountered. They may be treated as Wall Lizards as far as their care and breeding are concerned.

A small number of Wall Lizards from the USSR are known to be parthenogenetic; i.e. they develop from unfertilised eggs. In these populations only females occur, and their care, although similar to that of *P. muralis,* is simplified by the absence of aggressive male behaviour. One species, *P. armeniaca,* lays clutches of 2–5 eggs during the summer, which require 40 days at 30°C to develop. Biologically, these are exceedingly interesting, but so far little-known, lizards.

Family Teiidae - Tegus and Whiptails

This New World family seems to have filled the same evolutionary niche as the Lacertidae has in the Old World, and many similarities exist between them, both in appearance and in habits. Their care in captivity is based on hot, dry vivaria with good basking sites. Small species may be treated in the same way as the Wall Lizards (*see* pp. 239–40), but several species attain greater sizes, and these require large, easily cleaned enclosures. All are carnivorous, the small species eating mainly insects, whereas the larger ones also take small vertebrates such as rodents and birds. All species lay eggs.

Ameiva species

CENTRAL AND SOUTH AMERICA

To 60 cm. Well-built lizards with pointed heads, several of which are superficially similar to the Green Lizards (*Lacerta viridis* and *L. trilineata*) of Europe. They are rather aggressive and prone to panic in captivity, and for this reason must be kept in large vivaria with plenty of hiding places. As a rule they lay several clutches throughout the year, each numbering 2–4 eggs.

Cnemidophorus sexlineatus   Six-lined Racerunner

NORTH AMERICA

To 20 cm. A slender, streamlined lizard with a very long tail. The body is brown with, predictably, six cream stripes along its back and on to its tail. The front part of the body has a greenish-yellow wash, and the male's throat and belly blue.

These are fast-moving, diurnal lizards from arid regions. They require dry vivaria with a substrate of sand or fine gravel, and hiding places constructed from rocks or dead boughs. They are insectivorous. Two or more clutches of 2–4 eggs each are laid in the summer.

Several other Racerunners, sometimes called Whiptails, occur in dry areas of North and Central America. All are rather similar in appearance except that some are spotted rather than striped, and certain tropical species are very brightly coloured in brilliant blues and greens. The care of all of these is as for *C. sexlineatus.* A group of species, including *C. exsanguis* and the well-named *C. uniparens,* are parthenogenetic. The few details of these which are available indicate that they may reach maturity in one year or less, and their eggs have an incubation period of 2–3 months at approximately 23–28°C.

Tupinambis teguixin   Tegu

SOUTH AMERICA

To 150 cm. A large, powerful lizard, attractively marked with bands and stripes of white on a glossy black background. The long tongue is bright red.

Tegus are nervous, aggressive lizards which can give a painful bite. Large examples are not easily handled, and they are therefore more suitable for zoos than private collections. They require very large, strongly made enclosures with a powerful heat source and a sizeable water container. Food consists of dead mammals and birds such as chicks. Chopped meat is also taken. Young animals may be fed on large insects. No records of captive breeding have been traced. Wild females often lay their eggs in termite mounds, where they become sealed until they hatch.

Family Anguidae - Slow-worms, Glass Lizards and Alligator Lizards

In this family there is a strong tendency towards a reduction or complete loss of the limbs. Examples may be found in America, Asia, Africa and Europe, but species are not numerous.

A range of climatic zones and habitats are utilised by the various species and it is difficult to generalise on the subject of care. Some species lay eggs, others produce live young, and both diurnal and nocturnal forms exist. Most, however, are terrestrial, and all are carnivorous.

Anguis fragilis   Slow-worm (36)

EUROPE, NORTH AFRICA, ASIA

30–50 cm. Male Slow-worms are uniform brown or grey in colour, females and juveniles are often copper-coloured with dark flanks and a thin, dark vertebral line. The legs are entirely absent, but the presence of eye-lids and a rather stiff, smooth body distinguishes them from snakes. Their tails are easily broken, and specimens with regenerated tails may be in the majority in some populations, especially around towns, where they are frequently molested by cats and small boys, apart from natural predators.

A variety of habitats is used, including hedgerows, railway embankments and even rubbish dumps, but some moisture and plenty of cover are the most important elements. Their vivarium should therefore contain some leaf-mould or a piece of turf, with broken crocks, pieces of flat stone, or bark, under which they will spend most of their time. A temperature of 15–23°C is adequate in the summer, but basking should be encouraged by the fitting of a low-powered light bulb at one end of the vivarium. They thrive in outdoor enclosures. Food consists of soft-bodied invertebrates, especially slugs and earthworms, but larger prey can be tackled, including small lizards.

Breeding may take place in captivity, especially if they are given the relative freedom of a garden frame or reptiliary. 6–15 young are born alive towards the end of the summer after a gestation period of about 3 months. They measure 6–10 cm at birth and are a bright silvery colour.

Gerrhonotus coeruleus   Northern Alligator Lizard

NORTH AMERICA

To 30 cm. A slender, slow-moving species with a distinctly armoured appearance. A fold of skin starts just in front of the fore-legs and continues along each flank to the hind legs. The dorsal colouration is olive, with black mottling.

Alligator lizards prefer rather cool (18–25°C), humid conditions and like to clamber and climb among low branches and plants. They are mainly insectivorous creatures, preferring crickets and caterpillars, but will also take slugs and snails. The sexes are alike, but pregnant females become plump during the summer owing to developing young, which are born alive and usually number 5–10 per brood.

Gerrhonotus multicarinatus   Southern Alligator Lizard

NORTH AMERICA

To 30 cm. Similar to the above species in general appearance, but the markings tend to be arranged in bands, and there are rust-coloured blotches on each flank.

Care is as for the preceding species, but *G. multicarinatus* is oviparous, laying 6–15 eggs, each containing a well-developed embryo. They take about 6 weeks to hatch.

Ophisaurus apodus   Glass Lizard or Glass Snake

EUROPE, WESTERN ASIA

To 120 cm. Rather like an enormous slow-worm with a large head. The colour is plain brown, but juveniles are grey with brown blotches and bars. A lizard of dry, rocky hillsides, fields and waste ground, which may climb into low shrubs and bushes to bask. Despite its rather formidable appearance, it does not bite when handled, but attempts to twist itself free and may defaecate copiously. The common name alludes to its ability to discard its tail, but this rarely happens, even if it is picked up by that member.

This is an interesting exhibit, even if of rather unprepossessing appearance. It is most easily kept in large vivaria with newspaper for substrate and a jumble of rocks and branches for climbing among. Temperatures 23–32°C. It will eat large insects, snails and small vertebrates, and can be trained to accept strips of meat sprinkled with vitamin and mineral powder, but it is usually a shy feeder and should be left undisturbed at this time. Breeding in captivity has not been reported, but 8–10 eggs are laid.

Family Varanidae - Monitors

An Old World family which contains one genus and about two dozen species. The Monitors are mostly large powerful predators or carrion-eaters, and include the famous Komodo Dragon, the world's largest lizard, from Indonesia. Typically they have long back legs for running, and heavily-clawed front legs for tearing at their food. Their heads are long and pointed, and the sinuous, flickering tongue is deeply forked and snake-like in appearance and use.

In captivity, even the smaller species require spacious, strongly built cages if they are not to lead a life of abject misery. Newspaper is the only practical substrate, unless the means of washing large amounts of gravel at frequent intervals is available. Many species like to bathe, and a large water container is essential for these. All species need to bask beneath a powerful heat source in order to digest their often enormous meals, consisting of dog-meat, dead rodents and chickens, eggs and appropriate supplements. A daytime temperature of 30–35°C or more is required beneath the lamp.

The handling of large wild specimens can be exciting, to say the least, and in the main Monitors are more suitable for zoological gardens than for the collections of hobbyists.

Varanus niloticus Nile Monitor

AFRICA

To 200 cm. More slender than the following species, with a laterally compressed tail which is used in swimming. The young are

245

attractively marked with extensive black or grey reticulations, usually in the form of bands, on a white or yellow background. Older specimens are less distinctly marked.

Although they feed well, being particularly fond of eggs, and may thrive in captivity, Nile Monitors rarely lose their natural aggression and adults are not easily handled.

Varanus salvator   **Water Monitor**

SOUTH-EAST ASIA

To 200 cm. A large, heavy-bodied species, with rough granular skin. The colour is predominantly grey.

Care is as in the family description. This is one of the most commonly available species and it is tough and reasonably tractable in captivity in spite of its potential size. It requires an opportunity to bathe regularly, and will often defaecate in its water bowl or pool, making frequent water changes essential.

Family Amphisbaenidae

Amphisbaenians are secretive, burrowing, worm-like reptiles which are sometimes grouped with the lizards and sometimes placed in a sub-order of their own. They range from about 10 to 100 cm in length and their scales are arranged in rings around their cylindrical bodies, giving a segmented appearance. They are rarely kept in captivity, and little is known of their natural history.

They require a deep layer of slightly moist sandy soil, scattered with half-buried stones and logs, beneath which they will form chambers in which to live. The smaller species, such as the European *Blanus cinereus,* feed on invertebrates such as small mealworms, ants and crickets, which will live in the vivarium until eaten. Larger forms, such as the South American *Amphisbaena alba,* will tackle larger prey, even small rodents. Temperatures should be moderate, probably 20–28°C, but *B. cinereus,* at least, will stand cooler conditions. Once, while digging in my garden, I turned up an escaped specimen that had been at large throughout an English winter. Little is known about their reproduction, except that most species (but not all) lay a few, small elongated eggs below ground.

This is an interesting but neglected family of reptiles.

14
Order Squamata:
Sub-order Serpentes -
Snakes

The snakes, sub-order Serpentes, constitute the remainder of the order Squamata, and may be distinguished from the lizards and other reptiles by the following combination of characteristics: they have no limbs, they have fused eyelids, there is no external ear opening, and, internally, their left lung is greatly reduced whereas the right one is elongated.

Of all reptiles, snakes are undoubtedly the most repulsive to 'normal' people (i.e. non-herpetologists), and several reasons may be responsible for this infamy. Their biblical notoriety and the ability of several species to cause rapid and spectacular death through their venom are probably the most significant. Again, the great size attained by certain species, and the almost unbelievable capacity of their mouths and stomachs, no doubt play their part. For many enthusiasts, however, the fascination of snakes started a life-long interest in all reptiles.

Accommodation for snakes is quite simple; a rectangular cage with provision for heating, lighting and viewing form its basis (*see* Fig. 4), with modifications for some of the more specialised kinds. The cage need not be very large, as few species require enough space even to stretch out full length. They prefer to coil up in a corner, behind a log or stone, or in a specially constructed retreat. As an indication, a cage measuring 100 × 50 × 50 cm is big enough for a pair of average-sized (100–150 cm) snakes, although very active species may require rather more space than this.

Except for specialised types, such as burrowing species, by far the most satisfactory substrate is newspaper. This can be easily replaced when soiled, and abnormal faeces, often the first sign of disease, are easily examined on it. Other artificial substrates, such as shredded bark and wood shavings, are almost as good, but such materials as gravel and sand are better avoided if possible. If a natural appearance is essential, pine needles, dried bracken or dead leaves may be used with discretion, but soil is particularly unsuitable as it holds moisture and may harbour parasites. Exceptions may be necessary, however, in the case of certain arboreal species, for which the provision of living plants is often beneficial.

As a rule, snakes prefer a lower temperature than lizards, 23–28°C being satisfactory for most temperate species, and 26–30°C for most tropical species. Heat may be applied to one end of the cage to create a gradient, and certain species like to bask beneath a radiant heat source, especially when digesting a meal or if pregnant. A slight drop in temperature during the night is desirable, and seasonal fluctuations in light and temperature levels may be essential if breeding is intended (*see* page 81).

Without exception, snakes are carnivores, and include among their prey invertebrates (worms, slugs and insects), fish, amphibians, reptiles, birds, mammals and eggs. Prey is eaten whole, the flexible arrangement of the bones in the lower jaw enabling animals much larger than the head to be swallowed. Captive snakes often prefer dead prey, and this is to be encouraged for reasons of humanity, legal obligation and convenience. The digestive systems of snakes are very efficient. This efficiency, coupled with their low metabolic rate, enables them to maintain themselves with very little food, a good meal lasting from one to two weeks and fasts of much longer being possible under extreme conditions. It should be noted, however, that active diurnal species may require more frequent feeding, and that a long fast may cause parts of the digestive tract to atrophy, creating problems when normal feeding is resumed. In most cases, snakes refuse food when they are about to slough their skin. This pre-slough, or 'opaque', period may be recognised by a general dulling of the markings and the milky appearance of the eyes some four to five days prior to the actual slough (*see* Plate **41**). Newly sloughed snakes are often very anxious to feed. Pregnant or gravid snakes may also refuse food as their bodies become full of eggs or young, but will usually feed ravenously after egg-laying or parturition. Apart from the above causes, refusal to feed may be due, in order of importance, to: (1) too low a temperature; (2) an incorrect food item or incorrectly presented food; or (3) infection of the mouth.

Snakes may be oviparous or viviparous, and captive breeding may be reasonably expected if a pair is kept under good conditions and their reproductive cycles are investigated and, where possible, the important parameters simulated. Male snakes can generally be distinguished by the swelling formed by their inverted hemipenes. A few species show some degree of parental care, but by and large the eggs and young are deposited and then left. Baby snakes may have different feeding habits from adults of the same species, and some are so small that it may be necessary to force-feed them with small pieces of food until they grow sufficiently to handle complete prey items (*see* page 75). Most species grow rapidly under optimum conditions, and may be ready to breed at less than one year of age, but large species take two or more years to attain sexual maturity.

Almost all snakes are secretive by nature, and this dictates a low level of lighting and the provision of some kind of retreat or hide-box. This can be most simply a inverted cardboard box with a hole cut in one side for access. Alternatively, small snakes will enter an inverted clay flower-pot by the drainage hole or, if a more natural effect is required, a hollow log. A rock cave could also be used.

Clean fresh water must be available at all times — snakes will often refuse to drink foul or stale water even though they may be thirsty. Certain species like to immerse themselves completely in water, especially in preparation for sloughing. When this is necessary, sufficient room must be left in the vessel to prevent displaced water from overflowing and making the substrate damp — with few exceptions, *snakes must be kept on dry substrate*. Failure to do this will result in sores which may be difficult or impossible to cure. This point applies equally to 'water' or 'swamp' snakes, as well as to terrestrial species from dry habitats.

The care of venomous snakes, which is a specialised and hazardous pastime, is dealt with more specifically on page 279.

Families Typhlopidae and Leptotyphlopidae - Blind Snakes

Members of these two widely distributed families are small (20–75 cm) burrowing snakes, with covered eyes, shiny scales and cylindrical bodies. They are not frequently kept in captivity,

owing to their secretive habits and less than colourful appearance, but as far as is known they require a deep layer of firm
sandy soil, with scattered rocks or logs on the surface. Their
food consists of invertebrates such as earthworms, ants and
termites, and other burrowing forms.

Most species apparently lay eggs, although at least one,
Typhlops diardi, appears to be viviparous. Another species,
Typhlops braminus, which lays 2–7 elongated eggs, is almost
certainly parthenogenetic, as males are unknown. *Leptotyphlops
humilis* is shown in Plate **37**.

Vivarium-keepers could contribute greatly to the knowledge of
these secretive snakes.

Family Boidae - Boas and Pythons

Boas and pythons include amongst their ranks the world's largest
snakes, as well as a number of more moderately-sized species.
They are distributed throughout the tropical regions of the
world, and a few species range into subtropical and temperate
regions. The pythons are primarily Old World species, whereas
the boas are found mainly in the New World, with a few species
in the Old World. They are unique among snakes in showing
external signs of vestigial limbs, reduced to small spurs positioned on either side of the cloaca. In males these are often more pronounced, and may be used to stimulate the female during courtship and mating.

Care of the boas and pythons is essentially as for other snakes,
but, in many cases, on a much larger scale. Pairs of the larger
species require spacious vivaria, heated to 25–30°C, and a
regular supply of food — necessities that often lead to the
disposal of a pet which, after two or three years, has outgrown
the resources of its owner. It would be far more satisfactory if
smaller species were chosen in the first place.

The boas are viviparous, the pythons oviparous. In several
species of the latter, the female coils around her eggs, gathering
them into a conical pile. She remains around them for the
duration of their development, and in some instances elevates
their temperature slightly above that of their surroundings by
means of a physiological process which is not fully understood.
Eggs laid in captivity may be removed and incubated artificially,

but by so doing the keeper deprives himself of the opportunity to witness an unusual and fascinating aspect of reptilian behaviour.

Many species of Boidae are protected in their country of origin, and there may be additional restrictions on their importation into some countries. Captive-bred stocks of a few species are readily available.

Boa constrictor   **Common Boa, Boa Constrictor (38)**

CENTRAL AND SOUTH AMERICA

To 400 cm, usually smaller. The celebrated Boa Constrictor is a handsome silver-grey snake with variable black and reddish-brown markings on its head and along its length. A dark line passing through the eye is always present. Babies sometimes have a pinkish overwash, and in some forms the markings on the tail are bright red.

The Common Boa is partly arboreal in habit and it should be given quite a tall cage with some strong boughs arranged so that the snake can climb and rest among them. A temperature of 25–30°C should be provided — certainly not below 20°C at any time. During the day a heat-lamp may be used slightly to raise the temperature in part of the cage.

The main food is rodents (mice for juveniles, rats for adults) but large examples may also take rabbits or chickens. They are usually quite willing to accept dead prey.

Captive breeding is possible, but unpredictable; a pair may breed one year but not the next even though conditions may be identical. Sexual activity may be observed when the snakes are still quite small, but successful mating is unlikely to occur before they are at least 1.5 m in length. In captivity at least, mating and birth can take place at various times of the year. The gestation period is approximately six months, and a litter size of about 20 is usual for captive animals, although litters of up to 60 have been reported. The young are large enough to eat mice. They are rather prone to respiratory ailments if not kept in warm, dry, draught-free cages.

Chondropython viridis   **Green Python**

PAPUA NEW GUINEA, NORTHERN AUSTRALIA

100–200 cm. A very striking species, being bright green with a few patches of white scales along the dorsal midline, and white or pale yellow below. Rarely, the green colouration is replaced by bright blue! The young are totally different, being brick-red or bright sulphur yellow in colour, changing to green after about two years. Prominent heat-sensitive pits are situated *within* the labial scales.

This is a highly arboreal species and it must have a tall vivarium with horizontal branches available for resting on, and a temperature of 25–30°C. It will feed on any warm-blooded prey, including rats and mice. In general it is hardier than its 'double' the Emerald Boa (see below), and of somewhat better disposition, but it may be snappy and bad-tempered, especially when first obtained.

Breeding occurs, but rarely. It may be necessary to lower the temperature slightly to induce mating. The eggs, which may exceed twenty in number, are brooded by the female, the only time that either adult spends any length of time at ground level. It is not known whether she raises their temperature at this time or if she is merely guarding them. The humidity of the cage should be raised slightly by occasional spraying. The incubation period is about 50 days, and the hatchlings are large enough to take mice as soon as they have completed their initial slough.

A beautiful and highly-prized species which is protected in the wild – hopefully, the trickle of captive-bred animals will swell to supply the demand.

Corallus caninus   Emerald Boa

SOUTH AMERICA

150–250 cm. A spectacular arboreal snake closely resembling the previous species, a fine example of parallel evolution. The basic colour is bright green with a series of short white bars across the back. The chin and underside of the body is yellow. The juveniles are bright yellow, brick-red or reddish-brown in colour with the same white bars as the adults. It is most easily distinguished from *Chondropython viridis* by the position of its heat-sensitive pits – *between* the labial scales.

This species rarely if ever descends to the ground and requires a tall (minimum 1 metre) vivarium with several strong branches firmly attached in a horizontal position. The snake(s) will drape their bodies over this in exactly the same manner as *C. viridis*.

Water should be provided – the snakes will hang down from their branch to drink and also soak themselves prior to sloughing – and it may be beneficial to spray the cage occasionally to raise the humidity for a short spell. Their natural food is said to be birds and bats, but captives will usually accept mice and rats which should be offered dead – it may be necessary to hold these up to the snakes.

Breeding has been achieved on a few occasions. Up to 15 young are born after nine to ten months gestation, during which the females will usually refuse food. They give birth from high branches and the young may fall to the floor – it would seem to be advisable to provide a material which ensures à soft landing when a birth is imminent. Wild-caught adults are very aggressive – captive-bred young can be expected to be somewhat tamer.

Similar species: *Corallus enhydris cooki*, Cook's Tree Boa, is variable in colour, ranging from yellow to brown or grey, with or without black markings. It grows to 200 cm and its maintenance is the same as that of *C. caninus*. About 6–10 young are born after a gestation of slightly more than six months.

Epicrates cenchria Rainbow Boa

SOUTH AMERICA

To 200 cm. The Rainbow Boa is named for the multicoloured sheen which covers its body when seen in sunlight. Under artificial lighting it is a brown to orange snake, and there may be a series of connected dark rings along its dorsal midline (subspecies *E. cenchria cenchria*, Brazilian Rainbow Boa).

Its care is similar to that of *B. constrictor*, but its broods are smaller.

Eryx jaculus Sand Boa

EASTERN MEDITERRANEAN REGION

60–80 cm. A stout snake with a blunt tail and wedge-shaped head. The body is yellow or grey with irregular dark markings. A line runs from the eye to the angle of the mouth.

The Sand Boas, of which this species is the most frequently met, are secretive burrowing snakes that may be kept on a substrate of smooth or pea-gravel with flat stones placed on the surface, or may be provided with artificial 'burrows' in the form of dark boxes with small entrance holes, in which case the substrate may be newspaper. Food, consisting of young rodents or birds, is usually eaten inside the retreat, whether natural or artificial. No records of breeding in captivity have been traced, but in the wild about 12 (6–20) young are born towards the end of summer. They measure 12–15 cm at birth.

Lichanura trivirgata   **Rosy Boa**

NORTH AND CENTRAL AMERICA

70–120 cm. A grey or cream snake with blotches or longitudinal stripes of brown, maroon or orange. Three subspecies are recognised, of which the Desert Rosy Boa, *L. t. gracia*, is the most attractive.

Fig. 63 *Eryx jaculus*, a small species of Sand Boa.

Rosy Boas are partly arboreal, climbing into low bushes and shrubs in search of nesting birds, and are mainly nocturnal. Their extreme docility and adaptability make them good vivarium subjects, but they enjoy partial protection. They require a temperature of 23–28 °C, a retreat, and a few rocks or branches to climb among. Their food consists of mice, which should not be too large. Breeding in captivity has been achieved, but only on a few occasions. The gestation period is about four months, after which 5–10 relatively large young are born.

Python molurus   Indian Python

ASIA

To 600 cm. The Indian Python is one of the most attractive Boidae. There are two subspecies, *P. m. molurus*, or light phase, and *P. m. bivittatus*, or dark phase. The latter is most commonly kept, and its markings consist of a row of irregular dark brown blotches along its back, on a deep yellow background. Smaller brown markings occur on its flanks. The top of its head is marked with a brown arrowhead, and a brown line runs from the snout, through the eye, and to the angle of the jaw. *P. m. molurus* is similarly marked, but the colours are considerably muted, giving an over-all 'washed out' appearance.

Indian Pythons are tough, vigorous snakes, which thrive in captivity. They require a temperature of 25–30°C and very roomy accommodation. Their food consists of mice, rats and larger mammals, as well as chickens, but newborn chicks should not be used exclusively or vitamin deficiencies will result. They can easily be tamed, and can then be handled with confidence.

They appear to be among the easiest snakes to breed. Sexual maturity is attained at about 2.5 m (males) to 3.5 m (females). Mating invariably takes place as a result of decreased day-length in winter, usually in November, December or January. The eggs, numbering 20–50, are laid about ten weeks later, the female usually having fasted for at least the latter part of this time. As the eggs are laid, the female gathers them into a heap, and on completion of the clutch she coils around them to begin the incubation. During this time her body twitches every few minutes; this is believed to be associated with her attempts to raise the eggs' temperature. Some females may leave the eggs to drink or slough, but food is rarely taken at this time. At 30°C the

Fig. 64 *Python molurus*, the Indian Python, a frequently kept and bred species.

incubation time is 65–70 days, and as soon as hatching begins the female takes no further interest in the eggs. The hatchlings measure 50–60 cm and are lively and aggressive. They slough when 2–4 days old and usually begin to feed immediately afterwards. Growth may be extremely rapid, sexual maturity sometimes being reached in 18–24 months.

Python regius Royal Python

AFRICA

To 150 cm. The Royal Python is short and stout. Its basic colour is very dark brown to black, attractively marked with irregular cream and brown, or golden, blotches. When alarmed, it may hide its head amongst its coils, and for this reason is occasionally known as the Ball Python. This species is rather inactive, remaining tightly coiled for days on end. Its care is as in the family description, but it is a confirmed rodent eater, and occasionally goes on long, self-imposed fasts. Provided it has been well fed, and is in good condition, this should not give cause for alarm, although food should continue to be offered regularly. Breeding in captivity is very rare. A small clutch of eggs is laid, and there are no accounts of females brooding these.

Python reticulatus   Reticulated Python

ASIA

To 1,000 cm. Potentially the world's longest snake, the Reticulated Python has a series of diamond-shaped yellow patches down its back, its flanks being intricately marked with brown, black, cream and purple.

This species is usually irascible and untrustworthy, and as it grows it can become a most difficult animal to handle safely. For this reason it cannot be recommended for the private collection, although large examples make good exhibits for zoological gardens. It feeds well on rodents and larger mammals, pigeons and chickens. It is not easily bred, but clutch sizes of over 100 have been recorded for wild examples.

Python sebae   African Rock Python

AFRICA

To 900 cm, usually much smaller. A light brown or tan snake, with extensive markings and marblings of darker brown. These markings are often edged in white or buff. Old animals become darker, and their markings may become indistinct.

Care is as in the family description. Rock Pythons may refuse to feed during the winter, and become dormant. In fact, they can withstand quite low temperatures, ranging as they do into the cooler regions of Southern Africa. Breeding in captivity is possible, but unusual, most cases having been reported from African zoos. 20–70 eggs are laid and brooded in the same manner as *P. molurus*. At 30°C, incubation takes approximately 75–85 days, the newly-hatched young measuring 55–70 cm. They feed readily after their initial slough.

Family Colubridae - Typical Snakes

The Colubridae is by far the largest family of snakes, consisting of over 1,000 species. Most of these are harmless, although many may bite, and a relatively small number of species are capable of introducing venom through wounds made with small grooved fangs in the rear of their mouth, which are brought into play by chewing, rather than by striking. A few are dangerous to man and some of them are listed with the venomous snakes in Chapter 15.

The Colubridae includes small insectivorous and quite large constricting species, but most are moderate in size, 1–2 m being about average. The care of most species is as described in the introduction to this sub-order (pp. 247–9), with the more important variations noted under the relevant species. Several genera within this family, for instance *Thamnophis, Elaphe,* and *Lampropeltis,* have attracted an exceptionally large following owing to their colourful appearance and the ease of keeping and, in some cases, breeding them, and these are dealt with in more detail than other genera.

Arizona elegans   Glossy Snake

NORTH AMERICA

75–120 cm. A moderately slender species with a pointed snout. Buff or cream in colour with a series of slightly darker blotches down its back.

Care is as given on page 247. The Glossy Snake is a lizard-eater by nature, but some examples can be persuaded to accept small mice. It requires hot, dry conditions, 25–30°C during the day, cooler at night and in winter. 6–10 eggs are laid, incubation taking about 70 days, but captive breeding is infrequent.

Boaedon fuliginosus   House Snake

AFRICA

80–120 cm. A smooth, supple snake, and a powerful constrictor. It is uniform rich brown above, except for a cream line from the snout, through each eye, to the neck, and cream lips. Beneath, it is cream or pinkish, with a pearly sheen.

Care is as on page 247, temperature 22–30°C. House Snakes are very good vivarium subjects, readily feeding on mice of appropriate size. They may be aggressive at first, but soon become tame. An average of 8–10 eggs are laid during the southern spring or summer. Captive breeding is quite easy, but in the northern hemisphere imported animals may take several years to adjust their breeding cycle to the reversed seasons.

Coluber constrictor   **Racer**

NORTH AMERICA

To 200 cm. A slender species, which may be plain black, brown or olive above. Racers, of which there are several subspecies, are active diurnal hunters of lizards, frogs, rodents and invertebrates. Captive specimens are often nervous and aggressive, and frequently refuse to feed. Spacious vivaria with hot, dry conditions are essential. 12–24 eggs are laid, incubation taking approximately 60 days.

Coluber viridiflavus   **Western Whipsnake**

EUROPE

100–150 cm. This species is the commonest of several Old World Whipsnakes. Like the previous species, it is slender and fast-moving. It is brown to black, marked with a varying amount of yellow, sometimes arranged in bars or (on its tail) stripes. Examples from some parts of its range are entirely black.

Care is as on page 247. Usually aggressive when handled. A temperature of around 25°C is required and a diet consisting primarily of lizards, although young mice and invertebrates may be taken. Breeding in captivity is infrequent. 8–15 eggs are laid. Feeding the very small hatchlings is likely to present considerable problems.

Dasypeltis scabra   **Egg-eating Snake**

AFRICA

To 100 cm, usually smaller. A very rough-scaled species, which may be grey or pale brown in colour with a series of dark, square-shaped blotches down each flank. One or more V-shaped markings are present on the neck. The Egg-eater has a spectacular and unnerving aggression display when newly captured; it forms itself into a semi-circular coil, and by moving one loop of its body against another its rough scales produce a rasping or hissing sound. At the same time it lunges forward with its mouth wide open, behaving very like the similar, and venomous, Night Adder, *Causus rhombeatus,* with which it shares part of its range. In fact, the Egg-eating Snake is completely harmless, feeding, as one might expect, on eggs. This is achieved by stretching its jaws to such an extent that it can engulf eggs several times larger than its head. When the egg reaches the snake's throat, its shell is sawn through by several inward projecting vertebral processes, and the empty shell, characteristically folded, is ejected.

In captivity, Egg-eaters do very well if an adequate supply of eggs is available. Only the largest specimens can take hens' eggs, otherwise smaller birds' eggs must be provided. Alternatively, beaten egg can be fed via a short length of rubber tubing attached to a syringe.

12–15 eggs are laid in the southern summer, i.e. December–April, but no records of captive breeding have been traced. The young measure 20 cm and are very thin, making force-feeding obligatory for several months at least.

Drymarchon corais Indigo Snake

NORTH, CENTRAL AND SOUTH AMERICA

To 250 cm. Examples of the most popular subspecies of Indigo Snake (*D. c. couperi*, the Florida Indigo Snake) are completely glossy black in colour (apart from the chin in some specimens, which may be deep rose-red), and are among the most handsome of serpents. More southerly occurring forms tend to become brown or olive, especially towards the fore-part of the body. There is also a difference in temperament: the Florida form rarely bites, although it may hiss threateningly, but other forms are frequently bad-tempered and aggressive.

Indigo snakes require very large vivaria with plenty of hiding places. A temperature of 25–30°C is required during the summer, with a 5–10°C drop during the winter if breeding is to take place. Rodents are the most convenient prey for captives, although fish, amphibians, birds, lizards and other snakes are taken equally readily (in fact it may take some time to persuade newly-imported animals to accept mice and rats). Prey is pinned down with a loop of the body, or forced up against a solid object, and is normally swallowed live, although captives will usually take dead prey.

Males may fight during the breeding season, which in the case of North American specimens begins in the middle of winter, and they may have to be separated at this time to prevent serious injuries being inflicted. Up to 12 eggs are laid in spring or early summer, usually in May, and are large (6 × 4 cm) and have a granular shell. They require approximately 100 days' incubation at 26–27°C. The hatchlings, which measure about 45 cm, are speckled and often require fish or frogs for their first few feeds.

Elaphe guttata Corn Snake (42)

NORTH AMERICA

100–150 cm. Of the commonly available species of snakes, this species ranks among the most popular and most attractive. Its ground colour is pale yellow to grey, and a series of large red to brown saddles runs from the head to the tip of the tail, each saddle being edged in black. A prominent red line goes across the snout from eye to eye, and just behind this, on top of the head, is a V-shaped marking. The belly is chequered black and white, and contrasts strongly with the dorsal markings.

This species is usually quite docile and settles down to captivity quickly. It can climb quite well, but rarely does so, and its cage need not be very high. An adult pair will require a cage of about 100 × 50 × 50 cm, and as with most snakes this must be kept dry and clean, and contain a retreat for the snakes. Temperatures should be 25–30°C in summer, cooler in winter. The main food is mice, which are constricted, but lizards and frogs are also taken.

The Corn Snake breeds readily in captivity, usually in the spring, with up to 20, but more usually around 10, eggs being laid one month after mating. At 28°C these hatch in approximately 70 days. The young vary in size from clutch to clutch, some being large enough to take newborn mice straight away, others requiring to be force-fed with small pieces of fortified meat, mouse legs etc, until they have grown sufficiently to feed themselves. Under optimum conditions, sexual maturity may be reached in 8 months, but 2–3 years is more natural.

Elaphe longissima Aesculapian Snake

EUROPE

100–150 cm. A slender snake which is usually uniform olive green or brown in colour with white flecks on some of its scales.

The narrow head may be paler than the body, often yellowish brown, and the underside is cream. Juveniles are spotted, and have yellow and black markings on their head and neck.

European members of the genus *Elaphe* are similar in habits to their North American cousins, and may be treated similarly in captivity. The present species likes to climb and should have a branch in its cage. 6–20 eggs are laid in spring or early summer, and incubation takes about 50 days and 28°C. The young measure 20 cm.

Elaphe obsoleta   Rat Snake

NORTH AMERICA

150–200 cm. Several different subspecies of the Rat Snake are recognised, and as they differ from one another in colour and markings those most frequently met are described separately. Juvenile forms of all the subspecies are similar, being grey, buff or pale yellow, with large dark grey or brown blotches on their backs and tails.

E. o. lindheimeri, the Texas Rat Snake (**41**), is a dark form in which the blotches remain, but become less distinct with age as the background darkens. The areas between the blotches may be speckled with cream or pink.

E. o. obsoleta, the Black Rat Snake (**40**), is a shiny, jet black snake with a white chin. Some examples may retain faint signs of the juvenile markings.

E. o. quadrivittata, the Yellow Rat Snake, is a slender subspecies, yellow to brown with four dark lines running from the neck to the tail.

E. o. rossalleni, the Orange, or Everglades, Rat Snake, is similar to the above subspecies except that the yellow colouration is replaced by orange.

E. o. spiloides, the Grey Rat Snake, is the only form in which the juvenile markings persist throughout life.

All the above subspecies are strong, robust snakes, which constrict their prey, consisting of mice and small rats. All climb well and should be given a branch in which to rest, as well as a retreat. Temperature 25–30°C in summer, cooler in winter. Northern subspecies (*E. o. obsoleta, E. o. spiloides*), may be hibernated, the others require a 5–10°C drop.

Captive breeding is relatively easy. The eggs are laid in spring or summer, and usually number 6–12, but larger clutches, including one of 44 eggs, are on record. At 25–28°C they hatch after 70–80 days. The young are quite large and will normally take newborn mice. Sexual maturity may be reached in one year, but 2–3 years is more usual.

Elaphe quatuorlineata   Four-lined Snake

EUROPE

120–200 cm. Powerfully built, with a broad, triangular head, the Four-lined Snake is pale grey or brown with four dusky lines along its length. Its scales are heavily keeled, and this immediately sets it apart from the other striped *Elaphe* species (such as *E. obsoleta quadrivittata*, above). Juveniles are similarly coloured, but have strongly blotched markings, and examples from some parts of the range retain these throughout their life (*E. q. sauromates*).

The Four-lined Snake thrives in captivity, and may become very tame. Care as for the Corn Snake. Temperature 25–30°C in summer, cooler in winter. Captive breeding is rarely reported, presumably because this species is not often kept. 3–18, usually about 10, eggs are laid. The hatchlings are large, averaging about 35–40 cm in length.

Elaphe situla   Leopard Snake

EUROPE

60–100 cm. A beautifully marked little snake, of which two forms are known. The most common one consists of a series of black-edged red blotches on a yellowish or cream background, whereas the other is of two longitudinal black-edged red line running from neck to tail. Both forms exist in the same region, and may even be present amongst young from the same clutch of eggs.

Care in captivity is as for *E. guttata*. Small mice are the main food of adults, but the young may require lizards or force-feeding. Captive breeding is rare. 2–7 eggs are laid during June or July. At 26°C these hatch in 65–70 days.

Elaphe subocularis   Trans-Pecos Rat Snake

NORTH AND CENTRAL AMERICA

80–150 cm. An unusually slender species, with prominent eyes. Unlike other *Elaphe* species, the Trans-Pecos Rat Snake is nocturnal and has vertical pupils as a result. The ground colour is clear, pale yellow, broken by a number of H-shaped markings along the length of the snake.

Care is as for *E. guttata*. A temperature of 25–30°C is required, with a slight reduction in the winter. Captive breeding has been achieved on several occasions, 3–6 eggs being laid about one month after mating. At 30°C these hatch in approximately 70–80 days, and the hatchlings will eat newborn mice.

Elaphe vulpina   Fox Snake

NORTH AMERICA

80–130 cm. The Fox Snake is more heavily built than most *Elaphe* species. It is grey or pale brown with large chestnut brown saddles.

Care is as for *E. guttata*, but this is a more northern species and cooler conditions are more natural: 20–25°C in summer, cooler, preferably hibernation, in winter. No records of captive breeding have been traced, but in the wild 7–29 eggs have been recorded, with an average of 15 per clutch.

Heterodon species   Hognose Snakes

NORTH AMERICA

35–80 cm. Hognose Snakes, of which there are three species altogether, are rather similar in general appearance. Their most distinctive feature is a sharply upturned snout, and they are also characterised by a short, stout body. They are heavily spotted or blotched brown or grey snakes, and their scales are keeled.

When threatened, they may hiss loudly or lie on their backs and pretend to be dead. In fact they are docile and harmless, and soon become tame. As captives they have one serious drawback — they feed almost exclusively on toads, although *H. nasicus* will normally eat mice and this species is now bred regularly in captivity and is highly recommended.

Lampropeltis calligaster Prairie Kingsnake

NORTH AMERICA

80–120 cm. A variable species, but most commonly grey, with a number of bold chestnut-brown saddles along its back. Other forms are olive-brown with indistinct red-brown blotches, or brown with a very small number of widely spaced, indistinct darker blotches (subspecies *rhombomaculata*, the Mole Kingsnake).

The Kingsnakes are an enormously popular genus of North American snakes which are attractive and quite easily cared for. This particular species is no exception. Its general requirements are as described on page 247. It is a terrestrial species which climbs only rarely, so its cage need not be very tall, but a retreat is essential. Temperature, 23–28°C in summer, cooler in winter. Its prey consists of mice, but reptiles, including other snakes, may also be taken, and therefore it should not be kept with other species. Captive breeding has been achieved on several occasions. Mating takes place in spring, after a period of inactivity in the winter. 6–15 (average 11), eggs are laid, usually in June or July. Their incubation period is approximately 45–50 days. The young measure 20–30 cm at hatching and can deal quite easily with newborn mice.

Lampropeltis getulus Common Kingsnake

NORTH AMERICA

100–180 cm. A smooth-scaled, black and white species, which may be spotted, speckled, striped or banded. The most common subspecies are the following.

L. g. californiae, the Californian Kingsnake, has two phases. The most common one is ringed alternately with broad black and white (sometimes brown and cream) bands, and the other, by contrast, consists of a single white line running from neck to tail, on a black background. The latter form occurs only in the San Diego region.

L. g. floridana, the Florida Kingsnake, is basically black, brown or olive, with many partially white scales. These are usually arranged in bands across the body, but the subspecies is highly variable.

L. g. getulus, the Eastern Kingsnake, is black with narrow bands of white. Each band divides into two on the flanks to link up with the arms of the adjacent bands, so forming a chain-like pattern.

L. g. holbrooki, the Speckled Kingsnake, is black with a yellow or cream spot on every scale, giving an over-all speckled appearance.

Fig. 65 *Lampropeltis getulis californiae,* the Californian Kingsnake. The form shown is a typically banded example.

Fig. 66 *Lampropeltis getulis californiae* – an example of the striped phase.

All of these Kingsnakes require roomy cages heated to 25–30°C in summer, and with ample hiding places. They rarely climb. Their food in captivity is mice, which they constrict, but they will readily take lizards and other snakes, and so must not be kept with other species. Furthermore, large and small Kingsnakes should be housed separately and, even if of the same size, a close watch must be kept on them when feeding is in progress in case two specimens seize the same mouse and one proceeds to swallow the other. This applies particularly to groups of young Kingsnakes, which often feed voraciously. It may be prudent to separate them into small individual containers during feeding and for an hour or so afterwards.

Breeding is not difficult. Mating takes place in the spring, especially after a few months at a slightly lowered temperature or (for northern subspecies such as *L. g. getulus* and *L. g. holbrooki*) a short hibernation. Up to 17 eggs are laid, 6–12 being the usual range, and at 25–30°C these hatch in about 70 days. The young are boldly marked at hatching, and with *L. g. californiae* both striped and banded phases may be present in a single clutch, depending upon the origin and genetic make-up of the parents. The hatchlings measure 25–30 cm and are capable of taking newborn mice.

Lampropeltis pyromelana   **Sonoran Mountain Kingsnake**

WESTERN NORTH AMERICA

50–100 cm. This is one of a group of Kingsnakes known as tri-coloured species. It is banded in black, white and red, the black areas separating alternate red and white bands. Its snout is always white.

These beautiful snakes are secretive, semi-desert species which spend much of their time beneath rocks. They therefore require a cage that has ample hiding places and is warm and dry. A temperature of 25–30°C is required in the summer, dropping to 15–20°C in winter. Mating takes place in the spring, usually May or June, and 3–6 eggs are laid in July. At 25–30°C these hatch in 50–60 days, the hatchlings measuring 20–25 cm in length. Some will accept newborn mice as a first food, but most appear to favour small lizards.

Lampropeltis triangulum   **Milk Snake**

NORTH AND CENTRAL AMERICA

50–120 cm. Another variable species, of which many subspecies have been described. Apart from the commonest form, *L. t. triangulum*, the Eastern Milk Snake, which is beige with dark brown saddles, the rest of the subspecies may be loosely described as tricoloured. The pattern may consist of black-edged red saddles on a white or cream background, or of complete bands of black, white and red. The white bands always become wider on the flanks, which distinguishes this species from similar ones.

In captivity, the various forms of the Milk Snake require much the same treatment as other *Lampropeltis* species, although they are usually rather more delicate. Their food consists of mice, and their optimum temperature ranges from 22 to 30°C in summer, depending on their origin. Northern subspecies, such as *triangulum*, may be hibernated at 6–10°C, whereas subspecies from the southern United States and from Central America may be given a temperature drop of 5–10°C during the winter. Mating takes place in spring or early summer, and 3–6 eggs are usually laid in July. At 25–30°C these take 55–70 days to hatch, and the hatchlings measure 15–30 cm in length, depending on subspecies, and are even more colourful than the adults. They will usually feed on newborn mice.

A number of forms, mainly the more colourful ones, are now being bred on a regular basis by herpetologists in Europe and North America. Captive-bred hatchlings of these are frequently available during the late summer, *L. t. sinaloae* and *L. t. hondurensis* being amongst the most commonly offered (and prettiest). This source of high quality captive-bred stock should ensure a good supply of these snakes and is much to be preferred over wild-caught animals.

Lampropeltis zonata Californian Mountain Kingsnake (43)

WESTERN NORTH AMERICA

60–100 cm. Yet another brilliantly patterned tri-coloured snake, this species may be distinguished from the Sonoran Mountain Kingsnake by its black snout. Once again, several subspecies are recognised, but all are rather similar in appearance (red, white and black stripes) with only the relative widths of the bands varying. Occasionally, the red areas are very much reduced, or even missing altogether.

Care is as for other Kingsnakes. Clutches of eggs tend to be small, usually 3–6, but captive breeding is a rare event.

Natrix natrix Grass Snake

EUROPE, ASIA AND NORTH AFRICA

60–120 cm. Quite a variable species, but usually olive-green in colour with a white or yellow collar and black spots and/or bars on the back and flanks. This species is probably the least aquatic of the several *Natrix* species, often being found in quite dry habitats. The habit of smearing its captor with a foul-smelling fluid from its anal gland if seized is particularly well

269

developed in this species, although it is also practised by a variety of other species.

Care is as given on page 247, but some individuals do not adapt well. It is primarily a fish and amphibian eater, but examples from some parts of the range are said to eat mice. Up to 50 eggs may be laid, but a more usual number would be 20–30. These have a short incubation period of about 40 days at 25–30°C.

Natrix tessellata   Dice Snake (44)

EUROPE AND ASIA

50–70 cm. Usually grey-green in colour with distinct dark spots on the back and sides.

Care is as for *N. natrix*, although this species is naturally more aquatic. It feeds readily on fish and earthworms. 5–25, usually about 12, eggs are laid.

Natrix maura, the Viperine Snake, is similar in most respects but slightly smaller and less frequently available.

Nerodia erythrogaster   Red-bellied Water Snake

EASTERN NORTH AMERICA

60–120 cm. A large stout snake, which is brown above and plain red or orange below. The scales are heavily keeled, giving a rough appearance and feel to the skin.

The care of Water Snakes is much the same as for other medium-sized snakes, but it is worth reiterating the warning relating to substrate, which must be kept absolutely dry. Failure to do this will certainly result in troublesome sores on the ventral surface. Water may be provided in a small drinking bowl, or in a larger vessel in which the snake can coil up, but ensure that there is room to do this without flooding the cage; and there must be a bulb or lamp in the cage under which the wet snake can bask and thus dry off completely. Temperature 25–30°C in summer; cooler, or hibernation, in winter. The natural food consists of amphibians and fish. In captivity they will almost always accept strips of fresh fish, dead goldfish or small food-fish such as whitebait. If sliced fish is given, it must contain some bone, and also the viscera of the fish. (*See also* page 96.)

Despite a reputation for irascibility, most Water Snakes adapt well to captivity, and being diurnal, active and ready feeders they make rewarding vivarium subjects. At the present time, breeding them has been a neglected aspect of their care, and reports of captive breeding are few. All *Nerodia* species are viviparous. Mating takes place in the spring, and young are produced in late summer. The present species produces up to 27, average 15, young during September.

Nerodia sipedon   Northern Water Snake

EASTERN NORTH AMERICA

60–120 cm. A variable species which may be brown, grey or orange, with broad dark bands. In some examples the contrast between the bands and the background is very striking, but in others it may be difficult to see the markings at all.

Care is as for *N. erythrogaster*. Broods of nearly 100 young have been reported, but 20–40 is a more usual figure.

Several other *Nerodia* species are occasionally available, including *N. rhombifera* and *N. taxispilota*. Care and breeding are as above.

Opheodryas aestivus   Smooth Green Snake (47)

NORTH AMERICA

30–70 cm. A beautiful, slender green snake with smooth scales, some individuals being more brightly coloured than others. The head is narrow and the eyes are bright yellow with round pupils.

This small snake is an ideal subject for the vivarium, provided that its food requirements are met: it is unusual amongst snakes by being entirely insectivorous and requires constant supplies of adult crickets, grasshoppers, spiders and (sometimes) caterpillars and grubs. These it hunts actively, chasing them from beneath rocks and logs and pursuing them around the cage. In other respects it can be treated in much the same way as other colubrids but, being much smaller and therefore cleaner than most, it can be accommodated in a more natural type of set-up if desired. A substrate of gravel and a jumble of logs and branches suits it well, but care must be taken to ensure that moisture is not retained in any of these furnishings – the ventilation must therefore be good. It is a diurnal species which likes to bask in a warm part of the cage, preferably off the ground and under a spotlight or some other concentrated heat-source. A background temperature of 20–27°C during the day, cooler at night is sufficient.

Apart from the usual sex differences, males are usually shorter and more slender than the females. Mating takes place during the spring and 4–6 eggs are laid. Great care must be taken to ensure that uneaten crickets are not in the cage at the time of egg-laying or they will destroy the eggs – it is advisable to remove the female to a separate cage for egg-laying when she becomes heavily gravid, and withhold food altogether.

Pituophis melanoleucus   Bull, Gopher and Pine Snakes

NORTH AMERICA

100–200 cm. A large, heavy bodied species which comes in a variety of subspecies. These may be white, yellow or grey, blotched with black or brown. The most distinctive are *P. m. catenifer,* the Pacific Gopher Snake, which is yellow, with a series of regular brown blotches on its back and smaller brown markings on its flanks; *P. m. melanoleucas,* the Northern Pine Snake, which is white or yellowish, with a small number of large black or dark brown blotches on its back; and *P. m. sayi,* the Bull Snake, which is deep yellow or amber, covered with many small spots and blotches of rich brown or reddish brown.

All of these forms, and several other subspecies, make good captives, although they may be nervous and bad-tempered when first captured, in which case they hiss loudly and vibrate their tail rapidly when disturbed. Most of this is bluff — they usually calm down if handled gently.

Their care is as given on page 247. This is a species which may cease to feed in the winter, even if it is kept at an artifically high temperature. In this case it is necessary to allow it to hibernate in order to prevent it from using up its food reserves too quickly. Summer temperatures should be 25–30°C, and food consists of mice, although large specimens may take small rats and young chickens. Captive breeding presents few problems. Mating takes place in the spring immediately after hibernation, but the exact month may vary slightly according to the part of the range from which the specimens concerned originated. 20 or more eggs may be laid, although clutches usually consist of far fewer, 3–12 being most common. At 28°C, incubation takes 60–70 days, and the hatchlings, which are 40–50 cm in length, are particularly vigorous and usually begin feeding on newborn mice as soon as they have sloughed.

Ptyas mucosus   **Asian Rat Snake, Dhaman**

ASIA

150–200 cm. A moderately-built snake, notable for its very large scales. In colour it is uniform olive-brown or yellowish brown.

Being a tropical species, it requires a temperature of 25–30°C throughout the year, otherwise care is as on page 247. Its food consists of mice and small rats. No records of captive breeding have been traced, but in the wild it apparently breeds throughout the year, each female producing several clutches of about 10 eggs. Like many Asian snakes, this species is prone to parasitism, and new acquisitions should be quarantined and preferably screened for worm eggs etc until all danger of cross infection is considered to be over.

P. korros, the Indian Rat Snake, is sometimes available and is similar to *P. mucosus* in all respects.

Storeria dekayi   **DeKay's Snake, Brown Snake**

NORTH AND CENTRAL AMERICA

20–35 cm. A small, brown snake with two rows of fine black spots down its back.

This dainty little snake requires a small cage with an area of slightly moist sphagnum or similar material, without which it soon becomes dehydrated, even if drinking water is available. Ventilation must be sufficient to prevent the build-up of stagnant air, and a temperature of 20–25°C in summer, hibernation at 4–6°C in winter, is suitable. Its food consists of earthworms, slugs, caterpillars and other soft-bodied invertebrates. No records of captive breeding have been traced. About 12 live young, measuring approximately 10 cm, are born in late summer.

S. occipitomaculata is similar but slightly larger, darker, and has a red or orange underside. Its requirements are as for *S. dekayi.*

Telescopus semiannulatus   Tiger Snake

AFRICA

50–80 cm. A slender, strikingly marked species, being yellow, buff or pale brown above, with a series of black crossbands. Its head is large, flattened and very distinct from the neck.

Many Tiger Snakes are nervous and difficult to keep alive for any length of time. Others may calm down quite quickly, and although their natural food is lizards (especially geckos), they can often be persuaded to take newborn mice. They are very secretive and require a retreat or, better still, a completely darkened cage if they are to thrive. Temperature 25–30°C. Although they use a mild venom to subdue their prey, this is injected via their small rear fangs and is of no danger to man. Captive breeding has not been traced, although 6–10 eggs per clutch are reported.

Fig. 67 *Telescopus fallax*, the European Cat Snake.

T. fallax, the Cat Snake, which occurs in Europe and western Asia, is available very occasionally. It too is a lizard-eater and requires similar treatment to the above species.

Genus *Thamnophis*   Garter Snakes

The Garter Snakes, of which there are many species and subspecies, inhabit North and Central America. They are deservedly popular among reptile keepers, because they are common, docile and easily cared for, and between them they display a variety of markings, consisting in the main of a number of longitudinal stripes, the colours of which vary from species to species. All are slender, active and diurnal, and are usually associated with damp habitats, and their food (amphibians, fish, earthworms) is consistent with this. Some western forms, however, are found in drier surroundings, and their diet includes rodents and nestling birds. None of them should be fed entirely on fish unless ample vitamin supplements are given.

Garter Snakes' requirements are similar to those of most other species, but above all they must be kept on a dry substrate. They rarely climb, so their cage need not be tall, but hide boxes are much appreciated. Temperatures are dependent to some extent on the natural range of the species concerned, but in general should not be too high: 22–26 °C in summer, cooler, preferably hibernation, in winter. All species give birth to living young, usually in late summer.

Identification of several species and subspecies can be very difficult, and a good key is necessary. Only brief descriptions are attempted here.

Thamnophis elegans   Western Terrestrial Garter Snake

WESTERN NORTH AMERICA

60–100 cm. This species is more heavily built than most Garter Snakes, and has a pale dorsal line. The area either side of this is black, or red and black, depending on subspecies.

Care is as above. This species eats mice, but feeding the newborn young can be problematical as they are too small to take young mice and often refuse worms, fish-pieces etc. 6–16 young are born.

Thamnophis marcianus   Chequered Garter Snake

NORTH AND CENTRAL AMERICA

50–100 cm. A very attractive species. The ground colour is buff or olive, and the dorsal stripe is pale yellow. Black markings on either side of this are arranged alternately, so giving the chequered appearance.

Although this species inhabits arid regions, it is always found near water. It feeds readily on fish-pieces, worms and so on. 6–12 young are born.

Thamnophis radix   Plains Garter Snake

NORTH AMERICA

50–100 cm. Another colourful species, the Plains Garter Snake, has a distinctive bright orange dorsal stripe, either side of which is an olive area with small black markings, and the chin and lower flanks are yellow or orange.

This species is a good choice for the vivarium, as it feeds well (on worms, fish and amphibians) and is less nervous than some of the other species. Very large broods of young have been reported (up to 92) but 15–30 seems about average.

Thamnophis sauritus   Eastern Ribbon Snake (46)

NORTH AMERICA

50–80 cm. The Ribbon Snakes, of which there are several rather similar subspecies, are slender versions of the Garter Snakes. They are vividly striped with three yellow or orange stripes on a dark background.

In captivity the Ribbon Snake may be treated much the same as other *Thamnophis* species, but it rarely accepts earthworms as food and is on the whole a less satisfactory vivarium subject. Broods of young range from 3 to 20.

T. proximus, the Western Ribbon Snake, is similar but slightly larger than *T. sauritus.* Its requirements are the same.

Thamnophis sirtalis **Common Garter Snake**

NORTH AMERICA

50–120 cm. The Common Garter Snake is extremely variable and exists as several distinctive subspecies. The best known are as follows.

T. s. concinnus, the Red-spotted Garter Snake (*see* Plate **45**), is a very beautiful form, perhaps the best. The areas between the pale dorsal stripe and the lateral stripes are black with red bars. The top of the head is reddish, and the lips, throat and underside are suffused with blue. In some pale examples the red colouration is replaced by a pale salmon pink.

T. s. infernalis, the Californian Red-sided Garter Snake, is similar to the preceding form, but the red markings may run together to form stripes. There is much variation in the intensity of the red pigment, some specimens being exceptionally brilliantly coloured.

T. s. parietalis, the Red-sided Garter snake, is a dark subspecies with a pale yellow or cream dorsal stripe. The areas on either side of this are black with a variable amount of red, in the form of bars. These are frequently only visible when the skin is stretched; for instance, when the snake has recently fed.

T. s. similis, the Florida or Blue-striped Garter Snake, is a large

Fig. 68 *Thamnophis sirtalis sirtalis*, the Eastern Garter Snake.

277

subspecies. The dorsal and lateral stripes are pale, the areas in between are grey with black markings. The whole snake, including the pale underside, has a delicate overlying blue tint.

T. s. sirtalis, the Eastern Garter Snake, is most commonly brown or olive with three yellow or dirty white stripes, but examples may be green or even reddish in over-all appearance, and totally black (melanistic) specimens are not uncommon in certain regions.

Care of the Common Garter Snake is as for other *Thamnophis* species. Western forms, such as *T. s. concinnus* and *T. s. infernalis,* are terrestrial in habit and will often eat young mice as well as fish, amphibians and worms. They also tend to have small broods, about 8–12. The eastern subspecies, such as *T. s. sirtalis, T. s. similis* and *T. s. parietalis,* are more aquatic in habit and rarely feed on mammals. They have large broods of up to 100, but more usually 15–30. The young feed readily on earthworms, and soon learn to take strips of raw fish. They grow very rapidly if fed every one or two days, and can reach breeding size in less than one year.

Several other Garter Snakes are offered occasionally, sometimes turning up in consignments of other, more common, species from the same area. They incluce *T. butleri,* Butler's Garter Snake (which is very small and appears to eat only earthworms); *T. couchi,* the Western Aquatic Garter Snake; *T. cyrtopsis,* the Black-necked Garter Snake; and *T. ordinoides,* the Northwestern Garter Snake, which is notoriously difficult to keep. Apart from the latter, all make good captives and can be recommended. Their care and breeding are as described above.

15
Venomous Snakes

The keeping of dangerously venomous snakes is not a pastime for amateurs. Apart from endangering himself, the keeper also puts other members of his household, and perhaps the public, at risk. Instructions for the care of these species is therefore given mainly for the sake of completeness, and in the knowledge that there will always be enthusiasts unable to resist this interesting but hazardous aspect of vivarium-keeping. *The inclusion of a species in the following list in no way implies recommendation to keep that species.*

In many countries, including Great Britain and the United States, it is a legal requirement to be in possession of a licence before a dangerously venomous snake can be obtained. Before such a licence is issued, it will be necessary to demonstrate to the relevant authority that certain stipulations, regarding the construction of the cage and the room in which it is housed, are met. Apart from these legal requirements, certain other precautions can be taken in order to minimise the risks involved.

1) The vivarium should be strongly built and placed on a firm and solid base.
2) It should have provision for a padlock, and this should be fastened whenever the cage is not actually being serviced.
3) If possible, a competent second person should be available in case of emergency.
4) The room should have well-fitting doors and windows in case of escape. A glass inspection window in the door is of great value.
5) The appropriate antivenene (antivenom) should be available — if possible in the same building. It must be refrigerated, and renewed every few years depending on its shelf-life. It should not be used by the herpetologist, but taken with the patient to his doctor or hospital.
6) A notice must be prominently displayed on the vivarium

giving the species of snake, location of the antivenene, and the name and address of a doctor or hospital department where treatment can be carried out.

In the event of snake bite, stay calm, consult a medical expert, and do not attempt any heroic activities such as opening the wound with a blade. If the snake has escaped from the cage, try to confine it to one part of the room or building, and if this is not possible kill it before it can make off. Above all, do not panic.

Apart from these precautions, which are only common sense, keeping venomous snakes is no different to keeping other snakes, their main requirements being warm dry conditions, places to hide and a supply of suitable food. As with other groups, some species adapt to captivity better than others. Venomous snakes may belong to any one of three families: the Colubridae, which also contains many of the harmless snakes already described, the Elapidae (Cobras, Coral Snakes and Sea Snakes) and the Viperidae, or Vipers.

Family Colubridae

Details of this family have already been given. A number of its members use venom, and these deliver it via wounds made by fangs at the rear of their mouth, and so they have to chew their prey before the venom can take effect. Several species, however, are large enough to inject their venom into a human finger or hand, and a few have caused fatalities. Other back-fanged snakes may have potent venom which is unlikely to find its way into the human bloodstream because the fangs are small or are so far back that they cannot easily be brought into play, but even these species should be treated with respect, and bites from them should never be solicited.

Boiga dendrophila   Mangrove Snake

SOUTH-EAST ASIA

To 250 cm. A vividly marked snake, being glossy black with narrow, bright yellow bands around the body, and yellow 'lips'.

The Mangrove Snake is a rather bad-tempered but relatively harmless arboreal species, which prefers to eat lizards and small birds, but will usually take mice in captivity. A temperature of 25–30°C, and an occasional spraying to raise the humidity, is appreciated. A clutch of 6 eggs has been recorded, and these hatched after 107 days. The hatchlings measure about 30 cm.

Chrysopelea ornata

SOUTH-EAST ASIA

To 150 cm. A slender species, which is mainly green in colour with a black edging to each scale.

This tree snake, and other members of its genus, are remarkable for their ability to glide from trees by flattening their ventral surface as they launch themselves. This species is rather nervous in captivity and strikes and bites repeatedly, but its venom is unlikely to be injected. Its preferred food is lizards, but young mice are usually accepted. Breeding unknown.

Chrysopelea paradisi, the Paradise Tree Snake, is sometimes available. It is darker in colour and usually smaller, but its care is similar.

Family Elapidae - Cobras

Members of the Cobra family, which include the Mambas, Coral Snakes and Sea Snakes, are mostly medium-sized, agile and very dangerous to man. Their fangs are situated at the front of their mouths, but are small — their main danger lies in their speed of movement, and the toxicity of their venom, which is fast-acting and usually affects the nervous system. Typical Cobras are found in Africa and Asia, and often raise the front part of their body, and flatten their neck, when threatened. Some are able to spray their venom.

As captives, most species are difficult and dangerous to handle, requiring catching boxes and grab-sticks if this is to be done safely.

Micrurus species Coral Snakes

NORTH, CENTRAL AND SOUTH AMERICA

To 100 cm, usually smaller. The Coral Snakes are small, secretive, burrowing species, all of which are brightly coloured with bands of yellow, black and red (or occasionally yellow and black), superficially resembling certain species of the genus *Lampropeltis* and others.

Although small, the Coral Snakes are highly venomous. They require small vivaria with loose substrate and bark under which they can hide. Their food consists of lizards, frogs and probably some invertebrates. No records of captive breeding have been traced.

Naja naja Indian Cobra

ASIA

To 175 cm. Many subspecies of this widespread cobra exist. Most have white markings on the back of their hood, often in the form of a ring or 'spectacle'. The body is usually brown, and it may be indistinctly banded.

A common species in zoological gardens, *Naja naja* usually adapts well to captivity, and feeds on mice. Temperature around 25°C. The eggs, numbering up to 12, hatch in 65–90 days.

Naja nigricollis Black-necked Cobra, Spitting Cobra

AFRICA

To 200 cm. Variable in colour, but usually some shade of brown or olive. The underside is off-white or pinkish, except for an area of black beneath the hood.

A nervous species which rarely does well in captivity. It can spit venom accurately up to 3 metres, making it an exceedingly dangerous species. No records of captive breeding have been traced. 10–22 eggs are laid.

Fig. 69 Opposite: *Naja naja*, the Indian Cobra.

Fig. 70 An albino Indian Cobra (*Naja naja*) eating a dead rat (also an albino!).

Family Viperidae - Vipers

The Vipers may be found in both the New and Old Worlds, are the most advanced snakes, and have developed the most specialised venom-injecting apparatus — long, re-curved fangs, which are folded away into the roof of the mouth when not in use. Although many species are heavy-bodied and sluggish, they can strike with great speed.

Many adapt well to captivity and make splendid exhibits, but a few are notoriously difficult to keep, often because they refuse to feed. The great majority are viviparous, and many breed regularly in captivity. Therefore, great attention must be paid to security where adult females are housed, as: (1) newborn young are considerably smaller than their parents and may easily escape through cracks and ventilation holes which have been over-looked; (2) there is no way of knowing the number born, and escapees can be at large without the knowledge of the keeper; and (3) the newly born snakes are fully equipped with venom and fangs.

Three subfamilies are recognised, of which two contain species which may be kept in captivity.

Subfamily Viperinae

The True Vipers are restricted to the Old World and there are several well known species amongst them. Their care in captivity is as for snakes in general, but with the obvious extra attention to security.

Bitis arietans **Puff Adder**

AFRICA

To 180 cm. The notorious Puff Adder is a stout black or grey snake with a number of pale, curved, crossbands. Its venom is very powerful.

This species does well in captivity, feeding on mice and rats, and breeding quite regularly with litters numbering up to 100, but usually 20–40, young.

Fig. 71 *Bitis gabonica*, the impressive Gaboon Viper.

285

Bitis gabonica   Gaboon Viper

AFRICA

To 200 cm. This is another very heavily bodied species, and it has a remarkably flattened, wedge-shaped head. Its markings are complex and beautiful, consisting of triangular and diamond-shaped areas of buff, pink and brown, linked together in an intricate fashion.

The Gaboon Viper is one of the most awe-inspiring exhibits in zoological gardens. It is usually docile and even-tempered, and takes well to captivity, feeding on mice and rats. It requires a slightly higher humidity than many snakes, especially if breeding is planned, but should not be kept on a damp substrate. Up to 50 young are born, each measuring 25–30 cm, after a long gestation (possibly one year).

Bitis nasicornis, the Rhinoceros Viper, is, if anything, even more extravagantly marked than *B. gabonica*. Its care in captivity is similar.

Vipera ammodytes   Sand Viper (48)

EASTERN MEDITERRANEAN REGION

To 90 cm. The Sand Viper is easily recognised by its prominent nose-horn, coupled to the characteristic zig-zag marking found in many other *Vipera* species. The markings of the male show greater contrast than those of the female, a rare case of sexual dimorphism in snakes.

It is the largest, and probably the most attractive, of the European Vipers, and does well in captivity. It requires dry, warm (25–30°C) conditions, with rocks to hide among. Its prey is rodents and (especially when young) lizards. Up to 20 live young are born.

Vipera russelli   Russell's Viper

ASIA

To 150 cm. Usually brown, with a row of darker, rounded blotches down its back and down each flank. These are often edged in white, and those on the neck may be in the shape of an arrow-head.

Fig. 72 *Vipera ammodytes*, the Sand Viper, photographed as it begins to shed its skin.

Care and breeding are as for *V. ammodytes*. A good captive, but very dangerous, being rather more slender and active than many *Bitis* and *Vipera* species.

Other *Vipera* species are popular with zoos and serious collectors of venomous snakes. All do well under conditions similar to the above, with the exception of *V. berus*, the Adder or Northern Viper, which is notoriously difficult to feed in captivity (unless kept in spacious outside enclosures).

Subfamily Crotalinae - Pit Vipers

Members of this subfamily are known as Pit Vipers, due to the presence of a heat-detecting organ, called the loreal pit, situated below the eye and used in the detection of warm-blooded prey in darkness.

It is a large subfamily, represented in both the New and Old Worlds, and includes the Rattlesnakes, well-known North American species in which the sloughed skins are retained by a 'button' on the tip of the tail, eventually forming a number of interlocking rings which buzz when the snake vibrates its tail rapidly in warning or agitation.

Agkistrodon contortrix   Copperhead

EASTERN NORTH AMERICA

To 100 cm. An attractive species, boldly marked with wide crossbands of rich brown and orange or buff.

A dry substrate, and a temperature of 23–28°C is required. Mice, small rats, and birds are eaten. Litters consist of about 6 live young.

A. bilineatus, the Cantil, and *A. piscivorus*, the Moccasin, are occasionally available. The latter normally feeds on fish, but readily accepts frogs, mice, small rats and birds, in captivity, and both bring forth live young (certain Old World *Agkistrodon* species, however, lay eggs).

Crotalus atrox   Western Diamondback Rattlesnake

WESTERN NORTH AMERICA

To 200 cm. Highly variable in colour, but usually brownish, with diamond-shaped dorsal markings outlined in white. A heavy-bodied species, with a wide, blunt head.

Warm (25–30°C), dry vivaria are required, with a substrate of newspaper or clean gravel. Mice, rats and larger mammals, such as rabbits, are eaten. This species usually does well in captivity and may breed regularly, producing about 10 young.

Crotalus cerastes   Sidewinder

WESTERN NORTH AMERICA

50–75 cm. This small Rattlesnake has prominent 'horns' above its eyes. Its colour usually matches that of the sand or soil of the region in which it lives, and can be pale yellow, brown, grey or reddish. A row of dorsal blotches, often indistinct, is usually present. Males are significantly smaller than females.

Sidewinders live in loose soil or sand (their peculiar looping locomotion is an adaptation to this), and hide beneath its surface during the day. Their vivarium should either contain a suitable loose substrate or, if newspaper is preferred, shallow, crack-like retreats should be provided. Small examples may favour a diet of lizards, but many can be persuaded to take small mice.

Temperature 23–25 °C; above this they retreat to a cool part of their cage and become inactive. 5–15 live young are born.

Crotalus ruber Red Rattlesnake

WESTERN NORTH AMERICA

To 150 cm. This species has Diamond-shaped dorsal markings, but is distinguishable from other 'diamond-backs' by its over-all reddish hue.
Care and breeding are as for *C. atrox.*

Sistrurus miliarius Pygmy Rattlesnake

SOUTH-EASTERN NORTH AMERICA

To 50 cm. A pale species, usually brown or yellowish, with a single row of dorsal blotches. The tail and rattle are noticeably smaller than in other Rattlesnakes.
A temperature of 20–25 °C is required, and occasional spraying may be of value. The food is lizards, young mice, and frogs. About 7 or 8 live young are born.

Trimeresurus albolabris White-lipped Pit Viper

SOUTH-EAST ASIA

To 75 cm. A bright green snake with a red tip to its tail. A white line runs along the upper jaw, and in females this continues along each flank. The tail is strongly prehensile.
Arboreal Pit Vipers, of which there are several similar species, require tall cages furnished with an abundance of branches and twigs and, if they are to slough successfully, some degree of humidity, best produced by daily spraying with tepid water. Although some will accept baby mice, lizards and frogs are the favoured prey. About 5–10 live young are born, and these usually require small frogs as a first food.

T. popeorum, Pope's Tree Viper, and *T. wagleri,* Wagler's Pit Viper, are sometimes available. Their care and breeding are as for *T. albolabris.*

Appendix I

Laws pertaining to the Keeping of Reptiles and Amphibians

Several laws have a bearing on the keeping of reptiles and amphibians, the most important of which are summarised below. Note, however, that the following information is intended for guidance only and the possession of current information, obtained by reference to the relevant authorities, is always desirable.

International Treaties

In recent years, two important conventions dealing with the protection of wildlife have been drawn up. Both have a direct bearing on the keeping of reptiles and amphibians.

1) *Convention on International Trade in Endangered Species of Flora and Fauna* (CITES) 1973 — sometimes known as the 'Washington Convention'.

This convention (not ratified by the United Kingdom, but incorporated with modifications into the Endangered Species (Import and Export) Act 1976 sets out regulations whereby certain species which are considered to be endangered or threatened are protected through the co-operation of the party states by restricting their import and export.

The animals concerned are classed as 'threatened' (Appendix I), likely to become threatened (Appendix II), or subject to internal regulations in one or more of the party states. Import, export or re-export of the animals on these lists is possible only if import and export licences or permits are first obtained. These licences, where granted, are valid for one consignment within six months of issue and are applicable only provided that the animals are not obtained illegally, and that they are shipped in such a way as to minimise the risk of injury, damage to health, and cruelty.

Exceptions are made for animals bred in captivity (but if these are species normally listed in Appendix I, they are treated as though they were in Appendix II), animals loaned or donated between scientists or scientific institutions, and travelling zoos, circuses etc.

Where trade with non-party states is involved, comparable documentation will be accepted in lieu of the usual import of export licences or permits.

The animals listed in the Appendices include several amphibians and reptiles, for example, all Crocodilia, all land tortoises, all Monitor lizards and all *Python* species.

2) *Convention on the Conservation of European Wildlife and Natural Habitats* 1979 — sometimes known as the 'Berne Convention'

Under this convention (not ratified by the United Kingdom, but incorporated with modifications into the Wildlife and Country-side Act 1981) the contracting parties (most of Europe) agree to co-operate in protecting important natural habitats and listed plants and animals. Exceptions may be made for various reasons including: education; re-population; and the keeping, on a small scale, of certain species under supervised conditions. In addition, the parties agree to control the introduction of non-native species.

Appendix I lists 'strictly protected' plants; Appendix II lists 'strictly protected' animals (including all European turtles and tortoises, 13 lizards, 11 snakes (including 6 vipers) and 17 amphibians); Appendix III lists 'protected' animals, and all reptiles and amphibians not listed in Appendix II are automatically included here.

British Laws

CRUELTY TO ANIMALS ACT 1876
Under this Act it is illegal to carry out experiments on any living vertebrates except on registered premises and unless a licence is first obtained (from the Home Office).

PET ANIMALS ACT 1951
Under this Act it is illegal to sell animals except from premises

which are registered for that purpose by the local authority who will first appoint a vet to inspect them in order to ensure that they are suitable for accommodating animals in a humane manner, and that they meet certain other requirements. An exception may be made where the animals have been bred by the vendor.

DANGEROUS WILD ANIMALS ACT 1976

Under this Act nobody may keep a dangerous wild animal unless they have obtained a licence from the local authority. The licence application must specify the species and number of animals to be kept, and must be accompanied by a fee set by the local authority. The licence will only be granted provided that the applicant is aged 18 years or over, and is considered 'suitable'; that the authority is satisfied that the animal(s) will be placed in suitable accommodation and provided with adequate food, drink, bedding etc. Before a licence is issued, the premises will be inspected by a vet to ensure that the above conditions are met satisfactorily, and the applicant must also pay the fee for this inspection. In addition, the animals must remain at the specified premises and be kept only by the specified licence-holder and he must take out insurance against damage caused by the animal(s). Licences run for one year, and the premises may be inspected again at any time throughout the year.

Exceptions to the law are zoos, circuses, pet shops and premises registered for performing experiments on animals (see above).

The reptiles figuring on the list are: all Crocodilia, Helodermatidae (Gila Monster and Beaded Lizard), Elapidae (Cobras, Kraits, Mambas, Coral Snakes etc) and Viperidae (Vipers and Rattlesnakes). In addition, a number of back-fanged colubrid snakes have been placed on the list. These include the following three species which have commonly been available through the pet trade: Mangrove Snake, *Boiga dendrophila*; Montpellier Snake, *Malpolon monspessulanus*; Long-nosed Tree Snake, *Dryophis nasuta*.

ENDANGERED SPECIES (IMPORT AND EXPORT) ACT 1976

This Act incorporates the Washington Convention into British law (*see* above), and regulates the import and export of certain endangered and vulnerable species. It is re-enacted, with amendments, by the Wildlife and Countryside Act 1981 (*see* below). It states that the importation of listed species may only be carried out if an import licence is first obtained, and it may be necessary to have additional documentation from the exporting country. For animals imported without licences, i.e. excepted kinds, the customs authorities may ask for a declaration giving the full scientific name of the species concerned, and stating that its importation is not restricted under this Act. Importation may be restricted to specified ports, airports and border crossings, and licences may be issued on the condition that the animals are kept at specified premises.

An amendment to this Act gives power of entry to authorised persons in order to ascertain whether plants or animals are being kept illegally. A revised list of protected animals is given with the Wildlife and Countryside Act 1981.

ZOO LICENCING ACT 1981
Under this Act it is illegal to operate a zoo without first obtaining a licence from the local authority, who will first consider reports made by inspectors appointed for this purpose.

WILDLIFE AND COUNTRYSIDE ACT 1981
Among other things, this recent Act (which repeals the Conservation of Wild Creatures and Wild Plants Act 1975) gives total protection, against collection or disturbance, to four native amphibians and reptiles (Crested Newt, Natterjack Toad, Sand Lizard and Smooth Snake) and prevents the sale, or the advertising for sale, of any other British species, except under licence.

Licences may be granted in certain circumstances, e.g. educational or scientific circumstances, photography, preserving public health and safety etc.

It is also an offence to release or allow to escape into the wild any species which is not native.

The United States

In the United States the legal position is extremely complicated. The most important laws are the Federal laws, which apply throughout the country and which are enforced by the United States Fish and Wildlife Service. These laws are designed mainly to protect endangered North American species but some are also concerned with the importation of foreign species. (The United

States is party to the Washington Convention — see above.)

In addition, there are many state and city laws and regulations and these vary greatly. Some states have hardly any restrictions on the keeping of reptiles and amphibians but in others it is banned completely. City ordinances are concerned with such matters as the keeping of dangerous species, species which are likely to become pests if released and the welfare of captive animals. If such regulations are suspected, the relevant local authority will have to be consulted.

In addition to the references given at the end of this section, information may be sought through the various regional herpetological societies and through the Society for the Study of Amphibians and Reptiles (*see* bibliography), who publish details of recent legislation through their quarterly bulletin *Herpetological Review*.

Other Countries

Many countries, e.g. Australia, have a complete ban on the importation of exotic animals, and others prohibit the capture of native species except under licence. In almost every country there are areas set aside as national parks and regulations here will almost certainly restrict the collection of reptiles and amphibians.

If the reader is in any doubt as to the legality of collecting, importing, exporting or keeping reptiles and amphibians in his or her part of the world, the only recourse is to make enquiries through the government department or local authority concerned, or by joining a local herpetological society.

Information Sources

BRITAIN
The various Acts of Parliament are usually obtainable through local lending libraries or university libraries. Alternatively, they can be ordered through bookshops acting as agents for Her Majesty's Stationery Office (most large cities have one) or directly from HMSO.

Two other useful publications obtainable from HMSO are: *Convention on International Trade in Endangered Species of Fauna and Flora* (reference number Cmnd. 5459), and *Convention on the Conservation of European Wildlife and Natural Habitats* (reference number Cmnd. 7809).

A leaflet entitled *Notice to Importers and Exporters* gives information on the Endangered Species (Import and Export) Act 1976, and is obtainable from: Wildlife Conservation Licencing Section, Department of the Environment, Tollgate House, Houlton Street, Bristol BS2 9DJ, to whom applications for licences should also be made.

UNITED STATES OF AMERICA

'Federal Registers' give details of the various federal laws and are obtainable from: Federal Wildlife Permit Office, U.S. Fish and Wildlife Service, Washington DC 20240. Further information is contained in a book entitled *A Compilation of Federal Laws Relating to Conservation and Development of our Nation's Fish and Wildlife Resources, Environmental Quality, and Oceanography,* obtainable from: The Superintendant of Documents, U.S. Government Printing Office, Washington DC 20402.

A compilation of the various state laws is contained in a publication entitled *State Laws as they pertain to Scientific Collecting Permits*, published in *Museology*, Sept. 3, 1976, No. 2. This is available from: The Museum Shop, The Museum, Texas Tech University, Lubbock, Texas 79409.

Appendix II

Herpetological Societies

Many parts of the world have one or more societies catering for the needs of amateur and professional herpetologists. Some are international in appeal, others are local, but each provides a means of collating and passing on relevant information through its journals, bulletins and newsletters. With two exceptions, it is impractical to give the addresses of officials of these societies as they are subject to change, but details are usually available at libraries (which should also be able to obtain copies of the more important journals), zoological gardens, museums and reptile dealers. Back issues of journals and other society publications are usually available to members (and sometimes also to non-members), and these rate amongst the most valuable sources of information pertaining to the biology and the captive maintenance and breeding of amphibians and reptiles.

AFRICA

Herpetological Association of Africa (HAA). Publication: *Journal of the Herpetological Association of Africa* (2 per annum).

ASIA

Japanese Herpetological Society. Publication: *Japanese Journal of Herpetology* (4 per annum).

AUSTRALASIA

Australian Herpetological Society and New Zealand Herpetological Society. Publications: Apart from their individual newsletters, these societies publish a joint journal, *Herpeto-fauna* (2 per annum).

EUROPE

Association for the Study of Reptiles and Amphibians (ASRA), c/o The Cotswold Wild Life Park, Burford, Oxon, England. Publications: *The Journal of the Association for the Study of Reptiles and Amphibia* (once annually), and newsletters.

British Herpetological Society (BHS), c/o The Zoological Society of London, Regent's Park, London NW1. Publications: *British Journal of Herpetology* and *British Herpetological Society Bulletin* (2 of each per annum).

International Herpetological Society (IHS). Secretary: Mr A.J. Mobbs, Broadstone Avenue, Walsall, West Midlands. Publications: *The Herptile* (4 per annum), and newsletters.

Deutsche Gesellschaft fuer Herpetologie und Terrarienkunde. Publication: *Salamandra* (4 per annum). Most articles are in German but have English summaries.

Dutch Snake Society. Secretary: Jaap Kooij, Langervelderweg 137, 2211 AG Noord-wilkerhout, The Netherlands. Publication: *Litteratura Serpentium* (6 per annum), published as a Dutch or English edition, and including colour illustrations.

Nederlandse Vereniging voor Herpetologie en Terrariumkunde. Publication: *Lacerta* (12 per annum). Most articles are in Dutch but have English summaries – the excellent illustrations, often in colour, are a feature of this amateur-orientated journal.

UNITED STATES

Herpetologists' League. Publication: *Herpetologica* (4 per annum).

Society for the Study of Amphibians and Reptiles (SSAR). Publications: *Journal of Herpetology* (4 per annum), *Herpetological Review* (4 per annum), *Herpetological Circulars* (occasional). The various publications produced by this society cater for every taste, and are essential reading for all serious herpetologists whether amateur or professional.

REGIONAL SOCIETIES
Although regional societies exist in many countries, it is in the United States that they are particularly active. Most states have at least one society which holds local meetings and publishes a journal and/or bulletin. Several are large and may be of interest to herpetologists outside the immediate area. The best known of them are as follows.

Chicago Herpetological Society. Publication: *Chicago Herpetological Society Bulletin* (4 per annum).
Maryland Herpetological Society. Publication: *Bulletin of the Maryland Herpetological Society* (4 per annum).
New York Herpetological Society. Publication: *Herp* (4 per annum).

Glossary

Amplexus	The mating embrace of certain amphibians, in which the male grasps the female prior to egg-laying.
Bromeliads	Plants belonging to the family Bromeliaciae, often called Air-plants or Urn plants, many of which are particularly suitable for vivarium decoration.
Epiphytes	Plants which grow attached to trees without being parasites, e.g. various bromeliads and orchids.
Gravid	Strictly speaking, pregnant, but more commonly applied specifically to egg-laying forms.
Hemipenes	The paired mating organs of male snakes and lizards.
Herpetology	The study of reptiles and amphibians.
Hybrid	Offspring resulting from parents of different species or subspecies, often artificially produced.
Intergrade	An individual which is intermediate in appearance between two subspecies, usually originating from a region where their ranges merge.
Oviparous	Egg-laying, e.g. most amphibians and reptiles. Cf ovo-viviparous, viviparous.
Ovipositor	The tube from which eggs are extruded in insects and in a few amphibians, e.g. *Pipa pipa*.
Ovo-viviparous	Forms in which the eggs are retained inside the female until the point of hatching, i.e. the developing embryos derive protection, but not nutrition, from their mother's body, e.g. *Salamandra salamandra*. Cf oviparous, viviparous.

Parthenogenetic   Forms in which the female can reproduce without having mated. In some species males do not exist at all but in others normal reproduction may also take place occasionally.

Prophylactic   Medicine administered in order to prevent disease.

Protozoa   Microscopic single-celled animals, invaluable as food for newly-hatched newt and salamander larvae.

Scute   The horny (and often patterned) covering of each bony segment of turtles' shells, otherwise known as laminae.

Spermatophore   The jelly-like mass of sperm produced by male newts and salamanders.

Temperate   Regions (or species from those regions) which experience well-defined seasonal variations in temperature, i.e. not tropical.

Vermiculite   A form of expanded mica, produced for the insulation of buildings etc, which may also be used as an incubation medium for reptile eggs.

Vivaria   Containers for housing living things, e.g. aquaria and terraria.

Viviparous   Species which bring forth living young which have drawn nourishment from the mother's body during their development, e.g. some skinks. Cf oviparous, ovo-viviparous.

Bibliography

General Works

Bellairs, A., *The Life of Reptiles* (2 vols.), Weidenfeld and Nicolson, London (1969).

Carr, A., *Handbook of Turtles*, Comstock Publishing Associates, New York (1952). (This book deals primarily with North American species but the Introduction consists of an unrivalled account of the biology and natural history of turtles in general.)

Carr, A., *The Reptiles*, Life Nature Library, Time Inc., New York (1963).

Cochran, D. M., *Living Amphibians of the World*, Doubleday Inc., New York, and Hamish Hamilton, London (1961).

Duellman, W.E., and Trueb, L., *Biology of Amphibians*, McGraw-Hill Book Company, New York (1985).

Fitch, H.S., *Reproductive Cycles in Lizards and Snakes*, University of Kansas, Museum of Natural History (1970).

Gans, C., *Reptiles of the World*, Ridge Press/Bantam Books Inc., New York (1975). (This little paperback gives an excellent introductory account of the reptile kingdom.)

Goin, C.J., Goin, O.B., and Zug, G.R., *Introduction to Herpetology*, W.H. Freeman and Co., San Francisco (1978).

Phelps, T., *Poisonous Snakes*, Blandford Press, Poole (1981).

Porter, K. R., *Herpetology*, W. B. Saunders and Co., New York (1972).

Pritchard, P. C. H., *Living Turtles of the World*, T. F. H. Publications, Jersey City (1967).

Schmidt, K. P. and Inger, R. F., *Living Reptiles of the World*, Doubleday Inc., New York and Hamish Hamilton, London (1957).

Regional Identification Guides

Note: Some regions are far better represented than others — this is due more to the distribution of herpetologists than of reptiles and amphibians. For each region, only the most comprehensive guides are listed here; many others, dealing with smaller areas or groups of species, may be available.

AFRICA
Fitzsimmons, V. F. M., *A Field Guide to the Snakes of Southern Africa*, Collins, London (1970).
Passmore, N. I. and Carruthers, V. C., *South African Frogs*, Witwatersrand University Press, Johannesburg (1979).
Pitman, C. R. S., *A Guide to the Snakes of Uganda*, rev. ed. Wheldon and Wesley, England (1974).
Rose, W., *The Reptiles and Amphibians of Southern Africa*, rev. ed. Maskew Millar Ltd., Cape Town (1962).

ASIA
Loveridge, A., *Reptiles of the Pacific World*, The MacMillan Co., New York (1945). (Rather generalised, and out of date now, but the only volume dealing with reptiles from this very rich region.)
McCoy, M., *Reptiles of the Solomon Islands*, Wau Ecology Institute, Handbook No. 7 (1980).
Reitinger, F.F., *Common Snakes of South East Asia and Hong Kong*, Heinemann, Hong Kong (1978).

AUSTRALASIA
Cogger, H. G., *Reptiles and Amphibians of Australia*, rev. ed. A. H. and A. W. Reed, Sydney (1979).
Robb, J., *New Zealand Amphibians and Reptiles*, Collins, Auckland (1980).

EUROPE
Arnold, E. N. and Burton, J. A., *A Field Guide to the Reptiles and Amphibians of Europe*, Collins, London (1978).

UNITED STATES
Conant, R., *A Field Guide to Reptiles and Amphibians of Eastern North America*, rev. ed. Houghton Mifflin Co., Boston (1975).

Stebbins, R. C., *A Field Guide to Western Reptiles and Amphibians*, Houghton Mifflin Co., Boston (1966).

SOUTH AMERICA

Roze, J. A., *La Taxonomia y Zoogeographia de los Ophidios en Venezuela* (The Taxonomy and Distribution of Snakes in Venezuela), Universidad Central de Venezuela, Caracas (1966). (The only recent book dealing specifically with a group of South American reptiles — unfortunately in Spanish.)

The Care of Reptiles and Amphibians in Captivity

The International Zoo Yearbook, published annually by the Zoological Society of London, often contains papers on the care and breeding of reptiles and amphibians. In particular, vols. 9 and 19 (1969 and 1979) each devoted a whole section to the subject and are well worth reading. Two papers (see below) deserve separate listing due to their importance.

Cooper, J.E. and Jackson, O.F., *Diseases of the Reptilia*, 2 vols., Academic Press, London (1981).

Judd, H. L. *et al*, 'Determination of sex in the Komodo dragon, *Varanus komodoensis*', *International Zoo Yearbook*, vol. 17: 208–209 (1977). (A short paper which discusses the use of hormone measurements in reptilian sex determination.)

Kauffield, C., *Snakes: The Keeper and the Kept*, Doubleday and Co., New York (1969).

Murphy, J. B., *A Brief Outline of Suggested Treatments for Diseases of Captive Reptiles*, Society for the Study of Amphibians and Reptiles, Herpetological Circular No. 4 (1975).

Murphy, J. B. and Collins, J. T. (Eds.) *Reproductive Biology and Diseases of Captive Reptiles*, a collection of papers published by the Society for the Study of Amphibians and Reptiles (1980).

Peaker, M. 'Some aspects of the thermal requirements of reptiles in captivity,' *International Zoo Yearbook*, volume 9: 3–8 (1969).

Riches, R. J., *Breeding Snakes in Captivity*, Palmetto Publishing Co., Florida (1976).

Townson, S., and Lawrence, K., *Reptiles: Breeding Behaviour and Veterinary Aspects*, British Herpetological Society, London (1985).

Townson, S., Millichamp, N. J., Lucas, D. G. D. and Millwood, A. J. (Eds.), *The Care and Breeding of Captive Reptiles,* a collection of papers published by the British Herpetological Society (1980).

Other Useful Publications

Hay, R., McQuown, F. R., Beckett, G. and K., *The Dictionary of Indoor Plants in Colour,* Ebury Press and Michael Joseph Ltd., London, in collaboration with The Royal Horticultural Society (1974).

Jenno, A., *Aquarium Technology,* Barry Shurlock and Co. Ltd., Winchester (1976). (A good account of equipment and techniques for maintaining aquatic animals.)

Sterba, G., *Aquarium Care,* Studio Vista, London (1963). (Contains important sections on equipment and live foods for aquatic species, and a comprehensive guide to aquatic plants.)

Periodicals

No periodicals deal exclusively with reptiles and amphibians, although fish-keeping magazines occasionally include the odd article of interest to reptile and amphibian keepers. Two of the best known are the following.

Aquarist and Pondkeeper, Buckley Press, Brentford, Middlesex (monthly).

Tropical Fish Hobbyist, TFH Publications Inc., Jersey City (monthly).

Index of Scientific Names

Figures in **bold** refer to colour plates; those in *italics* refer to page numbers of illustrations

Index of Common Names

Figures in **bold** refer to colour plates; those in *italics* refer to page numbers of illustrations